THE LONG NIGHT

William L. Shirer and *The Rise and Fall of the Third Reich*

STEVE WICK

THE LONG NIGHT
Copyright © Steve Wick, 2011.

All rights reserved.

First published in 2011 by
PALGRAVE MACMILLAN®
in the United States—a division of St. Martin's Press LLC,
175 Fifth Avenue, New York, NY 10010.

Where this book is distributed in the UK, Europe and the rest of the world,
this is by Palgrave Macmillan, a division of Macmillan Publishers Limited,
registered in England, company number 785998, of Houndmills,
Basingstoke, Hampshire RG21 6XS.

Palgrave Macmillan is the global academic imprint of the above companies
and has companies and representatives throughout the world.

Palgrave® and Macmillan® are registered trademarks in the United States,
the United Kingdom, Europe and other countries.

ISBN 978–0–230–62318–7

Photograph and text permissions are from Don Congdon Associates Inc.,
and the Literary Estate of William L. Shirer.

Library of Congress Cataloging-in-Publication Data.

Wick, Steve.
   The long night : William L. Shirer and the rise and fall of the Third
Reich / by Steve Wick.
     p. cm.
   Includes bibliographical references and index.
   ISBN 978–0–230–62318–7 (hardback)
    1. Shirer, William L. (William Lawrence), 1904–1993. 2. Journalists—
United States—Biography. 3. World War, 1939–1945—Journalists—
Biography. 4. World War, 1939–1945—Press coverage—United States.
5. Fascism—Germany—Press coverage. I. Title.

PN4874.S49W53 2011
070.4′332092—dc22   2011005262
[B]

A catalogue record of the book is available from the British Library.

Design by Newgen Imaging Systems (P) Ltd., Chennai, India.

First edition: August 2011

10 9 8 7 6 5 4 3 2 1

Printed in the United States of America.

In memory of Lt. Michael Murphy
May 7, 1976–June 28, 2005

"We owe respect to the living. To the dead we owe only the truth."

—Voltaire

"The historian's task is not to disrupt for the sake of it, but it is to tell what is almost always an uncomfortable story and explain why the discomfort is part of the truth we need to live well and live properly. A well-organized society is one in which we know the truth about ourselves collectively, not one in which we tell pleasant lies about ourselves."

—Tony Judt

"What can I say? At least you opposed evil. You weren't corrupted. You and I and the many locked up here, and the many more in other places of detention, and tens of thousands in concentration camps—they're all resisting, today and tomorrow..."

"Yes, and then they will kill us, and what good did our resistance do?"

"Well, it will have helped us to feel that we behaved decently till the end. And much more, it will have helped people everywhere, who will be saved for the righteous few among them, as it says in the Bible. Of course, Quangel, it would have been a hundred times better if we'd had someone who could have told us. Such and such is what you have to do; our plan is this and this. But if there had been such a man in Germany, then Hitler would never have come to power in 1933. As it was, we all acted alone, we were caught alone, and every one of us will have to die alone. But that doesn't mean that we are alone, Quangel, or that our deaths will be in vain. Nothing in this world is done in vain, and since we are fighting for justice against brutality, we are bound to prevail in the end."

"And what good will that do us, down in our graves?"

"Quangel, I ask you! Would you rather live for an unjust cause than die for a just one?"

—From the novel *Every Man Dies Alone*, by Hans Fallada, page 430

CONTENTS

TIMELINE OF EVENTS

January 1933	Adolf Hitler becomes chancellor of Germany.
February 1933	The Reichstag burns.
June 1934	The bloody purge ordered by Hitler known as *Nacht der langen Messer* (The Night of the Long Knives) leaves hundreds dead, including Ernst Röhm, head of the SA.
August 1934	William L. Shirer and his wife Tess arrive in Berlin. Shirer goes to work for an American news wire service.
September 1935	The German government approves passage of the Nuremberg Laws. These laws codified who was Jewish in the new Nazi state and deprived those defined as Jews of their German citizenship.
March 1936	German troops sweep into the Rhineland, in violation of the terms of the Treaty of Versailles written in 1919, a year after the end of the Great War.
March 1938	The *Anschluss:* Austria is brought into the German Reich. Hitler arrives victoriously in Vienna.
September 1938	The Munich Accord is approved. It gives Germany the right to annex the Sudetenland, the German-speaking parts of Czechoslovakia.
November 1938	Synagogues are set ablaze across Germany and Austria in an outburst of government sanctioned violence against Jews called *Kristallnacht*.
March 1939	German troops invade Czechoslovakia and occupy the capital city of Prague.
August 1939	Germany and the Soviet Union approve a treaty of non-aggression between the two countries.
September 1939	German troops invade Poland. Great Britain and France declare war on Germany.
May 1940	Sweeping west, German troops invade the Low Countries. The Netherlands and Belgium surrender.

June 1940   The German army reaches Paris. France surrenders and
                   signs an armistice with Germany in the same rail car in
                   Compiègne, France, where the Germans surrendered in
                   1918.
December 1940   William L. Shirer leaves Berlin on a flight to Spain and then
                   Portugal, where he boards a ship for the United States.

LEAVING BERLIN

Berlin, December 5, 1940

S now had fallen all night, and as morning broke over the metropolis, Bill Shirer set out in a taxi from the Adlon Hotel for the airport at Tempelhof. He felt as if he'd been running nonstop for days or weeks or years. On top of the fatigue, he'd had too many whiskeys the previous nights as he planned his getaway, and this morning his stomach churned. The alarm that had overcome him in previous weeks grew more intense as the cab negotiated the snowy streets.

The final mile to the airport stretched on and on until finally there it was, dark buildings set against an overcast sky. Each night Berlin became a vast city of dark streets and dark buildings trying desperately to hide itself from British bombers, but the morning sun revealed all its secrets. Shirer was sick of being in a blacked-out city, sick of the darkness and the fear and the inability to live any kind of happy life. He missed the bright nights listening to great music. He loathed the government censors and the officious bureaucrats and the journalists who played along with them. On top of everything, he missed his wife, Tess, and their two-year-old daughter, Eileen.

He had not expected the weather to turn so bad. It only heightened his worry. Three big passenger planes had crashed in previous days because of icing problems. If the storm worsened, the plane would not take off and the airport would be shut down. He'd have to try again another day, and every day brought unexpected risks. If the plane did take off in the storm, he feared that the wings would ice up and the pilot would have to drop lower over the mountains. Anything could happen then. His friend Wally Deuel, in a panic after the three crashes, had left Berlin the day before on a train to Stuttgart, where he hoped to find a safe flight out of the country.

Shirer had decided to try his luck at Tempelhof after a friend in the Propaganda Ministry had warned him that he might be arrested as a spy. He feared she was right. But he didn't know. There was no way to pin anything down and to know what was rumor and what was fact, or to know who was lying and who was telling the truth. Maybe she was setting him up for arrest at the airport as he walked across the tarmac to the stairs leading up to the plane.

On top of all the worry about the flight being able to depart, he was concerned about the bombings. Some nights when he was coming from the broadcast center, he'd hear the alarms sound and he'd run headlong into a building where he knew there was a shelter as the air wardens waved their arms frantically and blew their whistles to get everyone off the streets. From underground, he could hear the bombs striking their targets—deep, heavy thumps, followed by bigger explosions as the attack moved closer to the city center, like the thunder of an approaching summer storm rolling across the plains of eastern Iowa near his childhood home. Tornadoes would tear up isolated farmhouses and old hay barns, and Shirer would read about the damage in the Cedar Rapids newspaper and imagine what it must have been like to live through it.

On nights the British struck Berlin, the alarms sounded and panic set in as people who were still outside ran for safety. The noise of the bombers sounded like racing trains passing overhead. Then the antiaircraft guns would explode and fires lit up the night sky. He'd heard of parts of wings, tail sections, and whole engines being found in fields. On some mornings, the city streets were littered with thousands of pieces of shrapnel. With the bombings of the city and surrounding areas, there were no guarantees he could get to the airport at all if he did not get out this morning.

In spite of the bombings, the government went about its business as usual. Uniformed Germans sat happily in restaurants and cafés in Paris. They visited nightclubs and museums, spending their marks like happy tourists. Shirer had arrived in Paris hours after the French surrender and walked the empty streets and stood with other correspondents in hotel lobbies, empty except for smiling German army officers and pompous government officials, while columns of French refugees poured south. He found it all too incredible. Hitler in Paris!

Shirer was relieved when he reached the airport terminal, but he was also profoundly worried about the trunks in which he had packed all his personal papers. So much of himself was in them. The letters he had received, all the letters to others he'd carboned and saved in his files, nearly a decade of his diaries, his clippings, practically everything he'd put on paper going back years— all packed into trunks that he feared customs officials would search before he could board the airplane.

Knowing he would attempt to leave this morning, he had spent the last few days going through his papers and diary entries, burning the ones he thought could hurt him or others. Sensitive papers that he did not want to burn he gave to friends who worked in different embassies in Berlin, telling them to smuggle them out of the country in official pouches so that he could get them later. He had packed his remaining papers at the bottom of two trunks and put routine papers and copies of his radio broadcasts on top of them, hoping anyone who searched the trunks would see there was nothing to be concerned about and not go any deeper. Then he had taken the trunks to Gestapo headquarters on the Alexanderplatz, told them he was leaving the country, and had them put their official exit stamps on them. With this he hoped to thwart customs officials from doing their own searches at the airport.

The terminal was crowded in spite of the snow. Anxious men in suits and ties and overcoats stood in tight clusters with women in their best dresses, shoes, and hats. Frightened children huddled next to their parents. They were getting out now when they should have left years earlier. But they were getting out, finally. No more excuses. No more thinking, *It will get better. It has to get better. Hitler can't last.* All they wanted was for the plane to be cleared for takeoff and to feel it mercifully lift off the ground, to fly south until it cleared German airspace—away from the Fatherland.

Seeing these men and women reminded him of the night in March 1938 when he had gone to the airport in Vienna to buy a ticket to London and could not find a seat on any flight. He'd gone person to person in a crowd of panicked Austrians, offering money to anyone who would sell him a seat. None had taken him up, so desperate were they to get out. When he finally found a plane that would take him to London—via Prague, Dresden, and Berlin—he kicked himself for trying to talk someone out of leaving. Had a man or a woman stayed back because of him—what would have become of them?

Shirer's plane, a thirty-two-seat Junkers owned by Lufthansa, sat on the tarmac just outside the terminal. If there were no problems with his trunks, and if the weather cooperated, he would board the plane for Spain. His great hope was to be in America before Christmas and to be reunited with Tess and Eileen. Once in Spain, if everything fell into place, he'd board another flight for Lisbon. There, he hoped Ed Murrow would be waiting for him.

He could picture Murrow sitting in the airport bar, wearing a suit and tie, smoking one cigarette after another, listening to the radio, following the German bombing of London. And wondering, as Shirer also wondered as he waited in Tempelhof for the snow to let up and the plane to be cleared for takeoff, what the world would look like when the war finally ended and Hitler was triumphant.

PART ONE

THE AMERICAN CORRESPONDENT

"As you may have heard, my seven years of foreign service with the Tribune have just been terminated."

—William L. Shirer, in a letter to a friend

The Writer

Lloret de Mar, Spain, Summer 1933

Every morning at 8:00 sharp, William Lawrence Shirer climbed the stairs to his study on the third floor in the big villa by the sea and took his seat at his desk in front of the typewriter. The desk was covered with books, his many files and manuscripts, and stacks of newspapers—from London, Paris, Vienna, and Spain. There were American magazines, too, that his brother and mother sent to help keep him informed on news back home. He could read about the Depression in the United States and political upheavals in London and Paris, and about the new government in Berlin that had come to power the previous January.

Every day that he sat at his desk, he followed a strict schedule, working faithfully from 8:00 A.M. to 1:00 P.M. He knew that a writer who wanted to be successful needed a routine that he stuck to as an article of faith, something never to be disrespected or cast aside. There was always paper in the typewriter and no shortage of ideas. There were his stories, a play about India, a novel, a memoir, and, of course, the letters to friends and the regular entries in his diary or those he typed on onionskin paper. He kept at it, day after day.

On sunny days when the air was warm and the sky a deep, rich blue, the big house filled with soft light soon after sunrise. It was the kind of light painters called "wet," the light diffused by salt water. At the end of the day when the sun dropped behind the mountains west of the village, the sea in front of the house turned colors, from a soft blue to a darker blue, and then darker still as the sun disappeared and the jealous sky reluctantly let go of the glorious light. With all the windows open on hot afternoons and a breeze off the

Mediterranean, Bill and Tess could sit almost anywhere in the house and smell the salt in the air and tell each other how lucky they were. They had both been born landlocked—he in the American Midwest, she in Austria. The sea was a marvel.

On some mornings, seated in front of his typewriter, Shirer listened to Andres Segovia practicing his guitar on the far side of the big house. The soft chords, filtered through the house's thick walls, pleased Shirer. Hearing Segovia play reminded Shirer of nights in Vienna, when he and Tess had gone to concerts to hear a Mozart work and, when it was over, moved almost to tears, had jumped to their feet and shouted and clapped their hands. Shirer acquired his love of music from his mother, who on afternoons in the living room of her house in Cedar Rapids, Iowa, sat enraptured in front of her radio listening to the opera broadcast from New York City.

"Had so much grand music on the radio today," she wrote her son one day. "Do not know as I can come down to earth enough to write. Heard three symphony concerts. Sunday is the greatest day for grand music…We get a full opera broadcast from the N.Y. Metropolitan. I just could not exist in this place if it were not for the radio."

Shirer felt lucky to have discovered the village and the house and thought it a stroke of good fortune when the Spanish guitarist rented one side of the villa to enjoy the summer months on the Costa Brava. A small fishing village, Lloret de Mar hugged the Mediterranean Sea north of Barcelona, its back to the mountains that pushed north to the Pyrenees and the high, rugged frontier with France.

Unwilling to impose on Shirer and disturb his daily writing ritual, Segovia had told him he would practice as far away from him as he could. Shirer appreciated the kindness. Truth be told, he did not mind at all, nor did the guitar disturb him as he sat at the desk trying to write a future for himself. The three-story seaside house at Calle de San Bartolome 14, a double-sided villa with high ceilings and large rooms and a kind of shabby gentility, was big enough for both of them.

Bill and Tess had found the village, with its population of three thousand, by accident and then lucked out when the house was available. It was far too big for them, but it was cheap, the rent just $15 a month, its owner a doctor in Barcelona to whom Shirer had taken an instant liking. The year he hoped they could spend productively in the village would cost them a few hundred dollars a month, at most. They had less than $1,000 when they arrived soon after stepping off a ship that had brought them from the Italian coast. Hoping for the best, Shirer had paid the landlord the full year in advance, so he knew they would have a roof over their heads until April 1934. He gave himself twelve months to gain some traction on his writing goals. If he failed, he would have to begin aggressively looking for another reporting job.

He was well into a novel and a stage play about India. One of the characters was Gandhi, whom Shirer had met two years before. He posted query letters to New York editors nearly every week. He could not have been busier, but it was the busyness of a man anxiously looking for direction and so far not finding it. Still, he kept to his daily routine: at his desk from 8:00 A.M. until early afternoon, then sitting on the beach with Tess and Segovia or other friends like John and Frances Gunther if they were in town, reading from a bag of books he had assembled before they arrived. Evening found them having supper in the house, often freshly caught fish sold by the local fishermen, and afterward sitting in the living room and listening intently to Mozart, his favorite composer. Shirer sat quietly smoking his pipe, a book or a newspaper on his lap.

The newspapers brought word of growing unrest across Spain. Shirer feared that the Republican government would almost certainly fall. In Germany, Hitler was halfway through his first year as chancellor. In America, the economy was in a shambles. Certainly his brother, John, kept him up to date on that news. Shirer knew, as his and Tess's money slowly ran out, that it would be next to impossible to find another job in journalism. So deep was his despair that he began to accept the unthinkable: he might never again work as an American correspondent based in Europe.

Some days he felt overwhelmed with the sickening weight of failure and the great fear that the life he wanted for himself had been thwarted. E. S. Beck, the managing editor of the *Chicago Tribune*, had fired him the previous October, for reasons Shirer could still not get his mind around. He believed it had something to do with his crossing the paper's imperious publisher, Colonel Robert McCormick, but in any case he'd had no success in joining the staff of another paper. Now, so much depended on his writing efforts to bring in the money they needed to get by.

"McCormick's a contemptible son of a bitch," Shirer told Tess.

*　*　*

On a warm spring day in May 1925, in Cedar Rapids, a growing city in eastern Iowa that served as the business hub for the region's farm belt, Shirer walked across the campus of Coe College on graduation day feeling confident about himself and the road that lay ahead of him. At twenty-one years of age, with a boyish face and light brown hair he often parted down the middle, Shirer acted like a much older, more worldly man, one about to step out of rural Iowa and through an open door into his future.

His four years on the campus were over, finally. While he would remain cynical in many ways about his college experience, he had had several excellent professors and he felt more than well prepared. He was buoyant, self-assured, looking out across his own horizon and seeing nothing but great promise.

Just before graduation he had borrowed $100 from his deceased father's brother, Bill, who worked on the business side of publishing in Chicago, with the goal of using it as seed money to go to Paris to look for a job on the reporting staff of an American newspaper. He was certain that, if he got there, the pieces of the life he envisioned for himself would click together. Beginning during his last years at Coe College, while he was a reporter on the campus newspaper, no place tugged at Shirer's imagination more than Paris. It was everything he wanted. On top of that, he saw no future at all for himself in Cedar Rapids, whose small-city ways had long bored him half to death and about whose leading lights, in business, politics, and religion, he had grown increasingly cynical.

Not a religious man in the formal sense—he, his sister, Josephine, his brother, John, and their mother, Elizabeth (Bessie), were Presbyterians in an overwhelmingly Protestant part of the country—Shirer nonetheless believed in the essentially Calvinist notion of fate. It was not a religious conviction as much as a profoundly personal one. He saw a role for himself in the world. He had carried with him since his teen years a strong sense of his own place and the kind of life he wanted. It was a life in large part drawn from his readings while still in high school and later in college. The adventures of the journalist John Reed had captivated him. Reed's book on witnessing the Bolshevik revolution in Russia, *Ten Days That Shook the World*, knocked Shirer for a loop. He couldn't imagine seeing what Reed saw and writing it all down in a popular book. This pivotal role of the journalist as an eyewitness to history, as a keeper of the record and a sounder of alarms, informed Shirer's view of the world.

He also had a habit from childhood of reading the Chicago newspapers, the *Tribune*, which billed itself as the "World's Greatest Newspaper," and the *Daily News*. Even before Shirer began reading newspapers on his own, his father would read stories out loud to his family, excitedly relaying the big news of the day. Everything the papers represented in a free society fascinated Shirer—from the rough-and-tumble ways of the reporters' work in a corrupt society to the images they conveyed of a writer seated at his desk in a loud, busy newsroom, typing out a story.

Shirer's reading habits and fascination with daily events came to him from his father, Seward Shirer, a Chicago federal prosecutor who involved himself in his community and read avidly in politics and history. In 1904, the year Shirer was born in the family home at 6500 Greenwood Avenue, Seward Shirer was a sergeant-at-arms at the Republican National Convention in the city. He watched as Theodore Roosevelt was nominated for the presidency. A political moderate, the senior Shirer was close to many of the city's most influential citizens, including the attorney Clarence Darrow, a champion of the poor and of the city's embattled labor unions.

Seward Shirer died on February 18, 1913, when his son Bill was eight years old, after his appendix burst and his doctors were unable to stop a severe infection from spreading through his body. His death at age forty-two forced his widow, with only the proceeds of a small insurance policy, to move with her three young children from Chicago to her parents' home in Cedar Rapids. Bessie Shirer had grown up in the city, attending an elementary school also attended by Orville and Wilbur Wright. There was considerable history on both sides of the family in Iowa. Seward Shirer had been born in 1871 on a farm in Black Hawk County, and he stayed in Iowa to attend the Methodist-affiliated Cornell College.

Years later, the young Shirer would remember stepping off the train at Union Station in Cedar Rapids with his sad mother, brother, and sister, to be greeted by his anxious maternal grandparents. The city's skyline was dominated by the grain elevators of the Quaker Oats cereal company. From the train station he could see a large sign "meant to catch the eye of the tens of thousands who passed by on the passenger trains of the four railroads: CEDAR RAPIDS SUITS ME! IT WILL YOU!"

With his mother's encouragement, Shirer again read the newspapers. He appreciated that his mother had the *Chicago Tribune* delivered to the house. That way, Shirer could keep up on developments in the city where his father had worked. As she and her husband had done in Chicago, Bessie also talked with her children about art and books and writers. It caught on with Bill. "Something in the literary ferment in Chicago, a constant subject of talk in our household as I grew up, must have brushed off on me so that a little later, in Iowa, I felt it in my bones," Shirer wrote.

The young boy read the papers closely, taking particular note of the bylined stories of the correspondents who sent in their dispatches from across Europe. Often, he spoke with his mother about the accounts of the Great War that had begun the year after the family moved to Cedar Rapids. He knew the reporters' names, read their every word, and followed battlefield developments on maps printed in the newspapers. He was enormously relieved to read one day that Paris had not fallen to the advancing Germans.

Certainly before his eighteenth birthday, when he graduated from Washington High School and enrolled at Coe College near the family's home for his freshman year, he was sure he wanted to be a part of the rarefied world of these correspondents whose lives he romanticized. As he made clear to his mother and friends, staying in Iowa after college was not an option. Chicago, maybe, but not Cedar Rapids. The world was divided between doers and phonies, and he knew what side of the line he wanted to be on.

Besides a strong desire to get away, Shirer was less than enthusiastic about the citizens of Cedar Rapids. An exception was the painter Grant Wood, who lived with his mother in a house on Fourteenth Street and later built a studio in an old barn across the street from the Shirer home. The two came from different worlds—Wood's early life was marked by extreme rural poverty—and they were more than ten years apart in age. The two saw each other occasionally in Cedar Rapids, at a time when the artist had not yet caught on, and Shirer saw him as an example of an artist pursuing his passion through thick and thin.

Because he saw himself as a budding writer and journalist whose words would one day mean a great deal, Shirer in his late teens began recording his thoughts in diaries and journals and, later, on typed sheets of onionskin paper. Like any diarist, Shirer did not know what lay ahead. A historian works in hindsight, examining a record and knowing full well what would come; a diary exists only for the moment it is written and knows nothing of the future.

Similarly, a man living in Germany, Victor Klemperer, determined to "bear witness" in his diary, could sit at his writing table on an August day in 1933—when Shirer and his wife might have been on the beach in front of their villa, happily reading and chatting—and observe without any knowledge of what lay ahead: "I simply cannot believe that the mood of the masses is really still behind Hitler. Too many signs of the opposite. But everyone, literally everyone cringes with fear. No letter, no telephone conversation, no word on the street is safe anymore. Everyone fears the next person may be an informer."

Soon after enrolling at Coe College in the fall of 1921, Shirer and other students interested in journalism fell under the spell of one of the school's brightest lights, a dedicated professor named Ethel R. Outland. She had graduated from Coe in the class of 1909, had gone east to Radcliffe to attend graduate school as had many of Iowa's brightest, and returned to teach at her alma mater. In addition to teaching classes, she oversaw the staff of the campus newspaper, the *Cosmos*, whose reporters and editors prided themselves on their independence from the school.

Photographs of Outland taken at the time show a small, serious woman, single then and for the rest of her life, who was all about her work. She was one of those professors students always remembered—dedicated, very good at her chosen field, blunt in her criticism of work she considered inferior, a grammarian who knew the rules of the language and expected everyone else to know them as well, and someone who introduced her students to the wider world available to them if they applied themselves.

"She could not stand sloppy thinking and especially sloppy writing," Shirer wrote. She read books, attended plays, was worldly in a Midwestern city not noted for its worldliness, and kept up on the news of the day locally, nationally, and internationally. For Shirer and several other students who went on to find careers in journalism, she was a transformative figure. For him, his four years at Coe would largely come down to everything he learned from Ethel Outland.

While attending classes and writing for the *Cosmos* as well as one of the Cedar Rapids newspapers, Shirer began looking ahead to his graduation in 1925. He kept in touch with Coe graduates who had found work on the staffs of newspapers around the region. A friend who wrote for an industry newspaper in Chicago called the *Manufacturer's News*, which came out every Saturday, advised Shirer to reach out to H. J. Smith, the news editor of the Chicago *Daily News*. In addition, the friend urged Shirer to write to R. J. Finnegan, the managing editor of the *Chicago Journal*, and to James P. Bicket, the news editor of the *Chicago American*. Shirer had a special connection to Bicket, who had been a good friend of his father's.

"The city editors of the Post, Examiner and Tribune I do not know," the friend wrote. "With the City News Bureau, see Mr. Walter B. Brown, manager. As you suggest, I believe you would learn more by going direct to the City News Bureau, for it would give you an opportunity to learn Chicago, from a newspaper viewpoint, which you might be expected to know at once if you made a connection with a newspaper at the start.

"My suggestion to you," the friend went on, "would be to see both Mr. Brown and Mr. Bicket anyway, and take in Mr. Smith of the News, too, for good measure. Be sure to let me know when you come up here and I will be glad to see that you get in touch with the newspaper editors in the right way."

* * *

His graduation in the spring of 1925 fresh behind him, Shirer prepared to drive out of Cedar Rapids with his uncle Bill Shirer, a flesh-and-blood connection to the father the young Shirer had barely known. He was very fond of his uncle and enjoyed his company. Bill Shirer had stayed close to his deceased brother's family, helping them when he could and driving to Cedar Rapids for family celebrations as a stand-in for Seward Shirer.

Before leaving the campus for the drive to the senior Shirer's home in Chicago, Shirer boldly approached the college president, Harry Morehouse Gage, shortly after the commencement ceremony and asked to borrow $100 to finance his trip to France. With that and $100 from his uncle, he felt confident that he would have enough to stretch out a stay in Paris for several months. To his surprise, the president quickly agreed, a sure sign to Shirer that others whose opinions he respected saw in him a young man with a bright future. He now had his bankroll.

While his first stop was Chicago, to meet newspaper editors and introduce himself as a young, promising journalist, Shirer had a far grander plan: he would head east to New York, introduce himself to people who really mattered, and from the East Coast board a ship to France. He had already made contact with the owner of a freighter that transported cattle to Europe and was promised a berth, provided he would help shovel manure overboard. A few days after arriving in Chicago, Shirer said goodbye to his uncle and set out for New York.

In the train, smoking a pipe, which made him look older and more worldly, he read a dispatch in the morning's *Tribune* filed by the paper's correspondent in Morocco, Vincent Sheean, who Shirer knew was based in the Paris bureau. Sheean's was a byline Shirer had long followed, tracking his datelines across Europe and North Africa. As the train sped east, Shirer thought about the life of these journalists, reminding himself again of the stories he had read as a teenager by the journalists in France covering the Great War.

"They had struck me as a romantic tribe, dashing from one battle to another, from one revolution to another, from one international conference to another, hobnobbing with the great who made the headlines," Shirer wrote in the first volume of his memoirs. "But their exciting world had seemed to be far beyond my chances of entering. It was so terribly distant from the placid Iowa cornfields in which I had grown up."

As the train moved east to New York, Shirer read in the newspapers sold on the platforms of the stations where the train stopped to pick up and discharge passengers the coverage of the so-called Monkey Trial, soon to be under way in Tennessee. The story seemed too absurd to be spread all over the front pages of serious papers. A high school biology teacher was to be put on trial for violating the state's anti-evolution law. It was heresy to teach that man descended over millions of years of evolution from apes. Religious fundamentalism, as Shirer saw the controversy, trumped science. The teacher, John Scopes, had been put under arrest like a common criminal.

Shirer, ever the careful reader of the press, could not get enough of the coverage. William Jennings Bryan, a man Shirer had long admired, as had his father before him, and a man who had unsuccessfully campaigned for president on the Democratic ticket, stood as the prosecutor in the case. Clarence Darrow, the fabled defender of the anarchists Leopold and Loeb and his father's friend, sat at the defense table.

As Shirer saw it, the drama unfolding in Tennessee in anticipation of the upcoming trial was reason alone to take leave of his country. "I yearned for some place, if only for a few weeks, that was more civilized, where a man could drink a glass of wine or a stein of beer without breaking the law, where you could believe and say what you wanted to about religion or anything else without being put upon, where inanity had not become a way of life, and where a writer or an artist or a philosopher, or merely a dreamer, was considered just as good as, if not better than, the bustling businessman."

The career of a friend's friend named Bill Bridges, who had graduated from a small college in Indiana and was now working on an American newspaper in Paris, was one of the stories that inspired Shirer to dream that he could find a way, somehow, to stay in France. But, once contacted, Bridges had put a damper on the fantasy, telling Shirer that the city was overflowing with American college students and experienced newspapermen looking for work. Openings were few and far between.

Shirer arrived in New York on a hot summer afternoon. He bought a copy of the *Sunday World* newspaper and scanned the headlines of the city's other papers while standing in front of bustling newsstands, the sidewalks teeming with crowds. For a week he roamed Manhattan, overwhelmed by the city's "sheer electricity." He saw a Broadway play, *What Price Glory*, about soldiers in the Great War and thought it a more honest representation of the war than the patriotic speeches and triumphant parades he had witnessed in Cedar Rapids featuring returning veterans of the trenches.

During the day he tried to talk his way past the receptionists at the *World*, the *New York Times*, and the *Evening Post*, but he never reached the newsrooms. One night he attended a party in Greenwich Village, where everyone was expecting Edna St. Vincent Millay, whom Shirer had met the year before when she came to Coe for a poetry reading and afterward spoke to a group of students. She never arrived.

At the end of the week, Shirer boarded a train to Montreal, arriving on the afternoon of July 4 and meeting a Coe College friend, George Latta, with whom he was to take the cattle boat to Europe. It was a hot, humid day, and Shirer hoped they could board the boat the following morning and begin their cross-Atlantic journey. An aspiring artist, Latta brought with him painting supplies, with the idea that he would paint until his money ran out and he had to return to the Midwest to attend art school.

They found cheap rooms to rent, and each morning went to the docks, only to be told that the boat would not be leaving as scheduled. Shirer feared they were getting the runaround. It was the same day after day, with, Shirer noticed, a growing number of other young men hoping to get on the same boat for France. He wondered if he had been taken by the ship's agent, who had already pocketed his $10 deposit.

"Morning after morning, soon after the crack of dawn, we lugged our bags on a streetcar down to the wharves only to find either that no ship was sailing or if one was we were not to be on it," Shirer wrote. " 'Tomorrow morning, for sure,' the burly agent would assure us, and wearily we would take up our suitcases, board a streetcar and return to the drab rooming house."

Careful to husband their limited resources, the pair lived off bread and cheese and ate on park benches to avoid the steaming rooms they had rented. Some days they walked over to the campus of McGill University to kill time. On July 13, Shirer had had enough.

"After nine days of waiting, we decided we had been duped," he wrote. "There was nothing else to do but go home. We rode down to the docks without our bags and asked the agent for our money back. 'Tomorrow morning for sure,' he said, but his eyes seemed shifty to me. 'And be sure you are here at six o'clock sharp,' he added as a parting shot. 'Boat sails at seven.'"

The following morning, July 14, a freighter packed with one hundred head of cattle slipped away from the wharf and floated down the majestic waters of the St. Lawrence River. Shirer and Latta began their assigned duties—feeding and watering the herd and cleaning up after it.

HIS LUCK HOLDS

When they reached Paris, Shirer and Latta found a cheap room at 85 Boulevard Port-Royal, a short walk from Montparnasse, the mythical place that had fired Shirer's imagination since he had first begun to think of going to Paris to make his way as a journalist and writer. He was overjoyed. Any reservations that had occupied his mind on the train ride from Chicago to New York, any fears that he was making a mistake, were now gone like wisps of smoke.

It was as if the twenty-one-year-old, just months out of his college, was somehow far older and far wiser in ways that were impossible for a young man from the American Midwest on his first trip to Europe to have been. He was now footloose in Paris, where not even seven years had passed since the end of the Great War, its impact seen in the young, crippled men who walked the city's beautiful streets on crutches.

Their new landlady was, like so many in her country, widowed from the war. Nearly 1.4 million Frenchmen had died between the start of fighting in 1914 and the moment the curtain was abruptly brought down on the slaughter, at the eleventh hour on the eleventh day of the eleventh month in 1918. More than four million had been wounded. The landlady's husband had died in one of the many battles on one of the many slaughter fields. Alsace and Lorraine, taken by the Germans after the French defeat in the Franco-Prussian War just two generations earlier, had been returned by the terms of the Armistice, carried out in a railroad car in the French village of Compiègne.

In large part, Shirer and his good friend felt at home in their rented room because others from Cedar Rapids, and even from Coe College, had stayed in the very same place. Teachers from Coe had stayed in the rooming house while on sabbaticals. Shirer and the landlady could exchange familiar names. Their first nights in Paris, Shirer and Latta strolled the Boulevard Montparnasse, stopping for dinner at small restaurants where a fine meal could be had for a few American cents. They were surprised to discover the restaurants filled with young Americans, many speaking with Midwestern accents. The two men were awed by everything around them. Once, seated at a streetside café filled with Americans, they spotted the dancer Isadora Duncan.

They drank wine with their meals and had after-dinner drinks and late-night coffee and cognac and were soon joining in conversations with perfect strangers and introducing themselves as a writer and an artist. From guide-books bought in bookstores, the pair sought out the city's great sights. Shirer had brought with him some recommendations. Grant Wood had studied the artistry of stained glass windows on a visit to Paris and told Shirer to make sure to see the windows in a number of cathedrals. They visited the Louvre, pausing, Shirer wrote, "like all the other tourists, before the obvious things, the Winged Victory, the Venus de Milo, the Mona Lisa, the paintings of Rembrandt, Titian, Giorgione, Caravaggio, Van Dyke, Rubens."

Each new day in Paris was a blessing. Whether seated on a bench near the Arc de Triomphe watching the pedestrians, riding the Metro, or gawking at the "ribbons of light [that] ran up the Eiffel tower," Shirer felt he had arrived in the center of the universe. Every day he felt more and more certain that he was where he should be and that, somehow, he would find a way to make it last.

*　*　*

After settling down at the end of his first week in Paris, Shirer set out to look for a job. His hope was to find something on one of the two American newspapers in Paris, the *New York Herald* and the *Chicago Tribune*. He quickly learned after short trips to the papers' city rooms that there were no jobs at all. One of the editors at the *Herald*, Eric Hawkins, went so far as to show Shirer a folder filled with applications. There were maybe a thousand names in the file, Shirer guessed.

"I'm sorry," Hawkins said as they sat in his office crowded with stacked newspapers and file folders. "But I don't see the slightest chance for you."

David Darrah, the editor at the *Tribune*, wrote down Shirer's name but offered no hope that a job would open up. There were just too many names. Shirer took note of his journalistic shortcomings: "Editor of a small college paper. Two summers on a small-town daily. French inadequate. Age twenty-one." There was one conclusion: it was hopeless.

With this in mind, Shirer counted his money, calculating how many more days or weeks he could afford to stay in Paris and still make it back to Cedar Rapids with pennies to spare. The goal had always been to hold out for two months. He resigned himself to the knowledge that he had never really believed he could stay in France and work as a journalist. Latta, unlike Shirer, had never thought of staying permanently in France. However long his money would last, he vowed, he would paint and get better at his art—and then go home. He was here to learn, not to dream of the impossible. So each day Latta would leave Shirer and go off and paint. At nights in their room he would often write his fiancée back home and, it seemed to Shirer, look askance at Shirer's nightly trips out into the city to meet and talk to people and finish off the day with a drink or two.

On one of those nights, Shirer found himself in a cabaret off the Boulevard Saint-Michel, hoping to meet a woman with whom he could spend time and take the edge off his loneliness. He met several women and danced with them, inviting them back to his table in a far corner of the club. He quickly discovered they were prostitutes, "rather too coarse and too willing."

With only so much money in their pockets, Shirer and Latta arrived at their last night or two in Paris. They would soon have to retrace their steps back to the coast and find a freighter to take them to Montreal. They had enough francs for a night on the town, including a trip to the Folies Bergère, where the entertainer Maurice Chevalier was to perform. Drinking champagne at each stop, they moved from cabaret to cabaret, arriving back at their boardinghouse as a new day was dawning over Paris. They would pack up their few belongings in the morning.

Reaching their room, Shirer spotted an envelope addressed to him under the door. Too tired and too drunk to read it, he washed up and sat on the bed. When he bent to pick it up, he saw on the envelope the imprint of the *Chicago Tribune*, 5 Rue Lamartine, Paris. By the address was a scrawled name: Darrah.

> *Dear Mr. Shirer:*
> *If you still want a job, would you be kind enough to come*
> *in to see me some evening about nine?*
> *David Darrah*

It was far too good to be true. He read it out loud to Latta, thinking perhaps his brain had mangled the words and that what it really said was something far different.

"You're not going to take it, are you, this last second when we're all set to go home?" Latta said. Shirer watched as Latta nonchalantly packed his belongings.

"You think I'm going to give up a chance like this?" Shirer asked.

"It doesn't sound like a very definite offer to me."

Excited, Shirer said, "I'm going to take a chance on it."

"It'll be a shock to Eleanor if you stay," Latta said, referring to Shirer's Coe College girlfriend, whom he had left behind in Iowa.

"If I get the job, I'll send for her."

His mood suddenly somber, Latta could not believe he was leaving and his friend staying. "He finished packing in silence, and I paced the room, brandishing the letter, rereading it and savoring the miracle of its coming at this very last moment," Shirer wrote.

When Latta finished packing, Shirer accompanied him to the Gare du Nord to meet his train for the coast. The whole way there, Latta argued that Shirer was making a fundamental mistake in not returning to Iowa. Shirer shook it off, confident in his ability to choose his own path. Returning to the rooming house, he tried to sleep. His head pounded and his stomach churned from the effects of drinking late into the night on what was to have been his last night in Paris. He was far too excited to sleep. So he cleaned up and dressed in his best clothes and set off for the *Tribune* offices on the Rue Lamartine. He walked through the Luxembourg Gardens and set off down the Boulevard Saint-Michel, stopping at newsstands to read the Paris dailies and the latest edition of the *Tribune*. He didn't want to sound like an uninformed idiot in the newsroom and give Darrah an excuse not to hire him.

At almost 8:00 P.M. he stopped at a small café for a light dinner. He found himself too nervous to eat, so he caught the Métro to the station nearest the *Tribune* building. He was early, so he walked around the block a few times until 9:00 P.M. sharp, when he climbed the stairs to the newsroom on the crowded third floor.

Darrah sat at a small desk in a corner of the newsroom, where the copydesk editors, recently arrived for work, had already set up, the air over their heads swirling with thick clouds of tobacco smoke. Darrah, busily supervising the work going on around him, asked Shirer if he had any experience on a copydesk. Yes, Shirer answered, two years. It was a fib, certainly, since his copyediting experience was confined to a short period when he was the editor of the *Cosmos*, his work supervised by Edith Outland.

"How's your French?" Darrah asked.

It was poor, he told Darrah. He'd have to work on it.

"The pay isn't much," Darrah said. "Twelve hundred francs a month. That's only sixty dollars."

A month, Shirer told himself silently. "It came to fifteen dollars a week, I quickly calculated. I had made fifty dollars a week on the hometown newspaper," he wrote.

"I guess I can get by on that," Shirer said.

He knew that this was no time to argue over money. He was being given a great gift, and he was bright enough to know it and to show his gratitude. Darrah thought for a long, silent moment. Around them copy editors ran pencils over sheets of paper and puffed on cigars and pipes. The room looked like a steam pipe had burst.

"When can you start?" Darrah asked.

"Right away," Shirer said.

One of the first editors on the copydesk to introduce himself to Shirer was James Thurber, "a lanky, owl-eyed man with thick glasses" who introduced Shirer to everyone else. Another one of the editors was Elliot Paul, a budding novelist. Two others were poets. "There was an Englishman who spoke in a thick Oxford accent and seemed rather learned; an Irishman with an equally thick brogue and a jaunty lilt of speech who told me during the evening that he and his novels were banned in Ireland," Shirer wrote.

When the copydesk broke up in the wee hours of the morning, Shirer, Thurber, and a group of others walked out into the night, crisscrossing the city, moving from bar to bar. Before dawn, Shirer found his way back to his room, now empty of George Latta's belongings. Beaming with joy at his great luck, Shirer tried to fall asleep, anxiously looking forward to returning to the newsroom the following evening.

* * *

The city was a thriving colony for American expatriates, artists, and writers, would-be and accomplished. The real and the pretenders were all at home. Shirer could hardly get his fill of it. Some of his colleagues on the *Tribune* night copydesk dropped names of writers they had met in bars or cafés. Thurber told Shirer of the young American writer Ernest Hemingway, who had come to Paris as a foreign correspondent and was working on a novel.

"Most of the American writers on the Left Bank, one soon learned, merely talked of writing—they were going to get down to serious work on 'the book' next week or next month, but they never did; they never got beyond sitting on café terraces and at bars—but Hemingway, everyone said, worked hard and took his writing with deadly seriousness," Shirer wrote.

Along with two other copydesk editors, Shirer one night ran into Hemingway at a small café called the Closerie des Lilas. "He was sitting with Ezra Pound, of whom I was somewhat in awe since he already had a reputation as one of the best American poets and he was only the second great poet, after Edna Millay, I had ever met," Shirer wrote, recalling the reading Millay had conducted at Coe College.

"Hemingway did not join in the discussion," he wrote.

Somewhat to my surprise, after all I had heard of him, he did not look or talk much like a writer. He was big and athletic, with a ruddy complexion and bright, lively eyes. Turning to me he began to talk of sports: the six-day bicycle races at the Velodrome d'Hiver, the fights at the Cirque de Paris and a new French middleweight boxer he thought might make it, the tennis and Suzanne Lenglen, the graceful, vivacious French champion.

He was playing a lot of tennis, he said, and doing even more boxing—he was even trying to teach Ezra Pound the art—and when he ran out of amateurs he took on the pros at a nearby gymnasium where he could pick up ten francs a round sparring with them before their fights. I wondered how he found time to write. He said not a word about writing, which I was hoping he would, for like most of the young Americans in Paris I was already trying to write poems and short stories and finding it more difficult than I had anticipated.

Some nights after work, Shirer shook off invitations to go out with colleagues and instead retreated to his room to write letters to friends back in Cedar Rapids. One friend, with whom Shirer had attended Washington High School and Coe College, was Charles Simon. Seated at a typewriter in his room, Shirer wrote Simon long letters, stopping mid-letter sometimes and leaving the paper in the typewriter as a reminder. Some letters he started while still in the newsroom, when his work had slowed and he was waiting to translate another cable from the French news service.

In one of his letters to Simon, Shirer explained his daily routine. "I have resigned myself to the simple life of reading four hours per day, studying French two, working six, eating and drinking and sleeping the rest," he wrote. He explained that his life was such that he had not "achieved a good drunk since embarking from the prairies of Iowa. Two or three times in Paris I have had enough good vin rouge in me to produce a feeling that life was worth living but never was as I used to be in C. R. and never have I worried over whether I was to wake up next morning and find myself blind."

He explained to Simon how hard it was to improve his French, and he mentioned the difficulty of translating a French wire dispatch about a storm that had ravaged Brittany "into the hard boiled English newspaper style." Then he went on to explain how great the bookstores in the city were. "Paris is loaded with bookstores and occasionally you find English translations at cheap prices," he wrote. "This afternoon, for instance, I ran into a Ruskin and also a Dostoievsky (*Crime and Punishment*) in a little shop by the Sorbonne and got both of them for 10 francs. Also there is an American library here which has a few fair books. So I am pursuing Mencken's *Prejudices*. . . . But in the meantime my mind seems a blank, that is, a blank as far as self expression, writing, for instance, is concerned. I have almost forgotten many of the ideas I cherished as a radical back on the steppes."

In his letters, Shirer talked politics, expressing reservations about Woodrow Wilson's noble experiment, the League of Nations. Shirer doubted that it would do any good at keeping war in Europe from erupting again, as if the Great War had ended on false pretenses, to be picked up at a later date.

"Up north of Paris to the Rhine you will find all the restaurants clogged with French officers poring over military maps while the French annual military maneuvers are held in that territory," he wrote Simon. "They speak continually of the next war here and the Frenchmen seem to admit that it is only a question of time, only a question of how long the Germans can be kept down by the French. But the French are determined that it will be fought on German territory and the Germans in the Rhine country know it and they seem resigned to the fact that it will come eventually."

One day at lunchtime, Shirer found himself in a restaurant where he spotted James Joyce, who had stopped in after a visit to the nearby bookshop owned by Sylvia Beach. Hoping to talk about writing, he walked over to Joyce's table and introduced himself as a journalist on the staff of the *Chicago Tribune*. To Shirer's disappointment, the two exchanged little more than hellos, but Joyce extended to Shirer an invitation to a reading in the backroom of Beach's Shakespeare and Company bookstore.

In his first few months in Paris Shirer had met the best journalists working in the city, along with artists, writers, and performers he encountered in the cabarets and in restaurants late at night. F. Scott Fitzgerald stumbled into the newsroom one night and drunkenly said, "Come on, boys. Let's get out the goddamned paper."

Seated at his desk, James Thurber made the introductions. *The Great Gatsby* had recently arrived in Paris's bookstores, and Thurber had earlier lent Shirer his copy of the novel. Shirer loved the book and was now face to face with the author, who was well into a state of momentous drunkenness. As Shirer and the other copydesk editors worked, Fitzgerald loudly sang songs.

* * *

After giving up his room in the boardinghouse, Shirer looked for a more comfortable place in which to live. The crowded rooming house had been fine for a while, but now, settled in as a working journalist with a regular paycheck, however small, Shirer wanted better. He found what he was looking for when he rented a room in the Hotel de Lisbonne. Other staffers on the *Tribune* had recommended the hotel, and a number of them also lived there.

"The rooms were rather spacious," he wrote. "In each was a large writing table and a bookcase well lit by French windows that extended from the floor to the high ceiling, a comfortable double bed, a dresser, a washbasin beneath a large mirror, and the inevitable bidet, which had to serve as a bathtub since there was no bathroom in the place. The wallpaper was atrocious in its loud, clashing colors and sentimental designs that jarred the daylights out of you until you stopped noticing it. Old and somewhat dilapidated as it was, the hotel had one modern convenience: central heating. The trouble was that it seldom went on, but when it didn't you could stir up some heat in a fireplace that burned coal."

Any homesickness Shirer may have felt reading letters from home disappeared during his first year. He was busy and found his work challenging; he was learning new skills, which thrilled him, and meeting fascinating people, and all in a society that encouraged creativity and freethinking. On a spring day in 1927, he sat in the amphitheater at the Sorbonne and heard H. G. Wells go on about the sad state of the world and the human race. He said only an elite class could save humanity, a notion that Shirer found absurd and bordering on the fascist.

The American Correspondent

At the beginning of Shirer's second year at the *Tribune* in 1926, he moved from the night desk to work dayside as a reporter. There were approximately twenty reporters on the paper's local desk and several more on the foreign staff, whom Shirer seldom saw. He knew that Henry Wales, the paper's bureau chief, only rarely plucked one of the local reporters from out of the mix and anointed him with a foreign assignment. Shirer didn't think Wales had any regard for him, so the likelihood of his moving into that world appeared distant.

Shirer's main focus was the city's large American colony, about twenty-five thousand strong. He covered talks and luncheons at the American Club, the nexus of US business interests in the city, but also dozens of other American-affiliated organizations, from the Rotary Club to the American Legion. The year's big event for the American Club was its Fourth of July dinner, a prestigious event that drew the biggest figures in French political, military, and cultural life. Less than a decade had passed since American troops had helped end the Great War, and a spirit of gratitude remained strong. At one of the Club's Fourth of July events, Shirer stood in awe of Henri-Philippe Pétain, a hero of the Great War.

Also among Shirer's reporting responsibilities was covering the large numbers of American tourists who came each year to Paris. That part of his beat he loathed, but he loved covering sports, particularly tennis, which the French dominated. The French newspapers gave heavy coverage to the tennis star Suzanne Lenglen, who had recently played and defeated the American

Helen Wills at a match on the Riviera that Thurber had covered for the *Tribune*. For the next few years, Shirer covered tennis in France and Britain, as well as the British Open golf championship, the 1928 Winter Olympics in Saint-Moritz, and the summer games in Amsterdam that same year.

Somewhere while he was reporting, or perhaps in the *Tribune* newsroom, he met a Parisian woman named Yvonne. She was, he recalled breathlessly, "chic, sophisticated, witty, bursting with energy and animation, and yet underneath rather contemplative, full of wonder about life, exhaustively curious about it but always skeptical, and determined to make the best of it that she could." She had black hair and dark eyes "that flashed and blazed and danced and laughed, but that also had some inexpressible depth that on occasion would indicate sadness and sorrow. It was her eyes that overpowered me from the first glance and remained forever a wonder and a mystery."

She was a freelance journalist and, at twenty-seven, five years Shirer's senior. He came unhinged when she told him she was married. She wanted both her husband and Shirer. The entire concept was over his head, but he wasn't able to pull away from her. She served as a fixer of sorts for other correspondents in the city, helping to arrange interviews and setting up appointments. She occasionally worked for Hemingway typing papers and answering his mail. She was the kind of woman—smart, pretty, dedicated to their common craft and to living the life she wanted, regardless—who Shirer sought out and fell hard for. In every category imaginable, as Shirer saw it, she was the complete opposite of every young woman he had known at Coe College. That she wanted to be with him made him feel that he had become a different sort of man from the wide-eyed American who had arrived in Paris fresh out of college.

Several times they left the city for weekends in the country. They went to the Alps together, and she traveled with Shirer when he was on assignment. He pushed her to divorce her husband and marry him. She refused. Then, abruptly, she changed her mind, but by then Shirer had found the strength to quit the relationship. Writing about Yvonne a half-century later, Shirer still gushed over her, unable through the years to completely shake her from his mind.

*   *   *

Around Shirer during the late 1920s were reminders that men with great talent were wrestling with how to achieve their goals. James Thurber, then in his mid-thirties, complained often to Shirer that he was getting nowhere as a novelist. Another one of the influential people in Shirer's life who was looking for personal direction was Grant Wood. He had been to Paris before to paint, and to Germany and Italy, but had always returned to Cedar Rapids. During

Shirer's second summer in Paris, Wood returned, funded with money he had borrowed from a real estate broker in Cedar Rapids. While Shirer worked at the *Tribune*, Wood went off and painted, and after several weeks he had enough paintings to arrange a show at a gallery in Paris.

When the show ended that summer of 1926, Wood and Shirer met in a restaurant, where Wood said he was so discouraged about his talent that he wasn't sure it was worth continuing to work at it. "Everything that I've done up to now [is] wrong," Wood said. Wood went on to denounce the French paintings he'd completed during his stay as revealing little talent on his part.

"All those years wasted because I thought you couldn't get started as a painter unless you went to Paris and studied, and painted like a Frenchman," he said. "I used to go back to Iowa and think how ugly it all was. Nothing to paint. And all I could think of was getting back here so I could find something to paint—those pretty landscapes that I should have known Cézanne and Renoir and Monet and the others had done once and for all."

Trying to cheer up his friend, Shirer said that Picasso was painting in the city, and Wood countered that it hardly mattered because the artist was a genius. "Maybe you'll be one," Shirer said. Then Wood said something that Shirer remembered decades later, re-creating a conversation that sounds too pat to be true.

"Listen. Bill. I think…at last…I've learned something. At least, about myself. Damn it…I think you've got to paint…like you have to write…what you know. And despite the years in Europe, here and in Munich and the other places, all I really know is home, Iowa. The farm at Anamosa. Milking cows. Cedar Rapids. The typical small town, alright. Everything commonplace. Your neighbors, the quiet streets, the clapboard homes, the drab clothes, the dried-up lives, the hypocritical talk, the silly boosters, the poverty of…damn it, culture…and all the rest. You know it as well as I. You grew up there, too."

"I got away," Shirer said.

"I'm going home for good," Wood announced. "And I'm going to paint those damn cows and barns and barnyards and cornfields and little red schoolhouses and all those pinched faces and the women in their aprons and the men in their overalls and store suits and the look of a field or a street in the heat of summer or when it's ten below and the snow piled six feet high."

Shirer did not fail to see the importance of the revelation as it applied to his own life. "Though I could not know it for sure, when we finally broke up after midnight, Grant had that August evening arrived at the great turning point of his life, as an artist," he wrote. "No doubt his decision had been simmering in him all summer. I'm sure he had talked it out with others, too—undoubtedly with a friend of his from Iowa, John Reid, a Cedar Rapids businessman, who was in Paris that summer and spent much time at the gallery during the exhibition.

"Later, Grant told me that on reaching home that year he had gazed at his mother standing to greet him at the door of his studio in the loft of the old coach house of the Turner mortuary. She was wearing a familiar green apron with jagged edges and at her neck an old cameo he had brought home to her once from Italy. Behind the wrinkled, weather-beaten face was a great radiance. He hastily made a sketch. Strange, he thought, that he had never seen in her a subject for a serious portrait."

* * *

Now a working reporter, Shirer began meeting other correspondents who were covering news across Europe. A number who were based in Berlin came to Paris on various assignments, and Shirer sought them out. Some of these journalists—Sigrid Schultz, who also wrote for the *Chicago Tribune*, Edgar Mowrer of the *Chicago Daily News*, and two others, H. R. Knickerbocker and Dorothy Thompson of the *New York Evening Post*—were very knowledgeable about German politics.

From where they watched events, these journalists wondered how long the Weimar Republic could possibly hold itself upright. When it fell, what would take its place? Under the assaults of economic turmoil, staggering inflation, and increasing violence, along with the growth of Far Right, nationalistic, deeply anti-Semitic political parties, the government seemed to tip ever more ominously toward collapse.

The journalists working in Germany whom Shirer met at this time saw events unfold before them. An unsuccessful putsch promoted by army officers in the winter of 1920 had given way to a sharp diminishment of the parties that formed the Weimar government in favor of conservatives and nationalists. Assassinations and terror tactics by the Far Right increased through the early 1920s. In 1922, Foreign Minister Walter Rathenau, a Jew, was murdered, while the year before an attacker had thrown acid in the face of former Chancellor Philipp Scheidemann.

A second effort to topple the government, known as the Beer Hall Putsch, had occurred in Munich in November 1923, this one led by Adolf Hitler and a group of Nazi Party loyalists. It had failed miserably, and Hitler and other leaders were jailed. Soon the myth of the putsch would become far more powerful than what had actually occurred, with Hitler as the centerpiece of the heroic narrative. At the time, the party had just fifty-five thousand members; that number would increase dramatically as the German economy hit bottom and inflation ruined the lives of everyday citizens.

Watching events unfolding in Germany from Paris, Shirer could only speculate on what lay ahead for Europe. He loved his encounters with these correspondents, seeing in them the personification of the journalists whose coverage of the Great War had been such a big part of his teenage years in Cedar Rapids when he sat on the living room floor staring at the battlefield maps printed in the newspaper. Shirer had grown especially fond of Sigrid Schultz, who spoke German fluently. Listening to her when she visited Paris was to understand how a journalist living in a foreign capital, covering a hostile government, could still do her job.

Talking to Schultz and the others who visited Paris, including the Moscow-based correspondent for the *New York Times*, Walter Duranty, and the *Chicago Tribune's* Floyd Gibbons, who had reached the status of legend for his coverage of the Great War (in which he had lost an eye and had worn a black eye patch since), reinforced in Shirer the long-standing goal of working as a foreign correspondent. He knew he would need the *Tribune's* Paris bureau chief to make it happen. As much as he liked interviewing Americans living in Paris, such as Isadora Duncan and Gertrude Stein and her partner Alice B. Toklas, this wasn't the kind of journalism he wanted to practice.

There were still important stories to cover, as when rioting broke out in Paris over the executions in America of the anarchists Sacco and Vanzetti, and the huge celebrations and the parade in the city to mark the tenth anniversary of the arrival of American troops in France as the Great War was entering its decisive, final year. For the parade, thousands of American soldiers marched down the Champs-Élysées, and Shirer spent several days covering their activities.

Hoping to make the move from a reporter on the *Tribune's* Paris staff to a foreign correspondent answering to an editor in Chicago, Shirer knew he needed events larger than the ones he had been covering in order to showcase his talents. His moment came on the afternoon of May 20, 1927, when a cable arrived in the *Tribune's* office with a startling announcement. The American Charles Lindbergh had, early that morning New York time, taken off from a grass strip on Long Island to begin a cross-Atlantic journey in his airplane, the *Spirit of St. Louis*. Shirer, preparing to cover a tennis match, quickly filed a story about Lindbergh's poor prospect for success and, realizing there was nothing he could do but wait out the news, went to the match, where five thousand people had gathered to watch the American Bill Tilden play a Frenchman, René Lacoste. Shirer ran into the American ambassador to France, who said he had heard about Lindbergh's flight.

Periodic updates throughout the afternoon and into the evening had the *Spirit of St. Louis* spotted near Newfoundland. The *Tribune's* managing editor, Bernhard Ragner, told Shirer he could cover the landing in Paris—if there was one—but only as the back-up to a more experienced reporter, Jules Frantz.

That night in the newsroom, Shirer and other staff writers studied maps in an attempt to figure out just where Lindbergh's path would take him. The bureau chief, Henry Wales, knew that if Lindbergh actually reached

Paris, it would be impossible for them to get their copy across the wires by either Western Union or the standard Press Wireless Service because everything would be jammed. He suggested they use another, less used service, Commercial Cable.

Instead of returning to the office to type out a story and then handing it off to a messenger who would take it through traffic to either Press Wireless or Western Union, where it would be typed out again for transmission, Wales would "install himself at the cable head in the Rue des Italiens and feed his stuff in short takes directly to the telegrapher with a direct line to Chicago." Wales ordered Shirer to "get the hell over to Commercial Cable and give me a hand" as soon as he could.

The next morning, a Saturday, Shirer returned to the office to monitor any cables to see if Lindbergh's plane had been spotted. A floor below him, in the offices of *Le Petit Journal*, the French reporters thought the lack of news was a bad sign. Still, the morning's French newspapers, Shirer thought, sounded optimistic that Lindbergh would make it. If he did, he might land in Paris sometime around midnight.

The day was beautiful, warm and sunny. The chestnut trees were in bloom, "their scent filling the balmy air." To kill time he went out again to watch the tennis, but he soon spotted activity in the American ambassador's box. When Shirer went to investigate, he was told the *Spirit of St. Louis* had been spotted over Ireland.

"I glanced at my watch," Shirer wrote. "It was a few minutes past 4 P.M. At a hundred miles an hour, Lindbergh could be here by ten, an hour after dark."

Back at the newsroom, Wales announced that Lindbergh had been spotted over Plymouth, England. "Let's get going!" Wales shouted, and he, another *Tribune* reporter, Jay Allen, and Shirer ran out into the street to hail a cab to take them to the airfield.

"Hardly had we got beyond the Porte de la Villette on the northeast edge of the city before we ran into a traffic jam such as none of us had ever seen before," Shirer wrote. "Ahead of us lay a solid line of cars, bumper to bumper, barely moving up the narrow two-lane road."

All the taxis and privately owned cars in Paris seemed to be heading to the air strip at Le Bourget. Giving up, the three men jumped out of the cab and "joined a sea of people who were making it on foot. By the time we got to the terminal, the largest crowd I had ever seen surrounded it and spilled off on the field beyond. It must have numbered more than one hundred thousand and before long, according to police estimates, it would reach close to half a million."

The three reporters pushed their way into the terminal and went to wait at the bar, where Shirer spotted Isadora Duncan drinking champagne and standing with a group of others who had managed to talk their way past the police. Some in the large crowd predicted Lindbergh would never make it—reports that he had been seen over Ireland or England had to be false.

Outside, as ten o'clock approached, Wales and Shirer stood by the landing lights. They heard a plane overhead. "A small searchlight picked it up," Shirer wrote. The *Spirit of St. Louis* dropped through the darkness, turned, and "came in gracefully between the runway floodlights, touching ground about two hundred yards from us. I glanced at my watch. It was 10:24 of May 21." As the plane's wheels hit the grass, a sea of people pushed past the police and a few soldiers and rushed toward the plane. It was so sudden, and with the plane's propeller still turning, Shirer thought someone would get killed. The plane stopped directly in front of Shirer and Wales.

A mob of people swarmed the plane, some pulling off pieces of fabric. A French airman jumped up on the wing and, reaching into the cockpit, "took Lindbergh's helmet from his hand and tossed it to the frantic crowd. Hundreds of screaming men and women tried to snatch it." While the crowd's attention was momentarily diverted, two French airmen pulled Lindbergh out of the cockpit and into a nearby car, and he was driven to a military hangar on the far side of the field. Jay Allen pushed his way across the field in an attempt to reach the hangar and interview Lindbergh, while Wales and Shirer set out for Paris. The road was a solid mass of parked cars.

"Willie, we've got to hoof it," Wales said. "I know some shortcuts." The two men ran down a narrow lane until they found a taxi heading back into Paris. They gave the driver a thousand francs to get them back to the city as quickly as he could.

The taxi dropped Wales off at the Commercial Cable office, while Shirer went on to the *Tribune* office to file a story for the local edition and to pick up any cables on the dramatic landing as well as early editions of the Parisian newspapers. When he reached his desk, Shirer learned that the earlier plan to have Frantz write the story had fallen through—Frantz was nowhere to be found—so Shirer was given the assignment. He quickly finished and headed back to the Commercial Cable office to assist Wales.

"Feed me all you can," Wales said. "And when you've finished get on the phone and find out where the hell the guy is. Allen should know by now." As Wales typed out the cable, Shirer handed him typed pages of his own.

Well after midnight, Allen phoned to say Lindbergh had made his way to the American ambassador's residence, where reporters were prevented from talking to him. Lindbergh was too exhausted to be interviewed. Angrily, Wales shouted into the phone for Allen to find some way to get to Lindbergh, even if he had to break into the building and push his way into Lindbergh's bedroom.

A few minutes later, to the surprise of the reporters who had mobbed the embassy, Lindbergh invited a dozen of them up to his room for a brief conversation. He'd been unable to sleep, he explained. As soon as Lindbergh stopped speaking, Allen raced to the Commercial Cable office to type out his report.

An hour before dawn, a cable came back from Chicago saying their stories had beaten the other wire services. Wales, exhausted, took Shirer and Allen to a nearby café for coffee and croissants. He praised Shirer for his work.

"Maybe I can find room for you," Wales said.

*   *   *

For some time, Shirer's stories had caught the eye of Colonel Robert McCormick, the *Tribune's* publisher, who was a close reader of his paper and a careful monitor of its tone and his editors' story choices. He had political issues he favored and many he loathed, and he wasn't shy about expressing himself and enforcing his vision for the newspaper. He kept a particularly sharp eye on the foreign coverage and the correspondents who filed stories. He was as suspicious of his correspondents as he was of what they wrote, always on the lookout for the kinds of writing and subject matter that offended his right-leaning sensibilities. He was the kind of man who smelled rats.

The reporters and editors in Paris spoke contemptuously of the man, and Shirer had heard enough to be concerned. They all knew that McCormick, who had spent many years as a young man living in Europe, regarded himself as an expert on foreign affairs. The publisher's mother, Katrina McCormick (whose father, Joseph Medill, had gained control of the *Tribune* in the mid-nineteenth century and was a friend of Abraham Lincoln), came frequently to stay in the Ritz Hotel in Paris, where a *Tribune* staff member was assigned to look after her needs. As with the others who came into contact with her, Shirer knew her as a person who "loved France and the French, disliked the British, as did her son, and had a distinct antipathy to Japanese, Germans, Jews and Roman Catholics."

Shirer knew McCormick handpicked his foreign correspondents, and in the aftermath of the Lindbergh coverage, he had been selected to move from the Paris staff to the Chicago staff. After several years of covering news and sports across Europe, Shirer was told to staff a bureau in Vienna, where McCormick's father had served as the American ambassador. It was a city the *Tribune* publisher thought he knew something about. In giving him the assignment, Shirer wrote, McCormick had issued a stern warning: "Don't fall for all those Socialists and Communists there. And don't let all the counts and countesses take you in. I know the place. I spent some time there in my youth."

Even as he picked Shirer to open the *Tribune* bureau in Vienna, he continued to hold deep-seated suspicions that perhaps the young man was not right for the job. McCormick had seen a long-winded story of Shirer's filed from Geneva about a meeting of the League of Nations and had been sufficiently upset at what he read to circle the first paragraph with a pencil and send it along with a note to Joseph Pierson, the paper's cable editor. In the note, McCormick wrote: "This guy Shirer is as heavy as a bride's cake." On the same note, he wrote: "Sentences so long I forgot what subject was by the time I made it through [a]string of modifying adjectives, adverbs and phrases."

In Vienna, Shirer moved into a room in the Grand Hotel. Soon he was receiving a steady stream of mail from other *Tribune* correspondents, as well as from others whose paths he had crossed covering various stories during the previous three years. Letters came from Wythe Williams, the Berlin correspondent for the *New York Times*, who advised Shirer on where to eat in Vienna and what to watch out for, and John Steele, the *Tribune's* correspondent in London. The American correspondents spread across Europe represented a tight club, and Shirer needed their guidance and expertise for story ideas, contacts, and advice on how to be effective in his new assignment.

Williams, who signed his typed letters "ww," went so far as to suggest women Shirer might take out on dates. He knew Vienna well but favored Berlin for the time being. "Vienna is a fine town alright in all ways that you suggest, but from the work point of view, I am glad I am here," Williams wrote in one letter to Shirer he addressed "Mon Cher Bill Shirer." In this letter, Williams said he thought the Grand Hotel was fine—"You can get away with murder in your hotel"—but said he preferred a smaller hotel run by a Frau Sachers. "Go there for the eats—best food in Europe outside of Paris," he wrote.

If Shirer had any doubts that his work was being closely scrutinized in Chicago, they were erased with the frequent letters he received from Pierson, the cable editor. He wrote often and critically, particularly if someone in Vienna had written to the paper complaining about a Shirer story. Each complaint produced a long typed account by Shirer to Pierson explaining his reporting on the offending story and reinforcing how diligent he was.

Once settled in as the Vienna bureau chief, Shirer met the newly arrived correspondent for the *Chicago Daily News*, John Gunther. He also met Vincent Sheean, the *Tribune* correspondent whose stories he had read while traveling on the train to New York from Chicago. All three men were Chicago natives and Gunther, like Shirer, had also arrived in Europe on a cattle boat hoping to find newspaper work, ultimately landing a correspondent's position with the *Daily News*.

Shirer and Gunther quickly grew close. As Shirer wrote, "John was a big, rangy man, bursting with energy and an enormous curiosity about life and people." He was also a published novelist, a real writer, and for this reason alone Shirer was smitten. At this moment in his life, he was a bold dreamer, seeing nothing ahead but good work and fulfilled dreams, with Gunther as a mentor treading the same path.

A Hungarian journalist in Vienna, Marcel Fodor, who had befriended Dorothy Thompson when she arrived in the city for her first newspaper job with the *New York Evening Post* not long after the end of the Great War, became friends with Shirer and some of his colleagues, especially Gunther. Fodor spoke fluent English and wrote for the *Manchester Guardian*. Like Shirer and Gunther, Fodor was a talker, a man who liked to stay up all night in cafés sipping drinks and going on about current events, often with his wife, Martha, a "dark-eyed Slovak," growing impatient at his side, Shirer wrote.

Others in Shirer's circle in Vienna were Whit Burnett and his wife, Martha Foley, who both wrote for the *New York Sun* syndicate and soon began self publishing a short-story journal they called *Story;* Webb Miller and Robert Best of the United Press; and William C. Bullitt, a Philadelphia-born "debonair man of forty" who had been sent by President Wilson to the peace conference in 1918 when he was only in his twenties and, the year after, to Moscow to meet Lenin. In 1923, seven years before he met Shirer, Bullitt had married Louise Bryant, who had been the lover of John Reed, whose book *Ten Days That Shook the World* had so captivated Shirer when he first read it in Cedar Rapids. Bryant and Reed had both covered the Russian Revolution, Bryant writing a series for the *New York American*. Shirer had caught a glimpse of Bryant in Paris where she lived with Bullitt after Reed's death in Russia.

Occasionally in Vienna were Dorothy Thompson and her husband, Sinclair Lewis, who won the Nobel Prize in Literature in 1930. In Shirer's view, she was among the very best foreign correspondents in Europe. He rated her and Sigrid Schultz as the two best female correspondents working anywhere. The couple held court at a nice apartment, where journalists, diplomats, "statesmen and what was left of the German, Austrian and Hungarian aristocracy" would regularly gather to talk politics.

That first winter in Vienna, Shirer skied in the mountains and skated in the city's many outdoor rinks when he wasn't covering stories. Spring came, and Shirer spent time with his group of regulars and, after breaking up with a Hungarian woman named Zora, "met a beautiful young Viennese girl, a budding drama critic and journalist" in her late teens named Tess Stiberitz.

Then, in August 1930, came a cable from McCormick: he wanted Shirer to go to India to write about Gandhi.

THE LONG TRAIN HOME

A few months after arriving in India, Shirer's work came to a halt. Gandhi and thousands of his followers sat in prisons across the country, and Shirer's cables back to Chicago covering the Indian political situation strained to report new developments. Worried, as always, about what the editors at the *Tribune*, and particularly McCormick, thought of his work, Shirer began looking for something else to write about that would justify his stay in India.

In October 1930, he attended a party in Bombay and, in a crowded room of Indian and British officials, was introduced to the crown prince of Afghanistan, Mohammed Zahir Khan, a haughty teenager who had been living in Paris, far from the hardships of his homeland. He was in India on his way to Kabul to celebrate his father's first year on the throne.

If Shirer could get the British to give him permission to travel to Afghanistan, he would have a story no one else was covering. There were good reasons foreign correspondents had not traveled to the country. While Afghanistan had not been stable for years, for the past year or more it had been even more unsettled. Nadir Khan had been on the throne for a year, a significant achievement in Afghanistan, and Shirer wanted to be there to cover the ceremonies.

Shirer needed British permission to travel through the Khyber Pass and permission from the Afghan authorities to go on to Kabul. Earlier that fall, he had tried without success to reach the Pass to report on the fighting between the Afghans and British and Indian troops. A new effort to win British approval would almost certainly be rejected again, so he lobbied the teenage crown prince to intervene on his behalf. The teenager, long away from his country, spoke French and very little English. Using his own French, Shirer asked if Khan would help him get a visa to travel to Kabul.

"No problem with the visa," Khan said. "I can arrange that. But with the British—that's more difficult. If you like, I can make you an official member of our party. We're already cleared to go through the Khyber."

After a train ride to Peshawar, Shirer boarded a caravan of trucks and cars to make his way to the pass. At a British checkpoint near the mouth of the Pass, the teenage prince negotiated permission for Shirer to proceed. Long caravans of camels loaded with trade goods slowly made their way through the Pass on the way to India. Shirer couldn't help but think about the adventure stories of Rudyard Kipling, but after two days on the road with the Pass still ahead of him, he failed to see any romance in the setting or the people with whom he traveled.

As they climbed higher, passing long columns of troops, they heard cannons and gunfire. Artillery pieces sat on every peak. After several hours of slow travel, they reached the Afghan border, where a sign warned Shirer that travel into the country was forbidden. In spite of that, the troops at a British outpost waved them through. Afghan troops lined the road on the far side of the border. As night fell, the caravan reached Jalalabad.

The city lay in ruins; a large palace where the caravan stopped was a mountain of rubble. Shirer tried to learn from his fellow travelers about the various Afghan tribes and their endless wars, but he could not keep the tribal names straight. Leaders were deposed so often and so violently—stoned, shot, and then whatever was left of the body hung from a pole—that Shirer could hardly come to any other conclusion but that the country was a sinkhole not worth a drop of foreign blood.

The group set up for the night in a part of the palace that still had a partial roof. "Soldiers lugged in a large wobbly table and some half-broken chairs for our simple dinner by the light of a couple of lamps, for there was no electricity," Shirer wrote. "Two orderlies spread bedrolls on the floor to sleep on. The prince apologized for the lack of plumbing, but the makeshift toilet did not bother me. It consisted of a hole in the floor in one corner of the big room in which we ate and slept."

Morning dawned hot and dusty, and after a make-do breakfast, the caravan proceeded on to Kabul, over an 8,000-foot pass where Shirer, who knew his history, recalled that a British army unit had been ambushed in 1842. They spent the next night in a tent on a hilltop above a ruined town, a company of Afghan troops posted above them. The following day they reached Kabul. In the bazaar they passed by a dozen bodies hanging stiffly from ropes, their hands tied behind their backs, their necks broken. They moved down unpaved streets, through crowds hastily assembled to greet the prince on his return to Kabul. It all seemed beyond strange—a teenage Afghan with royal pretensions who spoke fluent French waving to a crowd of tribesmen. Exhausted, Shirer found a room of sorts in a shabby hotel.

* * *

The problem with being the only Western correspondent in a far-off land, Shirer knew, was getting his stories out of the country. After all, the country was officially closed to foreign journalists; there was no infrastructure in place to assist their work, nor a body of officials whose job it was to help him or at least not get in his way. There were no telegraph lines, and no mail service that was anything but hit or miss.

Before leaving Peshawar in India, Shirer had put down a deposit at a radio station that he hoped could receive any dispatches he wrote from Kabul and wire them on to London. In Kabul he located a small radio station where he hoped he could send his stories on to Peshawar. No one at the station knew what he was talking about, but they wanted to be helpful. He wrote a lengthy account of the coronation celebrations and included with it a great deal of information about the country that few readers in America, or Europe for that matter, knew anything about. He hoped he would be able to wire it out of the country when the time came.

Over several days, he met an assortment of characters, including an American priest who was in the country to try to convert Muslims to Christianity; a deposed emir from a Central Asian country who had millions of dollars in booty and a harem and was living in squalor outside of Kabul, plotting to throw the communists out of his country; and a host of oddballs he could not imagine had any good reason to be in the country. Most came away thinking Shirer was a spy rather than a journalist.

Where it was safe, he traveled to towns around Kabul and, later that month, to the city of Paghman, where Nadir Shah had a palace. The king offered a lunch of lamb and no utensils. In the middle of the meal, the palace was attacked by mounted tribesmen with rifles, and the king and his guests fled in cars down a dirt road.

Shirer wrote a story about the interrupted lunch and, when he was back in Kabul, returned to the radio station to see if the operator could wire it to Peshawar. He said he would try. When Shirer returned the next day, the operator said he had had no success, as he could not reach anyone in Peshawar. A nightmare blossomed in Shirer's mind, in which his editors in Chicago, pushed by McCormick, came to the conclusion that their reporter in Afghanistan had fallen down on the job and should be sacked.

"Each day as I waited vainly for the Peshawar operator to receive my copy I had growing visions of suddenly becoming jobless in this out-of-the-way place, five thousand miles from my post in Vienna, nine thousand miles from home in America," Shirer wrote. "I realized I didn't have enough saved up to pay the fare back to Vienna, much less to Chicago. I would be stranded in the remotest land in all of Asia. There was no U.S. legation to appeal to for help; I could certainly not wheedle anything out of the British. The Russians had already turned down my request for a place on the plane that left Kabul for Moscow once a week."

Day after day, Shirer visited the radio station to watch the operator type out his story, hoping it would reach Peshawar. When it didn't, Shirer, more and more convinced that his head was on the block, returned to his squalid hotel room. In the room he would rewrite his dispatch, making it shorter and shorter, hoping that fewer words would get through more easily, and return the next day to the station. After four days, for unexplained reasons, the operator in Peshawar spoke into the radio and agreed to take the story. When he did, he wired it to London, which in turn wired it to Chicago. On October 20, the story ran—"in the first column on the first page," Shirer wrote.

He wanted to return to India and get back in touch with Gandhi as soon as he was out of prison and able to resume his revolution against the British. He saw several more weeks of work, then the long trip back to Vienna, where a life he had come to love—and his new friend, Tess—awaited him. Nearing the end of 1930, Shirer might have allowed himself the pleasant thought that the *Tribune* valued his services and saw his career at the newspaper on a certain and successful path. On December 29, the paper published an advertisement touting Shirer's work in Afghanistan: "Only One Correspondent, a Tribune Man, saw Nadir Khan become King!"

The copy accompanying the ad said that Shirer was the "sole representative of the world press" at the event. "Only by spreading its own writers over the world can the *Tribune* make certain of information uncolored by propaganda or external prejudice. Far flung, experienced, its staff ensures reliable news from foreign countries."

* * *

Safely back in India, Shirer resumed his customary task of writing letters to friends in Europe and America, keeping copies for his files. He wrote to his brother, John, who had graduated from Coe College in the class of 1928 and was living in Syracuse, New York. John sent his brother a copy of the Coe College *Courier*, an alumni newsletter that had been printed in November when Bill was in Afghanistan. Not one to shy away from praise, he was pleased to see his work extolled in it.

"William Shirer, '25, the only former editor in newspaper work abroad, is on the staff of the *Chicago Tribune*. He was formerly located in Paris, but his headquarters are now in Vienna. According to a recent issue of the *Tribune*, he was the sole representative of the world press at the recent crowning of a king in Afghanistan." The newsletter also mentioned Shirer's teacher at Coe, Ethel R. Outland, class of '09 and still teaching journalism, lighting candles on a cake at a school celebration.

After Shirer had returned to India, McCormick cabled him to reinforce how pleased he was with his work. One cable, addressed "Dear Shirer," read: "Your work has been very interesting." This was high praise from McCormick. By early January 1931, harsh economic conditions in America would begin to hit the *Tribune's* foreign staff. On January 9 (after Shirer had made his way back to Vienna) McCormick cabled his correspondents to tell them to cut down on expenses. Some wire services, such as the *New York Sun* Consolidated Press service, which maintained correspondents in Europe, closed up. Shirer's friend Whit Burnett lost his job. In a letter to a friend, Shirer wrote that Burnett "was left absolutely on his back with a three-month-old youngster and a wife to support." Shirer found it difficult to find stories to file; his health was failing, with complications from malaria and dysentery he'd picked up in Afghanistan. He desperately longed to get back to Vienna.

In addition to getting his good health back, returning to Austria would give him a new and important story to write. Economic conditions in the country brutalized millions of the country's citizens. Letters from friends spoke of severe hardships, both in Austria and across the border in Germany. Bread lines were common. In mid-September 1930, while Shirer was in India, elections to the Reichstag in Germany had completely recast Hitler's National Socialist German Workers Party.

Just two years earlier, votes for the National Socialists had totaled approximately 800,000, qualifying the party for twelve seats in the Reichstag, the national legislature. A year later the Depression hit Germany, sharply increasing support for the Far Right. Less than a year after that, on September 14, 1930, Hitler's party won more than six million votes, an enormous leap in voter support that qualified the Nazis for 107 seats in the Reichstag. With events in Germany changing rapidly, Shirer cabled McCormick directly to tell him of his plans to return to Vienna. He feared the publisher's answer, but to increase the chances for a "yes," he proposed returning to Austria overland, by way of Iraq, filing stories with exotic datelines the whole way. This appealed to McCormick, who cabled Shirer to return to Vienna "via Babylon." Pleased that he was going home, Shirer returned to Bombay and boarded a freighter bound for the port city of Basra.

After several days at sea, the ship reached Basra, where Shirer boarded a train to Baghdad. With stops in a place a sign said was "Ur" and in a little village in northeast Syria where he met a group of French army officers, the train eventually reached Baghdad. From there he proceeded to Kirkuk, where the line ended. Joining a party of mostly British officials, Shirer proceeded in a car caravan to Mosul. Days later he reached Istanbul.

From there Shirer boarded the Orient Express, hoping he would arrive in Vienna in time for Christmas. When the train reached Budapest, he was overjoyed to see Tess waiting on the platform in the early morning cold. "She was bundled up in a heavy winter coat but her head was bare, her face eager and beautiful in the dim light," Shirer wrote. "We fell into each other's arms. By the time we proceeded on to Vienna a couple of days later, we had decided to marry."

His Luck Holds Again

S oon after the start of the new year of 1931, Bill Shirer and Theresa Stiberitz stepped out of a taxi in front of the Rathaus in Vienna. While Tess had family in Austria, none came with her. Instead, they brought along Emil Vadnai, a mutual friend who wrote for the *New York Times*, and Vadnai's Austrian wife. They would be their witnesses when Tess and Bill stepped before the judge to recite their wedding vows. Shirer's German wasn't yet what it soon would be, and Tess prompted him when the official asked questions of both of them. Afterward the four went to Schoener's, "the best restaurant in Vienna," Shirer wrote, "for a festive lunch and champagne."

He was twenty-six years old and Tess just twenty. Overcome with the confidence he had always felt about his future, and profoundly in love, he was sure they had made the right decision. Within days of their wedding, a cable arrived from McCormick telling Shirer to return to India. The news broke both their hearts, and Shirer, knowing McCormick, felt certain he could not simply write the publisher and say he couldn't go, that he'd just gotten married. Gandhi, a growing figure on the world stage, was now out of prison, and McCormick wanted his correspondent back in India and writing about the man leading the revolution against the British.

The couple traveled to Trieste, where they boarded a passenger ship that stopped in Venice before heading to Bombay. Wanting to hold on to each other for as long as they could, they spent a day walking around the city and riding gondolas. They booked a hotel room for the night, and the next morning sadly walked back to the docks to say goodbye, neither knowing with any certainty when they would see each other again.

* * *

For ten long days, Shirer walked the deck of the freighter, reading newspapers and books, writing down his thoughts and story ideas, and planning for what he hoped lay ahead. Ever since leaving the port of Trieste, he had been thinking about India and what he would see there once he finally arrived in Bombay. He remembered it as a teeming city, unclean, smoke filled, extraordinary, packed with people and animals, vast and mysterious, its religions and customs smacking him in the face the moment he stepped off the ship.

Now, as the freighter navigated toward the Bombay docks, it hardly seemed possible that Shirer was about to step off the ship and enter this world. Once in the city, Shirer bought a ticket on the Frontier Mail for the journey to Delhi to meet Gandhi. Aboard the packed train he read the newspapers, talked to British officers sharing the train car, and prepared for his interview as best he could. Arriving in Delhi, Shirer made his way to the home of a Muslim doctor. Walking through the quiet house, he found Gandhi squatting on the floor of the verandah, spinning wool.

Shirer followed Gandhi to the Delhi train station, where a crowd of thousands surrounded the platform hoping to hear him speak. All the way to the city of Ahmedabad, as "the train crept hundreds of miles along a narrow-gauge track over the Rajputana plateau, thousands upon thousands rushed the rail stations en route and all but wrecked his dirty little compartment in their enthusiasm to get a glimpse of him…. All night long at every station stop hordes of villagers and peasants were waiting for him, swarming around the train until they found his compartment. Rail officials, police and soldiers exhorted the crowds in vain to step back so that the train might get under way. When it did manage to move, hundreds hung on the steps of the cars in order to ride on to the next stop with the Mahatma."

After months in India, while Tess was back in Vienna, Shirer worked up the courage to suggest to the publisher that he would like to leave India and get back to his new wife. McCormick's response was quick: no, stay where you are. So Shirer, frustrated and lonely, cabled Tess and asked her to take the boat from Italy to Bombay, where he would meet her. She arrived in June, when the weather was stiflingly hot, and she fell ill almost from the moment she landed. The air could not have been hotter and could not have held more moisture and less oxygen.

To help Tess acclimate, Shirer took her to higher altitudes far to the north of the country. There, feeling better, she settled down and began writing freelance travel stories for several Austrian newspapers and taking photographs. Prior to meeting Shirer, Tess had helped out in the Vienna office of the London *Daily Telegraph*. While nowhere near as experienced as her husband, Tess knew her way around journalists and how to report and write stories. She also wrote for *Drama*, a London magazine that specialized in theater coverage. At some point when she was covering the vibrant Vienna theater scene, Tess met a Viennese portrait photographer named Helene Katz, who maintained a studio at Stubenring 18, in a swank, touristy part of the city. Born into a Jewish family in Lemberg, Poland, in September 1899, Katz emigrated to Austria with her family when she was a teenager, during the ravages of the Great War. She attended a prestigious photography school in Vienna and, after opening her own studio, took portraits as well as teaching classes of her own. She soon developed a name for herself, signing her studio portraits of famous stage actors and conductors "Hella Katz." Tess no doubt learned a great deal about photography from Katz, who had a number of students.

In spite of the change in altitude and better weather conditions in the north of India, Tess soon became sick again, this time with dysentery. Shirer had, on and off, been in the grip of it too, along with bouts of malaria. Tess's condition, though, was far worse than Bill's. She had a high fever, and her body ached as if she'd taken a beating. By August, after weeks of illness, Shirer cabled *Tribune* headquarters in Chicago and, telling rather than asking, informed them that he was too ill to work and would return to Vienna. Besides, Gandhi planned to go to London for a peace conference, and the focus of Shirer's coverage in India would be gone.

On the train to Delhi, Tess collapsed. To Shirer's eye, she was "deathly ill," and an ambulance was summoned when the train reached Delhi to take her to the hospital. For days with the doctors unable to determine why she was so sick or whether they would operate, Shirer feared for his wife's life. Conditions in her room were abominable, with temperatures soaring above one hundred degrees by afternoon. The heat and humidity were more than she could bear. She found it difficult to breathe. "It was a damp, sticky, stifling heat," Shirer wrote. "I spent the whole day, from early morning until late in the evening, when the nurses asked me to leave, by her side, frustrated that there was nothing I could do except comfort her in her waking hours. The doctors seemed of little help, but they were all we had. At one juncture I proposed to take her back to Vienna. The physicians there were the best in Europe, and might save her. But the colonel-doctor said Tess was much too weak even to make the train journey to Bombay."

Finally, Tess recovered, and the couple made their way to Bombay and then by ship to Italy for the train ride north to Vienna. When they arrived in the city, they quickly packed up again and retreated to the Alps for several weeks before Shirer went off by himself to meet Gandhi in Marseille to travel with him to London for the peace conference.

* * *

In Vienna, the Shirers lived a comfortable life, with Bill traveling frequently and Tess doing occasional writing and photography assignments. The couple loved living in the city. They loved the Alps, too, and spent as much time as they could in the mountains. In the spring when the weather began to warm, Bill, Tess, and Bill's friend, John MacCormac of the *New York Times* and his wife, Molly, went on a ski trip in the Austrian Alps, where Shirer stumbled trying to avoid another skier. As he fell, the grip end of the ski pole struck his right eye, and he instantly went blind. Tess and MacCormac led Shirer down the hill to find a doctor, who "washed away the blood and bandaged my face. Vision in my left eye had come back partly. I could see blurred figures," Shirer wrote.

After two weeks in a Vienna hospital, the doctors removed the bandages. The vision in his left eye, while blurred, was better than he had hoped. But a blood clot had formed behind his right eye. "When the bandage was taken off, I could see light through it, but that was all," he wrote. "By midsummer, though not abandoning hope that someday the clot might disappear, I became reconciled to seeing through one eye."

More frequently than he would have liked, Shirer heard from editors at the *Tribune* about his work. Any sort of complaint from a reader set them off. A lawsuit against the paper had been filed by a woman named Anna Wong whom Shirer had supposedly libeled in an insignificant story about an accident in Vienna. And Shirer knew that McCormick had also fumed over a story he had written about Vienna workers. On October 16, 1932, E. S. Beck at the *Tribune*'s office in Chicago telegrammed Shirer the blunt message that he was fired. "Shirer this notification your services with Tribune terminates today October sixteenth stop you will be paid one month's salary covering to November sixteenth. E. S. Beck Tribune." Shirer read it over and over in disbelief. He dashed off a letter to McCormick, asking why he had been terminated.

"Dear Colonel McCormick: Mr. Beck's cable last night discharging me did not state any reasons for this action. Undoubtedly there were reasons, but I am not aware of them since neither you nor Mr. Beck had ever written complaining of my work, with the exception of the Anna May Wong story about which you asked an explanation without giving me the opportunity to explain. Would it be too much to ask why I was fired?"

On the same day, he wrote Beck, as he would again over the coming days and weeks, demanding an explanation. "Since your cable received yesterday did not state the reason for my discharge, may I enquire why?" Also on the same day, he wrote Sigrid Schultz, the *Tribune* correspondent in Berlin, telling her, "On the memorable day of October 16, 1932, I was fired off the greatest newspaper in the world. I know not why...." He said he and Tess would stay in Vienna for a while. "I want to master this damn language and read all the books which have been piling up these many years and hear some music."

He also wrote his friend John Steele, the *Tribune* correspondent in London, in a letter that showed, as always, that he was thinking and worrying about his future. "At 28 I cannot convince myself that I am finished yet."

In January, three months after the firing, the idea blossomed in Shirer's head that they should leave Austria and try to shake off their malaise. Now was the time for him to be the writer he wanted to be. Tess agreed with him and welcomed the change.

In a letter to his friend Nicholas Roosevelt, who worked for the US State Department, Shirer explained his and Tess's plan. "We are leaving Vienna toward the end of next month—for England or Spain, probably Spain, or at least I hope so. I don't like England. I've outlined some studies for myself, bought the necessary books and with some writing, already planned, I hope to be very busy by myself for the next twelve months. After that, there will be time to look for a job, if there are any by that time, which I doubt. . . . I don't feel lonely at all about being out of a job. There are so many of us."

Henry Wales, the Paris colleague on the *Tribune* who had given Shirer his big break on the Lindbergh coverage, had been fired months earlier while on assignment for McCormick in Asia. A number of American papers with correspondents in Europe were laying off staff. He and Tess would take their savings—a total of $1,000—and head to a place where they could live cheaply.

The same week he wrote to Roosevelt, Shirer sent off a letter to Claude R. Dawson, the American consul general in Barcelona, to ask how to find a house he and Tess could afford to rent for the next year. "We are thinking of only a simple, inexpensive house or part of one along the coast or up in the mountains that is not too primitive. . . . Are any accommodations available say, for $25.00 a month or thereabouts? And what would a good pension cost? And do you get a sirocco there and is it too hot in the summer to work? And are there malaria mosquitos?"

*   *   *

Soon after arriving in Lloret de Mar, Shirer wrote in his diary: "A little fishing village of some 3,000 souls, perched along a half-moon, wide, sandy beach between two rocky promontories. Back of us the mountains, rising gently toward the snow-capped peaks of the Pyrenees, the slopes terraced with vineyards and olive groves and tracts of cork-oak trees."

It was ideal for an out-of-work journalist who wanted to be a writer. The villa—three stories, with rental units on both sides—sat on the beach. It had ten rooms on the half the Shirers rented, "a large living room with fireplace, a spacious dining room, seven bedrooms and two baths—and there was central heating. The living room had been beautifully furnished by a Catalan painter, and the other rooms tastefully done. When the proprietor, a genial Barcelona physician and a professor on the faculty of the university medical school, told us the price would be fifteen dollars a month, furnished, we hid our pleasant surprise and promptly forked over the rent for a year, somewhat to his surprise.

At least we would have a roof over our heads for the next twelve months.... We soon calculated that, if we were careful, we had enough to tide us over to the end of the year."

In the villa, Shirer stuck to a daily routine of writing. The goal was fiction, a great novel. When his writing failed to catch the eye of a single interested editor, he pitched news stories to the New York magazines. They also failed to garner any attention. He wrote one friend, "I've finished the play on India, started a book and on off days do short stories. If nothing I write sells, I won't be the surprised one."

A letter to Shirer from his brother, John, who was then living in New Jersey, suggested magazines that might be interested in Shirer's freelance work. John Shirer volunteered to pay for a three-month subscription to the Sunday *New York Times*. If Bill liked it, he'd be glad to extend it. He told Bill their mother was sending him a three-month subscription to *The Nation* magazine. Life in America was deeply troubled, John wrote, noting that, on the day the letter was written, the US dollar went off the gold standard. Millions were unemployed.

"Roosevelt is making desperate efforts to salvage the creaking structure and one must admit that he has a fairly good chance of succeeding," John Shirer wrote. "But by the time he gets through he is likely to wind up with a virtually fascist state, though I hope we may be spared its more idiotic manifestations."

Even as he tried to write, Shirer spent a considerable amount of time at his desk in the Lloret de Mar house writing friends to inquire about job possibilities. He could see the handwriting on the wall and feared that his short-lived journalism career, notwithstanding how brightly it had burned the past seven years, had been extinguished with his cold-blooded firing from the foreign staff of the *Tribune*. The months were passing and no money was coming in; without finding a job, he did not see how he and Tess could possibly take care of themselves. No one was hiring, and he needed friends who were still working to tip him to any openings.

Frederick Birchall of the *New York Times* wrote from the paper's London office, "I cannot hold out any hope to you at present." A friend at the *Chicago Daily News* wrote that there was nothing at his paper, and he did not expect that to change anytime soon. Harold E. Scarborough, the London correspondent for the *New York Herald Tribune*, rejected Shirer's suggestion that the newspaper could use his services as a correspondent in Spain. No such opening existed, he told Shirer.

One letter went out to J. David Stern at the *New York Evening Post*, which Shirer characterized as a "fighting, liberal newspaper." He informed Stern that Europe was a "powder keg"—growing unrest in Spain and Hitler's coming to power in Germany were just two of the flashpoints—and that he, above anyone else who might express interest, could cover the unfolding drama that lay ahead. Other letters went out to Edwin L. James, at the *New York Times*, volunteering to come back to the United States "if you have anything there for me." There was nothing anywhere.

Other letters continued to go out to book agents in New York City, as well as to literary and other publications, as Shirer reached for something that could pull them through. But rejections continued to fill up his files. Shirer wrote to John Gunther, asking if he could recommend a New York book agent who could help him launch a writing career. In the same letter, Tess sent Frances Gunther directions on how to find the Lloret de Mar house when they next came for a visit: take the train from Paris to Toulouse Orleans, then on to Empalme, a junction near Barcelona. There, take the train to Blanes and the bus to Lloret.

Letters also came in from friends across Europe, such as one from Newell Rogers at the *Herald* in Paris. Rogers was a fellow graduate of Coe College and another of the journalists trained by Ethel Outland. "Paris has become the most expensive place in the world," Rogers wrote. "I'm paying 5 francs for pasteurized whole milk on which to keep fat. A half pound of steak at the market costs 8 francs. You can realize with what envious eyes we regard your $14 a month house, six bedrooms, two baths—my god—mountains, sea, what not."

Every time a job opened up at the *Herald*, Rogers wrote Shirer. "Are you interested in temporary job possibility here," read one telegram. Shirer responded in a one-sentence telegram: "Interested if job not too temporary could come immediately thanks. Bill." A friend who worked in the Paris office of the *Chicago Daily News* tipped Shirer to a possible job opening on that staff, which prompted Shirer to write to Hal O'Flaherty in the paper's main office: "If ever there is an opening, I would like very much to work for the *Daily News*."

Fearful of his and Tess's future, Shirer wrote to McCormick, imploring the man he despised to rehire him. "I can make Central Europe interesting, if you give me a chance.... Why should I fade out as a European correspondent? I don't want to. I won't. And I can prove it to you, if you want me to." In a letter written on a summer morning in 1933, Shirer told McCormick: "Being unemployed is no life for me and I would like to get back to work. I know I made mistakes when I was with the *Tribune*, but for seven years I gave you all I had, good and bad, and at the time you said some of it—my work in India, for instance—was good. May I have another chance?"

* * *

In spite of Shirer's dark mood about his and Tess's finances and his own future, he savored their sojourn in Spain. It was as if, somewhere in the back of his

mind, he knew that better days were ahead if he could just ride out this difficult period in his life. On top of that, he adored Tess and felt their time
together, after so much time apart, was a great blessing they would one day
look back on with fondness. They were a close couple, free spirited with each
other, and they shared many of the same interests—art, books, culture and
politics, artists and writers and musicians.

His mood improved by leaps and bounds when Andres Segovia, whom
Shirer had first heard in Paris and later in Vienna, moved into the other half of
the villa to spend a few summer weeks by the sea. Most afternoons Bill, Tess,
and Segovia sat in their beach chairs by the water, reading and talking. Shirer
had brought back musical recordings from India and Afghanistan, Iraq and
Turkey, and some nights Segovia joined Bill and Tess in their large living room
to listen to them. "The evening invariably wound up with Segovia playing some
of the works he had been practicing," Shirer wrote. He was astounded when
Segovia played Bach and Mozart on his guitar. Before Segovia left the house for
good, he gave Bill and Tess a Spanish edition of Cervantes's *Don Quixote*.

Other guests that summer were Jay Allen, then based in Madrid for the
Tribune and, like Wales and Shirer before him, soon to be fired by McCormick;
the Spanish painter Luis Quintanilla, who knew Hemingway and liked to talk
about bullfighting; and, before summer's end, Tess's brother, who came down
from Vienna, bringing news of German provocations against Austria along
with the alarming rise of an Austrian Nazi movement. As summer ended and
a beautiful Spanish fall arrived on its heels, Bill and Tess took jaunts around
the country, visiting museums and art galleries, awed by the paintings they
gazed at, husbanding their money as best they could while enjoying the lives
of tourists on a tight budget.

* * *

In Spain that fall of 1933, the one-year anniversary of Shirer's firing by
McCormick loomed in front of him. He knew they could not stay much longer. The country's unstable government was threatened by continued civil
strife and unrest. He and Tess put off a trip to Barcelona because of street
fighting "and bombs bursting all over the place." Elections in November,
marred by allegations of fraud, had seen 800,000 votes cast by the extreme
Right. Violence and street fighting broke out in several cities. Rail lines were
torn up, sending trains off their tracks. From their sanctuary along the sea
in Lloret de Mar, Bill and Tess wondered how much the political situation in
the country would deteriorate and if it would ultimately force them out of the
country. Their rent was paid up through the spring of 1934, but then, without
a dramatic change in their fortunes, they would not have the funds to keep it
going.

Even if it were financially possible to return to Vienna, where Tess might be able to find work, the political situation there was unstable and unpredictable. Paramilitary violence between Far Left and Far Right political parties had increased. Several political parties, including the Austrian Nazis, were pushing for a union with Germany. As in Germany, anti-Semitism was loudly and fully out in the open. In late July, an organ of a wing of the powerful Christian Social Party called for a major drive against Jews in the country.

"Very naturally every one is indignant at the expansion today of Jewish influence in every trade and profession, and the insulting behavior of the Polish Jews and at the uncontrolled conduct of the younger Jews," the *New York Times* quoted the organ as saying in a July 23, 1933, story. "The Jew is the principal demoralizing influence and only Christians are his victims. It is the Jew also who takes the lead in attacks on our Roman Catholic Church."

The organ went on to call for the expulsion of "surplus Jewish immigrants" from the country and the enforcement of "strict limitations of the Jews in the medical, legal and other professions." Three months later, in October, a Nazi sympathizer tried unsuccessfully to murder the country's chancellor, Engelbert Dollfuss.

As 1933 ended, and as winter began to show its ragged edges along the mountainous Spanish coast, Shirer sat at his writing desk in the villa and sent off letter after letter to friends at newspapers and wire services, hoping he would finally connect with a job. He now found himself in a situation not unlike that when he and George Latta were about to depart from their Paris apartment for the French coast to board a ship that would take them back to Canada and from there via train to Iowa.

Now, no rescue seemed imminent. In mid-December he wrote again to the *New York Times*, inquiring if anything might open up. In mid-January 1934, he wrote to Karl von Wiegand of the Universal News Service at Dorotheenstrasse 29 in Berlin. With so much going on, there just had to be work for a journalist in Berlin, if there was work anywhere. And what a city, and what a time, for a journalist like Shirer to be in Berlin. All he could do was hope for a positive response.

After introducing himself to Wiegand, he wrote: "I feel very much like getting back into newspaper work again and wonder if you are liable to have any openings in your organization within the next few months." Three days after writing that letter, he wrote C. R. Gratke, the European manager for the *Christian Science Monitor*. Were there any staff jobs? Neither Wiegand nor Gratke offered anything.

Early in January, Tess and Bill visited friends in Paris. His desperation had peaked, and their money was nearly gone. He visited with Eric Hawkins, who edited the American edition of the Paris *Herald*. While not offering anything solid, Hawkins held out the possibility that something might open up on the copydesk. If it panned out, Shirer would be back where he started. But it hardly mattered now. "I did not tell him—I was too proud—that I could not hold out for more than a month or two. We were down to our last one hundred dollars," Shirer wrote. "Hawkins would wire me, he said, if anything turned up."

January in Lloret de Mar was miserable. All the bright colors had been drained out of the village and the mountains above it. The midwinter weather was damp and cold, the sort that cut through clothing and thinly insulated walls and trampled optimism. Shirer's mood darkened. "We did not dare spend another peseta on coal for the furnace, so we tried to keep warm by donning extra sweaters and wrapping blankets around us on top of them, as the poor in Spain did when winter came.... We gave up eating meat, which was relatively expensive, and bought fish directly from the fishermen when they came in with their daily catch."

Seated in the living room, wrapped in their blankets, Bill and Tess thought that they would go hungry in Spain. Bill knew he could count on his brother John for loans, but how many times could he go to that well before his brother said enough? If Shirer decided they should return to America, he'd have to find money for the price of two tickets. And what would he find in America in the grip of the Depression? John Shirer, now living in Queens, New York, cautioned his brother not to think about coming to New York to live. "It's way too expensive for a writer's life," John wrote.

In mid-January, his gloom deepening, Shirer sat at his desk and wrote a long letter to Ethel Outland, the one person most central to his decision to pursue a career in journalism. Had his father not died young and his mother moved her children to Cedar Rapids, had Shirer not attended Coe, had he not signed up for Outland's no-nonsense writing and reporting classes, perhaps he would have pursued a far different life for himself. Now, he wanted to air his bitterness over his fate and his disappointment that he had failed to reach his lofty goals.

"For almost a year now we have been living here in this quiet little fishing village two hours north of Barcelona, watching the sea beat against our front door steps and in the evening hiking into the mountains back of the town, which rise up into the Pyrenees all snow covered and sparkling," he wrote her. "It has been a beautiful year, rich in the kind of development I wanted and needed, and fruitful too according to my own standards. And now it is almost over and I must go back to work, if there is any work, newspaper work."

Sounding a very bitter note, he went on to attack "all the bankers and bond and insurance salesmen" he was sure had wrecked America and brought on the Depression and crippled so many industries. "And they were the boys whom I was taught to look up to as God's own," he wrote. "They were the ones who endowed our colleges, made the commencement speeches, chased out 'radical' college editors and in general wove the patterns of our lives. And what a bunch of crooks they were."

A few days after his letter to his former teacher, the post brought a letter from Hawkins in Paris, offering Shirer a job running the day copydesk at the *Herald*. In an instant, the mood in the house shifted from somber to joyous. "We bought a hundred pounds of coal to heat up the house and a gallon of local wine to warm up our spirits," he wrote.

Seated at his writing desk, Shirer wrote in his diary a first draft of the history of his and Tess's year in Spain. Using words that showed how deeply he loved his wife—"we had time to know each other, to loaf and play, to [drink] wine and eat"—he wrote that the year in the fishing village had been "the best, the happiest, the most uneventful year we have ever lived together."

At the end of January 1934, a happy and much relieved Shirer boarded the train for the long ride to Paris to begin his new job at the *Herald*.

Gestapo at the Train Station

S hirer arrived in Paris at the end of January, found an apartment for Tess and himself, and reported for work on the copydesk at the *Herald*. He was glad for the job, greatly relieved to have a paycheck again, but he could not conceal his disappointment at the entry-level nature of his new employment. It felt beneath him. Nine years after his arrival in Paris as a naïve American, possessed with an overly developed sense of his own worth and looking for a bright future, Shirer was back working on a newspaper, but this time not as a staff writer or correspondent with all of Europe and Asia at his doorstep.

His first week at the *Herald* felt like his first nights on the copydesk of the *Tribune* back in 1925, meeting new people and introducing himself. He was far too experienced for his new job; he felt keenly that he was starting over. He did not wear his resentment well; the experienced journalist and foreign correspondent was now rewriting wire copy. He was determined that it would not last.

The Paris of the winter of 1934 was not the same city he had been introduced to in 1925. Nor was France the same country he had known nine years before. "I scarcely recognized them," Shirer wrote, his disappointment at the fundamental change in the city he worshipped for its culture, art, and sophistication profoundly embittering.

A curtain had fallen, and the stagehands had rearranged everything so that when the curtain was raised, nothing was recognizable. The country was sharply polarized, with hardcore Communists on the left and violent Fascists on the right. "Rancor and intolerance poisoned the air. Insults and threats were hurled at each other by the Right and the Left....I was astounded at the strength of incipient fascism in this democratic republic."

As France had been fundamentally changed by the world depression, Europe itself was in a political upheaval. Since coming to power in Germany, Hitler had brought out into full public view the program that mattered to him the most—the first forays in the war against the Jews, whose very presence on German soil (however Hitler chose to define "German soil") drove his agenda. There were of course other items on his plate—firmly establishing Germany's place in Europe and in eastern Europe, creating "living space" for the "Aryan" people, and getting rid of what he saw as the onerous conditions imposed on the country after 1918—but nothing burned so hot as Hitler's contempt for the Jews and his desire to physically remove them from society. While Hitler and those closest to him knew a second European war was inevitable—there was no other way for the Nazis to realize their goals—they placed the blame for it firmly at the door of the Jews. *They* would cause it. It would be the war against the Jews first and foremost, then against everyone else.

Victor Klemperer, in the home in Dresden that he shared with his wife, Eva, wrote early in February, days after Shirer's arrival in Paris, of his personal depression and the bleakness of their situation. "And my strength, all my physical and mental strength is increasingly exhausted," he wrote on February 7. Eight days later, on the fifteenth, he wrote of going to a meeting on the campus where he taught and being confronted by a student representative in an SA [*Sturmabteilung*] uniform. "But this arm raising makes me literally feel sick, and the fact that I always dodge it will cost me my neck one day.

"The hope that this state of boundless tyranny and lies must yet collapse at some time, never completely disappears," he wrote.

Klemperer, of course, saw only a small portion of the events unfolding all around him, just what was in his view, or relayed to him by Jewish friends, or what he read in the Nazi-controlled press. In France, as Shirer went about his new job at the *Herald*, he could only read about these events in the papers and in wire dispatches at his desk, or as he sat in cafés at night after work, and guess at where it was all headed.

In April 1933, after Bill and Tess had moved into their seaside home in Lloret de Mar, the new German government had organized official boycotts of Jewish-owned businesses—shops, department stores, factories, and a host of other businesses big and small. When these efforts were written up in foreign newspapers, government, business, and some church leaders denounced stories about assaults on Jews as so many lies meant to damage Germany's international reputation.

For Jews trying to go about their lives, the uniformed men attacking them and their businesses were straight out of another age. With some exceptions, non-Jewish Germans said nothing to protect businessmen they had known and bought from for years. Historian Michael Burleigh writes of a decorated Jewish war veteran who handed out leaflets protesting the boycott of his family's department store in the town of Wesel. The leaflets detailed his family's long military service to the country, going back to his grandfather.

"With such a record of past national service, do we now have to be subjected to public humiliation? Is this how the fatherland today expresses its gratitude, by placing huge pickets in front of our door with the demand not to buy from our house?" The leaflet went on to note that twelve thousand "German front soldiers of the Jewish faith" had given their lives in action during the Great War.

A year later, by the time Shirer was in Paris, official actions in Germany against the Jews included a newly passed law forcing Jews out of the civil service. Jewish lawyers were disbarred; Jewish judges were removed from the bench and Jewish prosecutors from their offices. Even before Hitler assumed power in 1933, the Nazis had begun an assault on newspapers across the country. There was one party-owned newspaper in Germany in 1926; there were ninety-seven by early 1934, with combined circulations of more than three million. Marxist newspapers were among the first victims of the Nazis. After Hitler came to power, SA thugs stormed some newspapers around the country whose policies and coverage they didn't like or that had published criticisms about the new chancellor. "Under heavy pressure, or facing economic ruin, many small and middle-size publishers sold their newspaper properties to the Nazi competitor," Oron J. Hale has written.

Moving to consolidate control, the government created a press leader to oversee the entire publishing industry; press organizations were also created whose memberships, including all editors and reporters, were strictly controlled by the government. Undesirables—leftists, Jews, Socialists, any journalists who opposed official control of newspapers—were purged.

Within weeks of Hitler's being named chancellor, an American named James G. McDonald traveled to Berlin as part of an official mission for President Roosevelt. McDonald was under consideration for the post of US ambassador to Germany—he would be named the League of Nations High Commissioner for Refugees—and he began the process of meeting high-ranking Nazis as well as other Germans to assess their goals and to learn more about conditions for Jews in the country. In Berlin on April 3, 1933, he visited the home of Siegmund Warburg, whose banking family had long been influential in both Germany and New York, at Tiergartenstrasse 2a, the lovely boulevard that ran along the edge of the Tiergarten.

Warburg was deeply worried about the Nazis' intentions toward his fellow German Jews and the impact of critical comments about Hitler's government made by Jewish leaders in America. At the meeting was an associate of Warburg's, a Dr. Melchior. "They were obviously much worried and concerned for themselves, their business, and their people," McDonald wrote in his diary. "I told them I was to dine later with Hanfstaengl. They said I might tell him that their people were considering a public statement signed by a hundred prominent Jews for the rest of the world to leave the [solution of the] problem to Germany."

That night, McDonald dined with Ernst Hanfstaengl, a top aide to Hitler whose job was to manipulate foreign journalists, who called him by the nickname "Putzi." He was a graduate of Harvard University and had met Franklin Roosevelt years before. His living in the United States had done little to make him a different sort of man. After meeting Hanfstaengl at his apartment at Friedrich-Ebert-Strasse 30 near the Reichstag building, McDonald walked with him to a nearby restaurant to have a meal and talk.

"Eventually we reached the subject of the Jews, especially the decree just announced for Monday's boycott," McDonald wrote in his diary. "He defended it unqualifiedly, saying: 'When I told Hitler of the agitation and boycott abroad, Hitler beat his fists and exclaimed, 'Now we shall show them that we are not afraid of international Jewry. The Jews must be crushed. Their fellows abroad have played into our hands.'"

As the two men ate their dinner, Hanfstaengl spelled out Hitler's plans, abandoning any effort to couch his words. He didn't go on about the humiliation of 1918 or the harsh economic climate after the Great War—he didn't touch on these subjects at all. "Then he launched into a terrifying account of Nazi plans: The boycott is only a beginning. It can be made to strangle all Jewish business. Slowly, implacably it can be extended with ruthless and unshakable discipline. Our plans go much further. During the war we had 1,500,000 prisoners; 600,000 Jews would be simple. Each Jew has his SA [storm trooper]. In a single night it could be finished. (He did not explain, but I assume he meant nothing more than wholesale arrests and imprisonment.)

"I protested the danger to Germany's economic life. He laughed: 'The Jews are the vampire sucking German blood. We shall not be strong until we have freed ourselves of them.'"

McDonald, who by then had made strong connections with the foreign journalists based in Berlin, particularly the Americans, brought up several of them whom the German government had openly harassed and were attempting to force out of the country. "About Mowrer he said, 'Of course, he is a Jew and so is his wife. So also Knickerbocker.' What of Enderis and Birchall? I asked. He answered, 'You know what hand feeds them.'"

Edgar Mowrer wrote for the *Chicago Daily News* and was president of the Association of Foreign Correspondents in Berlin, a position the German government wanted him to give up as a first step to leaving the country. Guido Enderis wrote for the *New York Times*, Frederick Birchall was the paper's Berlin bureau chief, and H. R. Knickerbocker wrote for the *New York Evening Post*. Hanfstaengl thought them all troublemakers.

* * *

In Paris, going about his new job with one eye on events unfolding in Germany, it was all Shirer could do to keep up on developments in the French government. He knew about conditions in Berlin for his colleagues, nearly all of whom—Mowrer, Knickerbocker, Birchall, and Sigrid Schultz—were close friends. For now he had to worry about his own work.

With all the political and cultural changes, it felt very much as if he were in a different country from the Paris he had lived in before. When he was in the city then, he wrote, "The theaters, concert halls, cabarets, restaurants, cafes were crowded. Prices were reasonable. The art museums and galleries attracted great throngs. Books poured from the presses and were bought and read.... Now, in the bleak January of 1934, that Paris, that France, seemed gone....Now, I found to my surprise that rowdy, antiparliamentary Fascist leagues had sprung up in France like mushrooms."

With fighting common in the streets between rival groups and members of Fascist organizations battling the police, Eric Hawkins decided to take Shirer off the night copydesk and put him on the Paris streets as a *Herald* reporter. Suddenly, the unhappiness that had gripped Shirer tightly over his job on the desk evaporated. He was a reporter again, and he was covering a major story. "To my utter astonishment it began to look to me as if France, which seemed so stable and peaceful...was drifting, like Spain, toward civil war."

The Depression had drained France of its economic vitality and its people of their savings and optimism. Among many groups that sprang up in the bitter atmosphere of economic fear, the financial collapse forged a deep-seated contempt for the government in power. With wages falling, as well as production in large industries, misery and resentment spread. In response, right-wing leagues sprang up, demanding an overthrow of the government. Right-wing newspapers advocated the establishment of a Fascist government built on the Mussolini model in Italy. One of the biggest organizations, Action Française, which published its own newspaper, sent out its members to storm government buildings. Another of the groups was the Solidarité Française, established by a perfume magnate. Shirer saw the group's shock troops in the street—"outfitted in blue shirts, black berets and jackboots, and their slogan, which they shouted in the streets, was 'France for the French.'"

Fueling the resentment even further were a series of financial scandals. "In the last years of the 1920's and stretching into the 1930's one financial scandal after another followed, all having the same pattern," Shirer wrote. "Crooks, with the aid of bribed cabinet members, senators and deputies, were able to set up in business, including banking, and then, when they were caught, evade trial or have their cases continually postponed or the charges quashed, sometimes by the minister of justice himself, who was in on the deal."

In December 1933, Shirer wrote, the newspapers reported the arrest of Serge Alexandre, a Russian-born Jew—as the papers noted—on widespread fraud charges. He'd been arrested several years earlier for bilking investors, and he had a long criminal record as well as an association with men in power. Nothing seemed to stick against Alexandre. Within a day, rioting broke out in Paris. A mob of several thousand stormed the Chamber of Deputies. Barricades went up in the streets. "They overturned newspaper kiosks and set them on fire," Shirer wrote. "They jammed the third-rail conduits furnishing electrical power to the streetcars, which, along with the public buses, were halted. A police report I saw a few days later described the damage as the worst in Paris in twenty years. The spirit of insurrection was spreading in the city."

Riots erupted almost daily toward the end of January. Covering the action in the streets, Shirer noted the injuries to police and reporters. He heard the mob shouting "Hang the Deputies" within earshot of government officials. The government teetered and then fell, pushed out by the revelation of yet another banking scandal, this one involving a top minister in the government. Forming a new government was the Socialist Édouard Daladier, whom Shirer met soon after he took over the government. Almost from their first meeting the two men hit it off. Daladier, a veteran of the fighting at Verdun, had been named premier just the year before, but his government fell within months. "Now in February, 1934, as the battles in the streets of Paris grew in intensity, Daladier appeared to many to be the man France needed."

On February 6, acting on instructions from Hawkins, Shirer went to the Place de la Concorde to cover a demonstration. By early evening the street was packed—"several thousand demonstrators who were standing their ground against repeated charges of mounted, steel-helmeted" police. "A mob was crowded behind the railings, pelting the police and Guards with stones, bricks, garden chairs and iron grilles ripped up from around trees," Shirer wrote, "the rioters were using sticks with razor blades attached to one end to slash away at the horses and legs of the mounted men, and they were throwing marbles and firecrackers at the hooves. A number of horses went down and their riders were mauled."

Shirer pushed his way through the mob to reach the Hôtel de Crillon and fled inside. Up on a third-floor balcony, a large group of frightened reporters had gathered to escape the violence. Shots were fired from the street, and a female correspondent standing immediately to Shirer's left collapsed. "When we bent over her, blood was flowing from her face from a bullet hole in the center of her forehead," Shirer wrote. "She was dead." He never learned her name.

Inside the nearby Chamber of Deputies, gunshots and the angry chants of the demonstrators could be heard. A mob grabbed Édouard Herriot, a former premier, and tried to throw him into the Seine. He was rescued by the police. At the Crillon, Shirer phoned in stories to the *Herald* newsroom. As evening settled over the city, thousands of war veterans took to the streets as well, carrying flags and banners demanding law and order. Shirer fell in with them and watched as they confronted police who blocked them from moving toward the Chamber of Deputies.

For the next several hours, a mob Shirer estimated at nearly thirty thousand tried to cross the bridges over the river and seize the Chamber. After more than a dozen attempts, the mob tried again, and wholesale gunfire broke out on the part of the police. The mob reformed, and, from Shirer's viewpoint, it looked certain that they would break through.

"Suddenly a large squadron of Mobile and Republican Guard cavalry, with drawn sabers, surged into the square, followed by several hundred police and foot guards brandishing their white batons. The surprised rioters gave way; they started to run. I could scarcely believe it. Within a few minutes the Place de la Concorde was cleared and the horse guards were chasing stragglers through the avenues that led from the square."

* * *

As preoccupied as he was with events in Paris, Shirer saw events unfolding in Germany and Austria as equally unsettling. In his wife's home country, on February 12, 1934, a week after the huge rioting in Paris, the chancellor, Engelbert Dollfuss, set troops against Socialists in the public housing projects—the very place Shirer had written about that drew the ire of Colonel McCormick. Hundreds were killed and injured. In his diary, Shirer wrote: "And there goes democracy in Austria, one more state gone."

In Germany at the end of June, Hitler set out to crush his own SA, arresting and killing many of its leaders, including Ernst Röhm, one of his earliest and most militant supporters. Even as he was repelled by the violence, Shirer saw in Germany a great opportunity for a correspondent. On the night of June 30, after hearing about the purge against the SA and Röhm's murder, Shirer wrote in his diary: "Wish I could get a post in Berlin. It's a story I'd like to cover."

On the afternoon of August 9, Shirer was sitting in the *Herald* newsroom going through a stack of Paris newspapers when his phone rang. It was Arno Dosch-Fleurot, who had covered the Great War and stayed on in Europe to write for the *New York World* newspaper. He now ran Universal Service, a news wire company owned by William Randolph Hearst. He offered Shirer a job in the service's Berlin bureau, named the salary, and Shirer quickly accepted.

Writing about the phone call years later, Shirer described Dosch-Fleurot as "a gentleman of the old school, courtly, wise, warm, with a fine mind and a passion not only for journalism but for history, literature and the arts." Overjoyed at the job offer, Shirer bolted from the *Herald* newsroom and into the bar of a nearby hotel, where he ordered a double cognac.

The next morning, a letter from Dosch-Fleurot arrived at Shirer's Paris apartment. The stationery showed that Universal Service Inc. had offices in Berlin, at Dorotheenstrasse 19, and in the World Building in New York City.

> *The job you have accepted is that of correspondent in Berlin of the Universal Service, that is to say, for the Hearst morning newspapers and other newspapers which buy the service. I was recently put in charge of the Universal Service for Central Europe with the title of "director of the Berlin bureau." That makes me automatically chief correspondent in these parts, so you are to be the second man in Berlin, except when I am away. Mr. Von Wiegand who has been the chief correspondent of the Universal Service abroad is often in Berlin also and, when here, is overlord of the whole show.*
>
> *Your pay will be sixty dollars a week with equalization. That is approximately one hundred dollars when it gets into marks.... The Universal Service will pay yours and your wife's...expenses from Paris to Berlin and will also foot your hotel and other living expenses for the first week in Berlin. You will find the work very interesting here. This is a really good opening and the Universal Service has a habit of keeping and looking after the men who serve it well.*

On August 18, Shirer wrote back to Dosch-Fleurot, informing him that he and Tess would arrive in Berlin by train from Paris on August 25. "Don't go to all the trouble of meeting us. We'll go to the Continental Hotel."

Soon after Shirer got the job, Jay Allen wrote Shirer to congratulate him. Now it was Allen who needed help finding work as a correspondent again. "I meant at once to congratulate you on your job with Hearst," he wrote. "As much as we dislike him we realize, don't we, that a job is a job, that a job with Dosch-Fleurot is a very good job, that a job in Berlin at a time like this is close to ideal."

Bill and Tess arrived at the Friedrichstrasse Bahnhof at ten o'clock on the evening of August 25. As they stepped off the train, two men greeted them as if they were on an official mission. One of the men, leading Shirer away from the train, shouted at him, "Are you Herr...?" Shirer could not make out the name and the man shouted it again. Alarmed, Shirer pulled his passport out of a coat pocket and offered it as evidence that he was not who the man was looking for.

"So," the man said, lowering his voice. "You are Herr Shirer."

"None other," Shirer said, "as you can see by my passport."

At the Continental, Shirer booked the biggest room available. He told Tess he'd come up with a pun that summed up the last months of their lives: "I'm going from bad to Hearst." Exhausted from the long train ride, he ached to sleep, to report fresh for work in the newsroom of Universal Service in the morning. He wrote in his diary: "Tomorrow begins a new chapter for me."

PART TWO

THE GOOD AMERICAN

Berlin and the World

Berlin in August was hot and humid, with occasional flashes of rain and thunder passing loudly overhead like harbingers of events to come. As new residents, Bill and Tess saw the city as big and colorless, nothing like Vienna, where they had met and been so happy, and certainly nothing like Paris. The couple could not help but look back with fondness on their lives just one year ago, when they lived in the villa on the beach in Spain, swimming on every warm day, chatting with friends like Segovia about events unfolding in Europe. But that was all just conversation—people pontificating, guessing, drawing information from newspaper accounts, and coming to conclusions based on little else. Now, Shirer was here, in Berlin, and there was no more guessing about what was going on. The reality of Germany under the Nazis was right in front of him like a giant billboard that listed, coldly and officiously, the rules of life in the new Germany. The two plainclothes policemen who'd confronted him when he stepped off the train, in his first minutes in Berlin, were certainly proof of that.

Within two days of his arrival, Shirer's friend H. R. Knickerbocker, who wrote for the *New York Evening Post*, told him that their mutual friend Dorothy Thompson had been ordered out of Germany at the demand of Ernst Hanfstaengl. Shirer had not yet met him, but had heard from other reporters that the man was a loudmouth, a buffoon, and a toady. He bullied reporters whose work and attitudes he did not like and was a fawning devotee of Hitler, quoting him liberally and predicting bold moves ahead that would surprise the world.

Shirer walked the streets every day, from his room at the hotel to the wire service offices on the Dorotheenstrasse, not far from where the fire-damaged

Reichstag stood, learning the layout of the government buildings and trying to understand how life in the city operated. One day a journalist took Shirer to a pub on the Friedrichstrasse, and afterward they walked by a building where the man said Jews had been tortured. You could hear them screaming, he told Shirer. Another day he and Tess went to the Berlin Zoo and lunched in a restaurant on the grounds. They tried different restaurants until they found one or two they preferred. As part of his job, Shirer introduced himself to the American ambassador to Germany, William E. Dodd, and through him Shirer met Dodd's daughter, Martha. She was a party girl in Berlin, frequently seen with high-ranking Germans in the government and playing the hostess at embassy parties.

Shirer was a keen enough observer to understand how the National Socialists, in power for nineteen months, controlled the lives of the city's and the country's residents. The red and black swastika flags flew from every government building, party buttons adorned lapels, and uniformed police and dour men in suits could be seen everywhere. Men in black uniforms congregated on streets and train platforms and in front of government buildings, watching and listening. There was no escaping their presence. Nor was there any escape from the mood of the city and the knowledge that the Nazis, holding the reins of government, were completely in charge of people's lives, down to the smallest detail. This was totalitarianism fully blossomed.

Shirer had never before set foot in a police state, and he found its boundaries tremendously confining. No one anywhere in the city or throughout Germany could openly say anything critical about Hitler or the Nazi Party; even talking in whispers in government hallways with bureaucrats with whom he sought interviews and general information was a hazardous affair. Most officials avoided him. No one he talked to said anything at all that deviated in the slightest way from the party's official pronouncements. When officials complained, it was always about how the international press failed to understand Hitler and what he was doing.

As a credentialed American journalist legally in the country and working out of a large office near the government buildings, Shirer was subject to German law, but not to the same extent that a citizen of the country was. He could be arrested, harassed, and followed by the police, but he believed there was only so much they could do to him—all far lesser measures than could be applied to any German. For the country's citizens there were the country's concentration camps, which were by no means any kind of official secret. Nor had they been constructed in remote places far from everyday observation. The populace knew where they were and who had been sent to them. They also knew, anecdotally and from accounts in the Nazi-controlled press, that these camps were teeming with Communists, Socialists, run-of-the-mill criminals, dissidents of all kinds, malcontents, political opponents as defined by the government, critics of any stripe, and Jews, although far greater numbers of Jews would be forced into the camps after the officially sanctioned attacks in early November 1938.

Shirer knew he could not be picked up and anonymously dumped in a camp, his name hidden away on a long sheet of paper somewhere. The government could expel him, a step he regarded as too horrible to be contemplated, but what else? It took him a while to fully come to grips with the delicacy of his reporting situation; he began to realize, through his own observations and in talking to other correspondents, that he could write the story he wanted to write and have it appear in American newspapers, as he did several times a week. But German officials in the United States read everything written about Hitler and the Nazis in the American press and reported back to Berlin. So if they saw something they did not like, there could be consequences.

* * *

The government's second party rally convened in early September in Nuremberg. "Five hundred trains carried a quarter of a million people to a specially built railway station," historian Richard J. Evans has written. "A vast city of tents was constructed to house the participants, and gargantuan quantities of supplies were brought in to feed and water them.... Outside the city, on the huge Zeppelin field, the serried ranks of hundreds of thousands of uniformed brownshirts, SS men and Nazi party activists took part in ritual exchanges with their Leader. 'Hail, my men,' he would shout, and a hundred thousand voices would answer back in unison: 'Hail, my leader.'"

For a foreign correspondent who had been in the country barely two weeks, Shirer's trip to Nuremberg to cover the party rally for the Hearst wire service was as big and as grand an introduction to Hitler's movement as could be imagined. He found its enormous scale, the use of searchlights splashing over hundreds of thousands of uniformed, precisely marching men, its over-the-top adulation of the Führer, to be both spectacularly mindless and brilliantly conceived. It was overwhelming, like nothing he'd heard of or read about or thought existed anywhere in the world. The German filmmaker Leni Riefenstahl captured the staggering dimensions of the party rally in her documentary *Triumph of the Will*.

On the town's narrow streets, Shirer worked his way into the huge crowds to see Hitler's entourage drive past "wildly cheering Nazis." He wrote in his diary, "The streets, hardly wider than alleys, are a sea of brown and black uniforms. I got my first glimpse of Hitler as he drove by our hotel, the Württemberger Hof, to his headquarters down the street at the Deutscher Hof, a favorite old hotel of his, which has been remodeled for him.... For the life of me I could not quite comprehend what hidden springs he undoubtedly unloosed in the hysterical mob which was greeting him so wildly."

That night, Shirer walked through the crowded streets to the Rathaus, where Hanfstaengl—"an immense, high-strung, incoherent clown"—spoke in fluent English to the foreign reporters. He lectured the correspondents on their responsibilities to report the greatness of Hitler. "Obviously trying to please his boss," Shirer wrote in his diary, "he had the crust to ask us to 'report on affairs in Germany without attempting to interpret them. History alone,' Putzi shouted, 'can evaluate the events now taking place under Hitler.'" Shirer knew what this meant: the correspondents were supposed to "jump on the bandwagon of Nazi propaganda."

As the night wore on, Shirer found himself in the packed lobby of the Deutscher Hof, where he watched Julius Streicher—"the number one Jew-baiter and editor of the vulgar and pornographic anti-Semitic sheet the Sturmer"—walk by him, brandishing a whip. To Shirer's relief, his friend Knickerbocker was also in town to cover the rally, and the two men met to talk quietly away from the crowds, each man performing the delicate dance of trying to report events without antagonizing the hosts to the point where they would follow Dorothy Thompson out of the country.

For seven days, Shirer immersed himself in the rally, introducing himself to midlevel government officials and other correspondents and trying, as best he could, to come to some kind of understanding of the man and his party. Perhaps it was the pageantry, Shirer wrote in his diary, or the introduction of mysticism and the nearly religious fervor it brought out in the Germans that was behind Hitler's great success. He could not explain it. One morning Shirer stood in the back of a grand, cathedral-like hall just outside the city and watched Hitler's entrance, staged brilliantly, with a marching band playing loudly so as to cause the crowd of thirty thousand to jump to its feet, right arms extended, shouting loudly. Behind the great man came the stout Hermann Göring, the small, clubfooted Joseph Goebbels, the tall, odd-looking Rudolf Hess, and the unimpressive Heinrich Himmler.

"Then an immense symphony orchestra played Beethoven's Egmont Overture," Shirer wrote in his diary. "Great klieg lights played on the stage, where Hitler sat surrounded by a hundred party officials and officers of the army and navy. Behind them the 'blood flag.'...Behind this, four or five hundred S.A. standards. When the music was over, Rudolf Hess, Hitler's closest confidant, rose and slowly read the names of the Nazi 'martyrs'—brown-shirts who had been killed in the struggle for power—a roll call of the dead."

Each day, Shirer watched the great spectacle. Thousands of goose-stepping, uniformed youths shouting their devotion to Hitler in the morning; at night there was a "great pageant" where more than 200,000 party officials holding "twenty-one thousand flags unfurled in the searchlights like a forest of weird trees" listened with great zeal and devotion to Hitler proclaim that their nation was strong and getting stronger. As darkness fell, thousands carrying torches paraded "through Nuremberg's ancient streets, Hitler taking the salute in front of the station across from our hotel."

On the morning of September 9, a number of the foreign correspondents were invited to a breakfast with Hitler. Shirer, perhaps because of his recent arrival in the country, was not among them. Later in the day he pushed his way through the crowd into a packed stadium where Hitler addressed the SA, whose leader, Ernst Röhm, Hitler had had executed the previous June. More than fifty thousand uniformed SA, in their brown uniforms, stood facing thousands of SS, who guarded Hitler.

The rally ended on September 10 with a make-believe battle on the Zeppelin grounds, guns and cannons firing, filling the air with the smoke of gunpowder. When the day ended, Shirer, exhausted, returned to his hotel. Before falling asleep, he sat for a moment at the desk and penned a few lines in his diary. "Shall sleep late tomorrow and take the night train back to Berlin."

Tauentzienstrasse

In early October 1934, Bill and Tess moved out of the Continental Hotel, where they had lived since their arrival in Berlin, and into a comfortable flat on the top floor of an apartment building on the Tauentzienstrasse, a handsome, tree-lined street running near the Tiergarten and within walking distance of the zoo, a number of big hotels, popular restaurants, and places favored by tourists and Germans visiting the capital.

Over weeks of searching they had examined a number of flats for rent, but rejected them out of hand because they were "furnished in atrocious style, littered with junk and knickknacks." The flat on the Tauentzienstrasse was by contrast tastefully furnished and in a lovely part of the city that was quiet at night. Settling into it gave them both the feeling that they could make a comfortable home in Berlin. On warm nights after an early supper, they walked toward the Tiergarten and sat on a bench and chatted, Bill smoking his pipe, or walked along the broad, grand promenade of the nearby Kurfürstendamm, the city's most popular boulevard.

In a very small way, the story of the studio flat was part of the ongoing narrative of Germany, circa fall 1934, a few months' shy of the start of the Nazis' third year of power. It was owned by a couple who knew they could not stay in the country. They were both Jews—he a sculptor, she an art historian of note who had lost her teaching post soon after the January 30, 1933, change in the government that brought Hitler to power. It was not just that they could not survive economically—he could not display his art in any "Aryan" gallery, and she could not hold a professional position—but also the ugly tone of government pronouncements and the mood across the land that Jews were to be restricted in every aspect of their lives.

The couple, who Shirer does not name in his diary, was in many ways representative of the country's Jews as a whole—well educated, successful, and very much a part of the country's professional class. Their extensive library, which they left behind in the flat as if they would return someday, reflected their literary interests and tastes and spoke to their love of German literature and history. But the handwriting indicating that they should leave Germany was writ large on the wall. Even before the end of Hitler's first year as chancellor, forty thousand Jews had fled the country. All the professional classes were being stripped of Jews. Nazi newspapers—all the country's papers, whether owned by the party or not, served the government's interests—trumpeted the news that Jews had become the country's untouchables.

Shirer wrote only a few sentences about the couple in his diary. Their abbreviated history begins and ends in a few lines—an anonymous couple abandoning their country and everything they knew for an uncertain future abroad. Realizing that the couple had lost everything when neither could work and that they were renting out their flat in desperation, Shirer arranged to wire them the rent payable in pounds sterling, which he knew was a violation of the German government's strict currency laws. He could just as easily have sent them nothing at all, and the couple would have had no recourse since they were out of the country. And they had no standing in any German court of law. The history of the fate of Jewish-owned properties in Germany during the period from the winter of 1933 to the late fall of 1938—from apartments to small businesses to department stories and factories—is filled with accounts of properties being sold for ten cents on the dollar, if that, with many rightful owners getting nothing at all after an approved "Aryan" (often a party member) assumed ownership. The Shirers, by contrast, chose to flout the law to help their landlords.

*   *   *

In Berlin, Shirer went about his business, trying to push a decent command of German into fluency. He spent a great deal of his time seeking out contacts— "with the Nazi officials who helped run the country; with German dissidents, if one could find them and win their trust; with German newspaper editors and reporters (all the good writers and artists had fled abroad); with the foreign diplomats and with my fellow foreign correspondents," Shirer wrote. "And a reporter had to go out into the streets and ride the subways, buses and streetcars to try to catch the mood of the people."

It is not clear, in Shirer's diaries or in his extensive letters and correspondence, when—or if—he met James McDonald, the high commissioner for refugees for the League of Nations, but it is very likely they did meet when Shirer went about searching for reliable contacts. All of the American journalists were on close terms with high-ranking officials at the embassy, and McDonald was one of those men in high office who liked journalists and socialized with them. He knew correspondents—Edgar Mowrer being one example—who were close to Shirer. Mowrer, eager to help out a friend and colleague, would have made the introduction. And Shirer, realizing very early in his tenure in Berlin that the German government would not tell him anything but lies, would most certainly have sought out diplomats in the country who could help him.

From his post, Shirer heard a great deal of speculation about Hitler's plans. It was impossible to get a grip on the truth, and to pursue it brought its own risks. As he wrote in his diary on November 28: "Much talk here that Germany is secretly arming, although it is difficult to get definite dope, and if you did get it and sent it, you'd probably be expelled."

In late fall, three months after his arrival in Berlin, Shirer began receiving invitations to government-sponsored events for the foreign press. Once a month, Alfred Rosenberg, the Nazi party's chief racial theorist, held beer parties for foreign correspondents. They were meant to be light events, all social, with lots of drinking and friendly chatter and nothing official or on the record. An early member of the party, Rosenberg considered himself one of the stars of the movement. His book, *The Myths of the Twentieth Century*, was nearly as popular as *Mein Kampf.*

Writing in his diary the night of the event, Shirer characterized Rosenberg's book as "a hodgepodge of historical nonsense." At the party, Shirer struck up a conversation with Rosenberg but found his German—Rosenberg was born in Estonia—difficult to understand. At Rosenberg's table, Shirer noted in his diary, sat the American ambassador, William Dodd. The Nazi minister of education was the speaker for the night.

In early December, a far larger, more important social event was held. This was the annual ball for the foreign press, held in a grand, high-ceilinged room at the Adlon Hotel, where some of the American newspapers kept their Berlin bureaus. The night before the ball, Shirer found a store on the Tauentzienstrasse that sold formal attire with tails, which was the required dress for the event. Tess had bought a new dress, and the couple left their flat on the night of the ball and took a cab that followed the edge of the Tiergarten into the heart of the city where the government buildings were clustered. The Adlon, a stout landmark built after the turn of the century, sat near Hitler's Chancellery, a short distance from the American embassy, and next door to the British embassy.

The ball was a long night of drinking and mixing with government officials and correspondent friends like Sigrid Schultz. She spoke fluent German and was very much in her element in Berlin, where she had a wide circle of contacts inside the government. At an event like the annual ball for the foreign press, Schultz mixed as easily with high government officials as she did with her colleagues. Shirer admired her and felt a close connection to her, in part because she worked for the *Tribune*, his old paper. Joseph Goebbels, the government's minister of propaganda, attended the ball, as did a top general, Walther von Reichenau, who, unlike Goebbels, felt comfortable in a room filled with journalists, Shirer noted later that night in his diary. Bill and Tess "danced and wined until about three" in the morning and went with a group of other correspondents and their wives to the Adlon bar for a breakfast of bacon and eggs.

Rosenberg held his last beer party of the year at the Adlon. To the American journalists, the party was a bizarre sideshow—men who they had reliably heard had been involved in the murderous purge of Röhm and his SA six months before during the *Nacht der langen Messer* (Night of the Long Knives) that began on June 30, 1934, were now dressed up in formal attire and shaking hands and selling their government like any good public relations staff. The room off the hotel's main lobby was festively decorated for the Christmas season.

After the party began with a round of beers for everyone, Heinrich Himmler arrived, dressed in a suit and looking annoyed and grim, out of place in a room full of prying foreign journalists who did not show him the deference he demanded of everyone else he encountered. To a government official who held life and death in the palm of his hand, smiling and pretending to answer questions about his government was a lie from beginning to end, nothing more than political theater. Himmler was followed by Field Marshal August von Mackensen, the aging legend of the 1914–1918 war, who was trotted out for the evening like a piece removed from a museum's display case, and General Werner von Blomberg, the minister of defense.

The guest of honor for the evening was Hermann Göring, who arrived with his outsized ego intact and wearing his status as a legend of the Nazi Party sewn to the sleeve of his gaudy, oversized military uniform. A large man with a huge head like a dark bowling ball, Göring glad-handed the reporters, speaking only in German. Shirer knew enough of recent history to understand that Göring had old connections to the party and had been wounded in the 1923 Beer Hall Putsch, the founding myth that had the party fathers battling the police in the streets of Munich for the soul of Germany. Wally Deuel, who wrote for the *Chicago Daily News*, Shirer, and certainly Schultz, who knew Göring well, believed that he had set up the government's terror apparatus and the concentration camps. They also knew he was a collector of big things—castles, for example, like Carinhall outside the city limits. He was a plunderer, a taker, and a spiller of blood.

To Shirer's eye, Göring was a hail-fellow-well-met, popular with the public—salty and crude, but exuding a "common touch." Seated at his table, Shirer hoped Göring would stand at the podium and speak about the new German air force. He didn't, but "he did not seem to mind our probing, though seri-ous questioning was rarely allowed German reporters." One of the reporters asked Göring if he would continue both the secret police and the concen-tration camps. Yes, he answered. Another correspondent, throwing caution to the wind, asked if it was true that Göring had set in motion the fire that had destroyed the Reichstag a month after Hitler came to power. No, he said, sticking to the party's myth, it was the Communists who did that.

After his talk, Göring went table to table to meet everyone. Earlier in the evening, Deuel had whispered to Shirer that Göring was a "blood swiller"—a prolific murderer—and now Göring took a seat at their table. Shirer asked him about his air force's violating the treaty, written after the war had ended in 1918, and Göring begged off answering. Then, as Göring got up to leave the table, he asked Shirer to come to his office during the week so they could talk. Shirer knew of other foreign correspondents who met privately with top government officials. In his view, the officials were merely using the reporters to float ideas and influence public opinion with planted stories. Shirer did not want that for himself, nor did he want to ask for a favor such as a tip ahead of everyone else. He did not want to be beholden. At the same time, working in the country was extraordinarily difficult. A government official who could tip him to something big about to happen would be welcome.

"I myself was never called in on such occasions," Shirer wrote. "More quickly than I had expected I was already becoming known in government and party circles as 'anti-Nazi' or, as some put it, 'unfriendly.' My access to news sources became more and more limited."

Later, when Shirer met with Göring, it was to discuss Göring's writing an occasional column for Universal Service that would appear in all the Hearst newspapers in the United States. Göring agreed, for a price, and the arrange-ment kept the two men in contact for several months. In return, Göring invited Shirer to a social event at the opera, which Shirer wisely skipped, and, at one point several years later, Göring tried to sell Shirer "some expressionist paint-ings he had confiscated from the museums and from Jews."

* * *

In Berlin, 1934 ended with Bill and Tess joining some of his colleagues for a New Year's Eve party with champagne. As the new year began, Shirer contin-ued to keep up on his personal correspondence. Letters were sent and arrived from his brother, John, living in New Jersey, his sister, Josephine, and his mother, who spent time with John Shirer but remained a resident of Cedar Rapids. In a letter, Josephine told her brother: "Mamie is sending you a copy of Time magazine for the interesting article about Grant Wood." She said the writer of the story had concluded that Wood was "the only American artist entirely free from French and Italian influence. And his greatest portrait is the one of John B. Turner. We were over to the Turners' Sunday for dinner and old Mr. T. never tires of telling how they gave their old barn to Grant Wood for his studio when he was too poor to rent one."

She went on to refer to "that bug" that sometimes struck her brother—melancholy, which she said she often suffered from herself, as did their mother. "It took me four years to get over mine," she wrote. "Maybe if you were in this country you could find someone who could help you. Did you ever try light therapy?"

A letter from his mother arrived in which she declined an invitation to travel to Berlin for an extended visit. She wasn't up to it. "I have been feeling terribly low for about three months but the last few days have felt better. It's sad to grow old, when your spirit is still young and feel yourself each year in a downward spiral."

She asked Shirer if he had a copy of "In Memoriam," written about his father at the time of his death. She did not want him to lose contact with his father's legacy or to have the memory of the man slip away. "If not I will send you a copy as it tells much [more] about him than I could tell you." she wrote. She said she'd received in the mail copies of some of Shirer's stories that ran in the New York newspapers, and she told Bill that Grant Wood was having his first show in a major New York gallery and that he'd married a woman who "looks old enough to be his mother."

To a friend, Shirer wrote that he wanted to stay in Berlin and had no plans at present to return to the United States. "Only a personal interest in the story here, the only one in the world outside America and perhaps Russia that interests me, made me decide to postpone the return a year or two. Berlin is cold and misty and ugly like Kansas City, but there is something in the air that takes the lead out of your behind. We both like it better than Paris, which was very decadent and depressing the six months we spent there.... The Nazis are Nazis still. Ebbutt still unearths amazing stories—and occasionally tips me off to them. The Taverne [restaurant] flourishes as of old, but the cutting off of registered marks has pretty much ruined the Adlon bar."

Ebbutt was Norman Ebbutt, the correspondent for the London *Times*, who Shirer regarded as the best correspondent in Berlin, and who, like Sigrid Schultz, had contacts deep in the government that allowed him to break stories. But like most other correspondents, Ebbutt walked on thin ice as he went about his work, waiting for the day when the propaganda ministry and the bureaucrats who managed the foreign press ordered him out of the country because of something he had written.

In late February, Shirer had written another friend with a very different kind of story: the Nazis had beheaded "two Prussian ladies" with an axe. "It was the first in the history of modern Germany in peacetime—but not the last,

I think," he wrote. The women were Benita von Falkenhayn and Renate von Metzner, executed after being tried and convicted in the People's Court on charges of treason. Falkenhayn had been married to Richard von Falkenhayn, the son of Erich von Falkenhayn, a fabled general from the Great War. Street posters announcing the executions had been put up across the city. "One of the important things to remember about national socialism," Shirer wrote to his friend, "is that it does seem to approximate what the majority of Germans want. Or to put it negatively, they don't mind having it." He went on to tell his friend that life in Berlin, notwithstanding the Nazis, was fine.

"We find life here in Berlin not so unpleasant as expected. The foreign correspondents are a nice lot and inclined to hang together more than in Paris. In Naziland you feel the need of it. Outwardly of course Berlin appears very normal, restaurants, shops full, scores of night clubs turning them away, etc. The theater is still pretty good, the actors, I mean, are good. Nazi plays are awful but rarely produced. 'Dosch' [Arno Dosch-Fleurot, manager of Universal News Service Inc.] is fine. His sense of humor saves him from the depression I get every once in a while."

In January 1935, Shirer had covered the plebiscite in the Saarland, a German-speaking region west of the Rhine where the voters overwhelmingly approved a referendum returning their territory to German control. The region had been given to the French in 1919, at least for fifteen years, with the future of its people to be decided by a vote when that period of time was up. When the vote occurred, more than 90 percent of the region's inhabitants voted to become German citizens, in part for economic reasons but also because the Nazis "exerted massive intimidation and violence behind the scenes to deter the opposition from voting against reunification with Germany."

In March, six weeks after the vote, German troops occupied the region. Along with a group of other correspondents, Shirer accompanied the Germans and watched as Hitler arrived to review a contingent of the *Schutzstaffel* (SS). In makeshift stands assembled so that pro-German crowds could see Hitler, Shirer stood with General Werner von Fritsch, the commander in chief of the army, who, as a Prussian, was known to have contempt for the Nazis. Standing next to the general, Shirer was taken aback by his candor. "I was a little surprised at his talk," Shirer wrote in his diary on March 1. "He kept up a running fire of very sarcastic remarks—about the SS, the party, and various party leaders as they appeared. He was full of contempt for them all. When Hitler's car arrived, he grunted and went over and took his place behind the Führer for the review."

Two weeks later, an official in the Propaganda Ministry called the Universal Service bureau on the Dorotheenstrasse, inviting Shirer to an important press conference at five that afternoon to be conducted by Goebbels. When Shirer arrived, he found a large group of foreign correspondents, which he estimated at one hundred, packed into a conference room. "Finally Goebbels limped in, looking very important and grave," Shirer wrote of the club-footed minister. "He began immediately to read in a loud voice the text of a new law."

With the stroke of a pen, Hitler had removed Germany's obligations to the provisions of the 1919 Treaty of Versailles that greatly limited the size and scope of the country's military. As Shirer tried to take notes—he would write in his diary that night that Goebbels was so excited that he read the announcement too fast—Goebbels explained that Germany was now restoring universal military service and would quickly form a standing army of twelve corps. Several of Shirer's colleagues ran for the telephones to call in the announcement. After the press conference ended, Shirer, Ebbutt, and Pat Murphy of the *Daily Express* walked up the Wilhelmstrasse. All three saw something ominous in the announcement. Shirer said goodbye when they reached the Dorotheenstrasse and ran inside to file his story. With his editor Dosch-Fleurot away, Shirer was in charge of the office. He put down his personal thoughts in his diary when he returned to his flat.

"It is a terrible blow to the Allies—to France, Britain, Italy, who fought the war and wrote the peace to destroy Germany's military power and to keep it down. What will London and Paris do? They could fight a 'preventative' war and that would be the end of Hitler.... To bed tired, and sick of this Nazi triumph, but somehow professionally pleased at having had a big story to handle, Dosch being away, which left the job to me alone."

Two days later, while Shirer sat at his desk in the office, a squadron of German airplanes flew in formation over the city.

The Watering Hole

The knock on the apartment door on the morning of April 11, 1935, startled Tess, who had not expected company. Her husband had left early for the Universal Service office and would not return until late in the day. Some nights he did not return until after midnight, preferring to go with his colleagues to the Taverne, an Italian-themed restaurant run by a gregarious German named Willy Lehman, that was the informal meeting place and something of a safe haven for Berlin's foreign correspondents. She was startled when she opened the door. Standing there was a man, an older gentleman. His face was bruised. When he introduced himself, Tess learned he was a friend of a friend. He needed help and a place to stay. Some biographical details followed: he was a distinguished veteran, having lost an arm and a leg fighting for Germany during the Great War; he was a well-known Berlin lawyer; he was a Jew.

When he wrote in his diary later that night, Shirer called the lawyer "Dr. S" to conceal his identity if the Gestapo ever searched the flat. On the morning he knocked on the door of the Shirer apartment, the lawyer had just been released by the Gestapo after several months in prison. Tess told her husband the man was "a little out of his head" and afraid to return to his family. Why the man had sought help from the Shirers is not explained in the diary, although Shirer wrote, "Many Jews come to us these days for advice or help in getting to England or America, but unfortunately there is little we can do for them." Perhaps the man went to the apartment because he believed the Jewish couple who owned it might still be living there.

Writing about the incident a half century later, Shirer expanded on his and Tess's assistance to Jews and to the lawyer in particular. "We foreign correspondents tried to help the Jews the best we could," he wrote. "Tess and I sheltered some we knew, who had gone into hiding, until they could escape abroad. We used our contacts at the embassies and consulates of the U.S.A., Britain, France and Switzerland to facilitate their getting visas.... Sometimes Tess and I would put up a Jewish friend, or a friend of a friend, who had come out of the jail beaten badly, caring for him until he recovered enough to return to his family without shocking them too much."

While in the diary Shirer wrote that Tess "fortified him with whiskey, cheered him up, and sent him home," he told the story another way years later and added two significant details. "The head of the Jewish War Veterans Bund, he had been incarcerated without any formal charges and given the usual treatment. When he came to us one morning he was so battered in body and spirit he did not dare to face his family. We hid him in one of the rooms of our spacious studio apartment until he was healed enough to go home. A few weeks later we were able to spirit him out to London."

Throughout the spring, Shirer, growing more comfortable in his role and speaking German well, covered several of Hitler's speeches, even though he was the number two man in the bureau. Dosch-Fleurot, Shirer's boss, covered one speech Hitler gave at Tempelhof airport, and later in the month Shirer packed into the Reichstag with the other correspondents to hear Hitler shout "Germany wants peace!" assuring the world that he had no interest in annexing Austria or amassing heavy armaments. "The man is truly a superb orator and in the atmosphere of the hand-picked Reichstag, with its six hundred or so sausage-necked, shaven-headed, brown-clad yes men, who rise and shout almost every time Hitler pauses for breath, I suppose he is convincing to Germans who listen to him," Shirer wrote in his diary.

Afterward Shirer ran back to his office to file his story. After drinks with his colleagues at the Taverne, Shirer went to bed, "tired and a little puzzled by the speech, which some of the British and French correspondents at the Taverne tonight thought might really after all pave the way for several years of peace."

*　*　*

On any given night, a dozen or more foreign correspondents gathered at the Taverne to talk about events and how to cover them, and to complain about the hardships they endured. Some nights the reporters brought their wives. Here they could meet, eat and drink, and talk amongst themselves without being bothered by Lehman and his Belgian wife, or feeling they were being spied on, or that someone was writing down what they said to each other and forwarding it to Gestapo headquarters on the Alexanderplatz. The fear of expulsion faded as the correspondents took their seats at their regular table and settled in for the evening. Nightly, the group had a corner table reserved just for

them—"and from about ten p.m. until three or four in the morning it is usually filled." Shirer went most nights after filing his story to compare notes with
the others and to see what they had written and what they had heard, but also
to drink, eat, and socialize.

The informal head of the gathering of American, British, and sometimes
French journalists was the Englishman Norman Ebbutt. Shirer regarded him
highly, and they usually sat together, talking and happily puffing away on their
pipes, filling the air over their heads with clouds of tobacco smoke. It was use-
ful for Shirer, who'd been in the country only since the previous August, to
associate with someone who had so rich and varied a list of contacts and who
knew so much about the players and the day-to-day routines and hardships
involved in covering the secretive offices of a police state. Ebbutt, Shirer wrote
in his diary, "has contacts throughout the government, party, churches, and
army, and has a keen intelligence."

On one of the nights when they sat together, Ebbutt complained to Shirer
that the London *Times* was not publishing all the stories he filed. He feared
that the paper did not want to print stories critical of the German government
and went so far as to suggest that Nazi supporters in London had acquired a
voice at the paper and were now asserting their views, steering the coverage
in a pro-German direction. "He is discouraged and talks of quitting," Shirer
wrote in his diary. Soon, Ebbutt began giving Shirer his tips, since he believed
that, if he wrote them up himself, his paper would not print them.

Others around the big corner table on most nights were Ed Beattie of the
United Press, "with a moon-faced Churchillian countenance behind which
is a nimble wit and a great store of funny stories and songs"; Fred Oechsner,
also of the United Press, and his wife, Dorothy—"he a quiet type but an able
correspondent, she blond, pretty, ebullient, with a low, hoarse voice"; Pierre
Huss, of International News Service, "slick, debonair, ambitious, and on better terms with Nazi officials than almost any other"; Guido Enderis of the *New
York Times*, "aging in his sixties but sporting invariably a gaudy race-track suit
with a loud red necktie, minding the Nazis less than most"; Al Ross, Enderis's
assistant, "bulky, sleepy, slow-going, and lovable"'; Wally Deuel of the *Chicago
Daily News*, "youthful, quiet, studious, extremely intelligent, his wife Mary
Deuel, much the same as he is, with large pretty eyes, they both very much in
love"; Sigrid Schultz of the *Chicago Tribune*, "the only woman correspondent in
our ranks, buoyant, cheerful, and always well informed"; and Otto Tolischus,
also of the *New York Times*, "complicated, profound, studious, with a fine pen-
chant for getting at the bottom of things."

At the Taverne on some nights was Martha Dodd—"pretty, vivacious, a
mighty arguer" and barely in her mid-twenties. She was a woman with close
friendships inside the German government and also with officials of other
governments with embassies in Berlin. Being the American ambassador's

daughter suited her well, and she played the part to the fullest. Others who came irregularly were Louis Lochner of the Associated Press, and John Elliott of the *New York Herald Tribune*, "a very able and learned correspondent, being a teetotaler and non-smoker and much addicted—as we should all be—to his books."

The true oddball among them all was Martha Dodd, who cultivated close relationships with the correspondents who also covered her father, and who always seemed to be privy to a wealth of information that she should not have had. She dropped names—of American officials, of Germans high up in the government, of other foreign officials in the tight diplomatic circle in Berlin, particularly Russians—and acted as though she were on intimate terms with some of them. Some of the correspondents steered clear of her, even as they needed to be on good terms with her father; Shirer did not mind her at all. She was a regular at press events, including the big yearly Foreign Press Ball.

Not long after President Roosevelt sent her father to Berlin to be the American ambassador, Martha set out to "capture Berlin," according to writer Shareen Blair Brysac. "Soon princes, the press, members of the foreign diplomatic corps, and acolytes of three secret services would be at her carefully shod feet." Brysac described Dodd's friendships back in the United States, including those with the film director Otto Preminger, the poet Carl Sandburg, who may have been her lover, and Thornton Wilder, along with a wide assortment of others from the worlds of high finance and academia who made up a Dodd "fan club." There was also a deserted husband in New York. "Martha was bright and talented," Brysac wrote. "She was also impulsive and indiscreet and would acquire a Byronesque reputation of being mad, bad, and dangerous to know."

Martha and her father hosted parties at the embassy that featured members of the "hard-drinking, fast-moving international set," Brysac wrote, along with journalists and people who liked to be referred to by meaningless royal titles. Her politics, if she had any, were bizarre to the extreme—she flirted with Fascism and later Stalinism. "Initially, Hitler's Germany impressed Martha," Brysac wrote. "Conditions had improved under the new regime. Her letters home, reflecting her father's initial optimism, were enthusiastic." Brysac quotes from one gushing letter, in which Martha praises the violent anti-Semite street brawler Horst Wessel, who had been killed in 1930 and was then elevated to sainthood by the Nazis: "The youth are bright faced and hopeful, they sing to the noble ghost of Horst Wessel with shining eyes and unerring tongues. Wholesome and beautiful lads, these Germans, good, sincere, healthy, mystic, brutal, fine, hopeful, capable of death and love, deep, rich, wondrous and strange beings."

Martha went dancing with the German foreign minister's son, Brysac wrote; she flew in the airplane of Ernst Udet, the great ace from the world war; Göring took her falcon hunting at his estate; she thought Goebbels "had a great sense of humor." In her private life, which wasn't so private, she "liked sleeping with attractive men, and that's how she learned about politics and history." At one point, Hanfstaengl tried to arrange a date between Martha and Hitler.

At a party given by Sigrid Schultz, which Shirer presumably attended, Martha met Boris Vinogradov, the first secretary in the Soviet Embassy in Berlin. He met her later at a nightclub, Brysac wrote, and they soon began a relationship—an official of Stalin's government sleeping with the daughter of the American ambassador to Germany. Their affair was well underway by the spring and summer of 1934 in the months before Shirer's arrival in Berlin. Martha also found a way to juggle relationships with a Gestapo official, whom Brysac identifies as one Rolf Diels. She had enough affairs in the American embassy that the embassy's butler referred to the building as a whorehouse.

*   *   *

For Shirer and his colleagues, gathering news that was not handed out as official truth was a monumental task. Trying to speak to anyone in the government was an act of frustration for Shirer and potentially dangerous for the official. Developing friendships with German journalists from the big newspapers was equally difficult and frustrating, since the papers had all been purged of anyone not racially "qualified," as well as of anyone not fully supportive of the Nazis. All reporters working for the German newspapers were members of the Nazi-controlled Reich Press Chamber. Large numbers of journalists who could not or would not meet the new requirements either quit and went into internal exile or fled to the West. Official harassment of foreign correspondents and their bureaus in Berlin was commonplace. In mid-1935 Shirer wrote: "We have been approached for commenting on the disappearance of *Der Tag* with regret. However, we lack all understanding for an attitude which welcomes conformity and monotony in the German Press."

In late August, Dosch-Fleurot wrote to Hanfstaengl to try to head off his criticism about a story Universal Service had filed that had run in the *New York American* on July 24. The tone of the letter is more than a bit groveling, as might be expected of Dosch-Fleurot, who was trying to protect his wire service from bullying by the government.

"Thank you for calling my attention to the Berlin dispatch in the New York American....As only a portion of this dispatch, and not the portion which you criticized, was sent by Universal Service, I have protested to New York against the use of the initials (US) on this story by the New York American. As a rule our papers do not change or add to Berlin dispatches, although they sometimes rewrite the 'leads' in a more sensational form than we cable. I shall always be very glad to have your criticisms of any news stories in the American newspapers accredited with Universal Service (US) or International News Service (INS)."

All the correspondents found it extraordinarily difficult to write the stories they wanted without the thought in the backs of their minds that they would be read in US papers and their contents reported back to Hanfstaengl. The writer could censor himself—not write anything that might draw criticism and threats of expulsion—or write the story he thought should be written and take his chances. Even more challenging was protecting those few sources of information from arrest.

While he was in Berlin, Shirer fretted daily that one of his sources—he had a number of them—would be arrested by the Gestapo and executed. Nowhere in the diary he kept in Berlin does he mention a name or position, fearing that the diary might be seized and used to incriminate someone. He wrote that he had been interrogated by the Gestapo, in his office and in the apartment, but he said little except that he offered them no help at all.

Years later, Shirer wrote that two influential sources of his had been arrested, and the effect was to sink him into despair. "When sometimes one of my sources did get nabbed and, in two cases, sentenced to death, I would walk the streets of the capital, dazed and despairing, searching my conscience and my memory to try to discover if anything I had done, any slip I might have made, could possibly have implicated him," he wrote.

In his writing a half century after the events recorded in his diary, Shirer identified one of his sources as a "fearless young Protestant pastor." They met after dark in the Tiergarten near Shirer's flat or on a busy street or at a railway station; other times, throwing all caution aside, the man came to Shirer's flat to talk. He does not name the pastor but says he was arrested and sentenced to death. Another was a journalist he identified as "X" in a January 1936 diary entry. The man was an editor of the *Börsen Zeitung* who secretly gave Shirer copies of Goebbels's daily instructions to the foreign press. In the January 1936 entry, Shirer wrote that the instructions from Goebbels "made rich reading, ordering daily suppression of this truth and the substitution of that lie."

Later, Shirer was greatly relieved when he learned that both the editor's and the pastor's death sentences had been commuted. They would spend the rest of the Thousand Year Reich in prison. Shirer vowed in another diary entry not to talk to anyone, or encourage anyone to work with him, if it risked the person's arrest and execution. Shirer knew that other German officials had provided him with information he was sure was wrong, and he suspected they were working for the Gestapo to try to entrap him. One, a young man in the Foreign Office, admitted to Shirer one night when they were drinking together that he had been assigned by the Gestapo to follow him. A very good and reliable source was a woman who held an important post in the radio division of the Propaganda Ministry. Shirer knew she loved a Jewish artist who had fled the country. She wore a party pin on her lapel as she went about her work, and Shirer came to both like and trust her. They met in secret, and she supplied him with information about the inner workings and plans of the government, at least as she knew them.

* * *

Early in the summer of 1935, Bill and Tess moved out of the flat on the Tauentzienstrasse to one in the Tempelhof district of the city. Neither wanted to be in the flat owned by the Jewish couple when the heat of summer arrived, as it was on the top floor of the building, just under the roof, and warmed up uncomfortably on sunny days.

If the owners of the flat were anonymous before, now, with the move, they disappeared entirely from the pages of his diary. However he felt about them as individuals, how he felt about their treatment by the German government, Shirer did not write down. If Shirer—and the other American and British correspondents who almost certainly had similar encounters, involving scores of other Jews in Berlin—felt a moral quandary as to what was the right course of action to take as they carried out their roles as correspondents, he did not write about it. Nor did he use his diaries or letters, at least the ones he saved, for a debate on the role of the journalist when watching injustice on a large scale take place right before his eyes. This is not to say he or the other reporters did not care about the dire conditions in which the German Jews found themselves; everything in Shirer's character, all the words he wrote about himself and his life, strongly suggests otherwise. He was in Berlin to report on the fundamental transformation of the German state and the movement toward a world war, after all, not to act as a lifesaver or advocate for a beaten minority. Nonetheless, the German government's war against the Jews went on without the foreign press getting its hackles up.

The Shirers' new landlord was a different sort of German—a flying ace from the Great War who Shirer refers to in his diary as Captain Koehl. As the first landlord was Jewish and had to flee the country, the new landlord was, as Shirer described him, something of a dissident. Koehl and his wife were acquaintances of some of Shirer's journalist friends, so Koehl, however critical of the government he may have been, seems to have moved in important circles. "He is one of the few men in Germany with enough courage not to knuckle down to Göring and the Nazis," Shirer wrote in his diary. "As a result he is completely out, having even lost his job with Lufthansa. A fervent Catholic and a man of strong character, he prefers to retire to his little farm in the south of Germany rather than curry Nazi favour. He is one of a very few. I've taken a great liking to him."

In an undated letter addressed to "Herr Koehl," Shirer wrote that he would soon be going to America on a trip and then referred to the mood of Germany in an unguarded way that might have gotten Koehl into trouble had the letter been opened. "Yes, the political situation is dark indeed. I suppose during 1936, though, there will be a decision one way or the other, for war or against." On a lighter note, he added, "Frau Hensel has been here for two days collecting your things."

As summer wore on, Shirer grew weary of the demands of his work and eagerly planned for a trip to America. He hoped to sail to New York in mid-September, which he knew was when the Nazi Party's Nuremberg rally was scheduled. It was more important for him to leave Germany for a brief respite than to attend what would have been his second party rally. In August he wrote a friend to explain why he was so eager to leave Germany.

"I've been in Europe with a year's interlude in the Near East and India, for ten years—since I was 21—with only two weeks off in America, and that during the fall of 1929 when the stock market was crashing and many of our citizens seemed stark mad," he wrote, forgetting his and Tess's extended stay on the Spanish coast. "And after ten years one can become very weary of the Old World and its quarrels and of the role of the eternal outsider, looked on suspiciously in the more pleasant countries, and regarded as an outright enemy and 'foreign liar' as in this country."

He wrote to his friend Nicholas Roosevelt, who lived on Long Island not far from the family estate of his distant relative Theodore Roosevelt. After a number of years in Europe, Nicholas Roosevelt was back in New York writing editorials for the *Herald Tribune*. In August, after learning from Shirer about the upcoming trip, Roosevelt wrote to say he wanted to get together with him when he arrived. Shirer also wrote his brother, John, to tell him when he would be in New York, and to make the sad point that he had not seen their mother since 1929. It was nothing to be proud of, not seeing his mother in six years, and Shirer felt the sting of it, wondering as he did on many occasions if he'd made the correct choices for his career. She was in her mid-sixties and lived in Cedar Rapids. He loved his mother, knowing full well what she had done for her children, and was haunted by the thought that she might die before he saw her again.

Tess stayed behind, to visit relatives in Austria, and also because the couple did not have enough money for tickets for both of them. Docking at Southampton in Britain, Shirer received word that Tess had come down with an acute attack of appendicitis while hiking in the Austrian mountains. "An ox cart, a bus and a train had just managed to get to Vienna in time for an operation that saved her life," Shirer wrote a friend. A few weeks later, Shirer wrote his brother asking for a loan of $100 to help pay for Tess's operation.

After he reached America on board the German liner the *Bremen* and visited his brother and mother—who had come east to see her son in New

Jersey—Shirer took the train out to Long Island, to Roosevelt's mansion, for a weekend in the country. He had last seen Roosevelt in Budapest, where he was stationed in the US Embassy. They were very different kinds of men—Shirer liberal and left leaning, Roosevelt conservative and outspoken—but they got along well and enjoyed each other's company.

Over the course of the weekend, the two men argued, not over European political developments but over domestic affairs in the United States, where Roosevelt was profoundly worried that the New Deal would crush the life and democracy out of the country. "He was too preoccupied with Franklin Roosevelt's 'dictatorship' to allow for much time to argue European affairs," Shirer wrote in his diary. Years later, Shirer wrote that Roosevelt behaved as if he thought FDR was "the devil himself, intent on leading the Republic to Bolshevik ruin. I could scarcely believe it. Indeed it seemed to me that Franklin Roosevelt had saved capitalism in America—despite the capitalists. We sat up arguing through the night, my good friend looking at me more and more as if I were crazy."

Shirer knew from reading the New York papers that the German Reichstag had met in Nuremberg while he was in New York and passed sweeping anti-Jewish legislation known as the Nuremberg Laws. The news barely registered in America. "No one, at least in New York, paid much attention," he wrote. "Most Americans I talked to that fall, even Jews, did not grasp the enormity of Hitler's crimes....I kept getting the feeling that they thought I was a bit 'emotional' and 'sensational' on the subject."

After the weekend was over, Shirer stayed with his mother and brother a few more days until he received an order from the Universal Service office in New York to return to Germany immediately on board the German liner *Europa*. Italian forces under Mussolini were threatening to invade Abyssinia, and Dosch-Fleurot was being reassigned to Rome. Seymour Berkson, head of the Universal Service office in New York, told Shirer that upon his return he would take over the management of the Berlin bureau.

THE DIRTY LIAR

S hirer arrived back on German soil at the end of September 1935, two
weeks after the close of the party rally at Nuremberg, to find the government even more secretive and more difficult to deal with than before. The
most minor requests to bureaucrats produced loud arguments. Officials in the
Propaganda Ministry who dealt with foreign journalists were more arrogant,
and the passage of the Nuremberg Laws had emboldened the wing of the party
that wanted to lower the hammer on the Jews. There was no time for Shirer
to pause and think back on the reunion with his brother and his mother or
to dwell on the thought that he should perhaps give serious consideration to
moving back to the United States. He and Tess would stay in Berlin as long as
they could.

There was a greater degree of concern among the foreign correspondents
that any wrong move—ask the wrong question, write the wrong story, speak
to the wrong people—would result in a visit from the Gestapo and an order to
leave the country. All feared that any Germans around them—housekeepers,
office assistants, part-time employees of any sort—were Gestapo plants listening to their every word. All worried that a vacation or an assignment outside
the country's borders could result in their being denied reentry. Beyond that
concern was a genuine worry that the government's efforts to punish them
could be far worse than expulsion, and that they—and the American Embassy
under Dodd in Berlin—would be powerless to prevent it.

For Shirer and a number of the correspondents who privately loathed the
Nazis, taking any sort of position, even a private one mentioned only among
themselves at the Taverne, could be a very bad move. They had all watched
with alarm as their colleagues—Edgar Mowrer of the *Chicago Daily News* in

1933 and Dorothy Thompson of the *New York Evening Post* in 1934—were ordered out of the country, while others were summoned to official offices, where they were berated and threatened. Their goal was to stay and continue to work, not to draw criticism and be expelled on short notice. They had to watch themselves, and that meant, to one degree or another, censoring what they said and wrote.

For his part, Mowrer seems to have been one of the only American correspondents in Germany, prior to his expulsion, to have referred to the Nazis' "barbarous campaign" against the Jews as a sign of far worse to come. In 1933, he used the word "extermination" as a possible future outcome. He was probably not using the word to suggest that the German government would round up its Jews and attempt to murder them all. Neither he nor any other observer could possibly have seen that coming. "Those who today claim that the world should have recognized from the outset in 1933 that the Final Solution was in the offing are using historical hindsight, a tool that was obviously not available to contemporary observers," historian Deborah E. Lipstadt has written.

As historian Michael Burleigh has noted, the Citizenship Law and the Law for the Protection of German Blood and Honour, together known as the Nuremberg Laws, satisfied those in the party who wanted to move aggressively against the Jews. They wanted a program, and new facts on the ground, and they got them. "Under the first law, Jews forfeited German citizenship, becoming 'state subjects,'" Burleigh has written. "The second law prohibited marriage and sexual intercourse between 'Aryans' and Jews; the employment of female 'Aryan' servants under forty-five years of age in Jewish households; and finally the hoisting by Jews of either German flag."

Those Jewish war veterans who had served on the western front during the Great War fell under the umbrella of the law. If the members of this group thought that somehow their service would allow them to fall between the cracks of government efforts against the Jews, the passage of the Nuremberg Laws dashed all hopes. The one-armed, one-legged veteran who knocked on the door of the Shirer flat looking for help was no longer a citizen of the country for which he had lost both limbs. These veterans could not fly a German flag, let alone the swastika flag, which Hitler now declared the national flag.

In late July, before Shirer had sailed to the United States on board the German liner *Bremen*, the ship had docked in New York Harbor. Passengers disembarked and supplies were taken on board for the return trip to Germany. Before the *Bremen* pulled away, a mob managed to get onto the ship's deck, where they pulled down the big swastika flag and tossed it into the Hudson River. In his speech at the party rally in September, Göring blamed this incident on "an impudent Jew, in his bottomless hatred" for Germany.

As 1935 came to a close, the tension between government officials and a number of foreign correspondents increased dramatically. For days running, Shirer found it hard to work and to write anything good enough to cable back to New York. There were few facts to find and fewer reliable people to discuss them with. Goebbels, whose Propaganda Ministry managed all the country's journalists and the news they put out, began calling out individual correspondents by name, using highly provocative language. He labeled H. R. Knickerbocker a "dirty liar." A second correspondent, Otto Tolischus of the *New York Times*, was threatened as well, as was Norman Ebbutt. Shirer's friend John Elliott, who wrote for the *New York Herald Tribune*, left Berlin for Paris out of sheer disgust at Goebbels and his staff and concern that he would be expelled.

Shirer made only one diary entry in December, on the thirtieth, when he jotted down a short paragraph in which he said that he and other American correspondents—presumably Wally Deuel and Sigrid Schultz—had gone to the American embassy to see Dodd and to meet the visiting US undersecretary of state, William Phillips. There was an urgent need for the meeting: Shirer and the others wanted Phillips's assurance that he would intervene if they faced expulsion. Their hopes were quickly dashed.

"We asked him what action Washington would take if the Nazis began expelling us," Shirer wrote in his diary. "He gave an honest answer. He said: None."

* * *

As the year came to an end, Shirer set out for the mountain village of Garmisch-Partenkirchen to write about planning for the Winter Olympics, which were scheduled to start in early February. Germany had been awarded both the winter and the summer games, and Shirer wanted to write about the preparations for the games as well as show how Hitler hoped to showcase his government's achievements and cast its actions in the best possible light. Three years had passed since he had been named chancellor; his government had opened concentration camps for political opponents, forced Jews out of their careers, and passed laws removing them as citizens of the country, but the world would arrive in the Bavarian Alps for the winter games as if none of this had happened in the country.

Making his way into the snow-filled Alps, Shirer noticed that the ubiquitous signs "Jews Get Out" and "Jews Unwanted" had been removed from the roadsides. He could think of only one reason for this: the government didn't want international visitors arriving for the games to see them. He did see one sign that read: "Drive Carefully! Sharp Curve. Jews 75 kilometers an Hour!"

but others were gone, as if an army of volunteers had fanned out across the country in the dead of night and taken them all down.

When Shirer returned to Berlin, he wrote a four-part series for the wire service on preparations for the games, noting in his final story that "All Jew baiting is officially off in Germany during the Olympics," and mailed it to New York. He had all but forgotten the series when, early on the morning of January 23, three weeks into the new year of 1936, the phone rang in the apartment. When Shirer, exhausted from a late night of work, picked up the phone, he heard the loud, angry voice of Wilfred Bade, a "fanatical Nazi careerist" in the Propaganda Ministry.

"Have you been in Garmisch recently?" Bade shouted.

"No," Shirer responded.

"I see," Bade said. "You haven't been there and yet you have the dishonesty to write a fake story about the Jews there—"

"Wait a minute," Shirer said, "you can't call me dishonest."

The line went dead as Bade slammed down the phone.

At noon, while Shirer was getting ready to go to the office, Tess turned on the radio to hear the announcer denouncing her husband by name. The stories, the announcer charged, were lies meant to embarrass Germany and force countries to boycott the games. That night, when he wrote in his diary, Shirer noted that the stories had also accused local Nazi officials of taking all the good hotels in Garmisch for themselves. Tess was horrified, but Shirer continued to dress, after which the couple shared a quick lunch and Shirer left for the office on the Dorotheenstrasse. He knew the dispute would not quietly go away. He was now in the spotlight.

Arriving at his desk, Shirer scanned the city's newspapers and saw he was being singled out "as a liar and a cheat and a 'German hater.'" His phone began ringing, one call after another from journalist friends advising him to ignore the attacks. It would blow over. To fight back would only push his name further up the list, surely kept on a desk in the Propaganda Ministry, of foreign correspondents to be ordered out of the country for their attitudes and dishonest reporting. The Germans who worked in the office and in the other newspaper offices in the building came to Shirer's desk to speak with him, expecting the Gestapo to show up and drive him to the airport.

With the arrival on his desk of new editions of the afternoon papers, Shirer grew angrier. He wanted to confront Bade. At this moment, seething over what they were saying about him, he did not care what they did in response. Picking up the phone on his desk, he called Bade's office and demanded to see him, only to be told he was not in. Every few minutes he called again, only to be told the same thing. Rushing out of the office, Shirer walked to the Propaganda Ministry building and, ignoring the rules of formality, entered Bade's office. He found him sitting at his desk. Shirer, his temper uncorked, shouted in Bade's face that he wanted an apology and a correction in the newspapers and on the next news broadcast. Bade lost any composure, shouting in Shirer's face that he would receive nothing of the kind and who did he think he was. Furious, Shirer spoke so fast most of the words came out in English and mangled German.

Hearing the commotion, several office workers opened the door and peered in to see if their boss needed any help. Bade waved them out and after the door was shut again, the shouting resumed. He slammed his fist on the desk.

Smugly, Bade told Shirer he would not be expelled.

Infuriated, Shirer dared him to try anyway.

When Bade did not react, Shirer turned and walked out of the office and back out into the street.

* * *

A week after Shirer's confrontation with Bade, he and Tess set out for Garmisch-Partenkirchen to cover the winter games. Although she wanted to be in the mountains and on skis herself, Tess also came along to help her husband cover different events going on at the same time. At the end of the day, she would give him her notes for his stories. As usual, she brought along her camera. The mountain village was filled with athletes from all over the world, and the German government was determined to play the good host. German soldiers and SS troops filled the streets. "On the whole the Nazis have done a wonderful propaganda job," Shirer wrote in his diary. "They've greatly impressed most of the visiting foreigners with the lavish but smooth way in which they've run the games and with their kind manners, which to us who came from Berlin of course seemed staged."

Among the visiting American correspondents was Westbrook Pegler, who had also written for the paper in the mid-1920s when Shirer was working for the *Tribune*. Now he wrote a popular column for the Scripps-Howard Syndicate. Each day, Tess and Bill, sometimes joined by Pegler, set out to cover the events—downhill skiing, what Shirer in his diary referred to as "bob races," hockey matches, and the thrilling Norwegian skater Sonja Henie.

On several days, when Hitler was in the stadium, Shirer, Pegler, and another American journalist, Paul Gallico, who covered sports for the *New York Daily News*, had confrontations with the SS troops guarding their leader. Pegler was irritated at their presence everywhere. Writing in his diary, Shirer said Pegler was particularly upset at a story in the Nazi newspaper the *Völkischer Beobachter* that quoted the *New York Times* reporter Fred Birchall as praising the games and going so far as to criticize American reporters who said the event was tinged with Nazi propaganda.

Shirer was upset enough at what he saw as the pro-German mood of visiting American businessmen that he organized a luncheon and asked a representative of the American embassy in Berlin, Douglas Miller, to address the visitors on the true nature of the Nazi government. As Shirer wrote in his diary, Miller barely got a word in edgewise. The businessmen were not interested in that side of the story.

Parading Down the Wilhelmstrasse

"This has been a day of the wildest rumors."
—William L. Shirer, diary, March 6, 1936

Among the American and British correspondents, who talked as much to each other about what might be going on as they did with the government officials they covered, the rumors centered on Hitler's abruptly ordering the Reichstag to convene on March 7, 1936. There was some sort of emergency—Germany was walking away from a series of treaties approved in the late fall of 1925 among France, Belgium, and Germany in the Swiss resort town of Locarno. The Locarno treaties had made formal the boundaries among the three countries as set by the 1919 Treaty of Versailles. The agreements signed at Locarno made permanent France's ownership of Alsace-Lorraine and required Germany to keep troops out of the Rhineland. Hitler was going to tear up the agreements and, if the rumors were true, order the German army into the Rhineland. The history of the end of the Great War, the terms laid down to the losers, was being cast aside.

An official Shirer knew well told him Hitler probably wouldn't send in troops—it was too provocative, and the French army could push them out easily if he did. The official—Shirer calls him an "informant" in his diary entry—said Hitler might just declare the German police in the Rhineland part of the national army, which, as Shirer noted that night, would have the same "practical effect" as sending in fresh troops.

Berlin was filled with government officials summoned for the convening of the Reichstag. Shirer found himself near the Foreign Ministry in a large crowd of Reichstag members wearing their shiny party pins on their lapels, along with uniformed troops and SS men. The mood was tense and defiant. Their Führer was a bold man! Shirer got the press chief at the Wilhelmstrasse, Dr. Gottfried Aschmann, on the phone, who denied vociferously that German troops would enter the Rhineland. (The Wilhelmstrasse was the name the reporters gave the Foreign Ministry, although other important party and government offices were also on the street, including the Propaganda Ministry.)

"That would mean war," Aschmann said, as if that were the last word on the subject.

Shirer of course did not believe Aschmann. He was almost certainly uninformed and under orders to say just that and nothing else. All the officials who dealt with the foreign correspondents were liars. That was their job. They made up stories. They bullied journalists to drive them away from the stories they were reporting on. They intimidated them so they'd stop asking questions the officials did not want to answer. They looked them in the eye indignantly and got theatrical about it: *Don't you believe me? Do you know who you are talking to? We don't lie. We're not like you.* Disgusted with Aschmann, Shirer rushed back to his office and typed out a dispatch and cabled it to the New York office, suggesting that German troops would not be sent into the demilitarized Rhineland because French troops could easily push them out.

* * *

As the sun rose the next morning, March 7, 1936, German troops marched into the Rhineland. Rushing to the Reichstag, which was meeting in the Kroll Opera House, Shirer found a seat in the press section and heard Hitler talk about peace in Europe and demilitarizing both sides of the Rhine. William Dodd, the American ambassador, was seated in the audience. General von Blomberg, whom Shirer had met at the Foreign Press Ball, was seated nearby, and to Shirer's eye looked pale, which Shirer interpreted as a lack of enthusiasm on the part of the regular army for their leader's escapades.

"Hitler began with a long harangue which he has often given before, but never tires of repeating, about the injustices of the Versailles Treaty and the peacefulness of Germans," Shirer wrote in his diary. "Then his voice, which had been low and hoarse at the beginning, rose to a shrill, hysterical scream as he raged against Bolshevism."

Shirer watched six hundred deputies—

personal appointees all of Hitler, little men with big bodies and bulging necks and
cropped hair and pouched bodies and brown uniforms and heavy boots, little men of clay

in his fine hands, leap to their feet like automatons, their right arms upstretched in the
Nazi salute, and scream "Heil's," the first two or three wildly, the next twenty-five in
unison, like a college yell. Hitler raises his hand for silence. It comes slowly. Slowly the
automatons sit down. Hitler now has them in his claws. He appears to sense it. He says
in a deep, resonant voice: "Men of the German Reichstag!" The silence is utter.

"In this historic hour, when in the Reich's western provinces German troops are
at this minute marching into their future peace-time garrisons, we all unite in two
sacred vows." He can go no further. It is news to this hysterical "parliamentary" mob
that German soldiers are already on the move into the Rhineland. All the militarism
in their German blood surges to their heads. They spring, yelling and crying, to
their feet. The audience in the galleries does the same, all except a few diplomats and
about fifty of us correspondents. Their hands are raised in slavish salute, their faces
now contorted with hysteria, their mouths wide open, shouting, shouting, their eyes,
burning with fanaticism, glued on the new god, the Messiah.

Hitler vowed that Germany would not yield to any army or force as it
went about the "restoration of the honour of our people," and he pledged that
Germany had no territorial demands to make on Europe and wanted only
peace. Shirer stood with the other correspondents and felt as if the intensity in
the room would lift the roof off the opera house.

After the speech, Shirer rushed outside to watch Hitler drive off with
his entourage. He and his colleague John Elliott, who wrote for the *New York*
Herald Tribune, walked across the Tiergarten to the Adlon Hotel for lunch,
both too overwhelmed by the speech to say much to each other. After lunch,
Shirer walked by himself back through the park and there ran into Blomberg
walking two dogs. It seemed so bizarre—the general walking his dogs in
silence after Hitler's speech. If Shirer toyed with the idea of stopping to talk
to him, he thought better of it, and instead proceeded to his office on the
Dorotheenstrasse. At his desk he typed furiously, stopping every few minutes
to telephone sections of the story to the office in Paris.

Shirer was surprised that the French did not immediately react to German
troops marching unmolested into the Rhineland. "It seemed incomprehensible they would not march with so much at stake," he wrote of the French
army. In his diary that night, he wrote: "Tonight for the first time since 1870
grey-clad German soldiers and blue-clad French troops face each other across
the upper Rhine."

As for Hitler's speech proposing peace for Europe, Shirer knew it was a
lie. He was disgusted with himself for not declaring it so flat out. But he knew
he could not, nor could he find a German outside the government to say it, and
the frustration ate at him. "The proposal is a pure fraud, and if I had any guts,
or American journalism had any, I would have said so in my dispatch tonight,"
he wrote. "But I am not supposed to be 'editorial.'"

As darkness fell over the city, Shirer stood at his office window and watched columns of storm troops parading down the Wilhelmstrasse, past Hitler's Chancellery, holding aloft burning torches. It was an extraordinary sight—thousands of uniformed men, their faces lit by the fires, marching in unison, a single, machinelike mass. Shirer dispatched a German office worker, who called back from the street that Hitler stood on this balcony admiring the parade with Julius Streicher next to him. A radio in the office broadcast that there were torchlight parades occurring simultaneously across the country. A correspondent working for Shirer in Cologne phoned to say that German troops had been greeted enthusiastically as they marched into the Rhineland. Women lined the streets throwing flowers at the soldiers. Reaching a government official on the phone, Shirer was informed that the Germans had sent in approximately fifty thousand men.

When he was done with his story, Shirer dashed to the Taverne to join a dozen or more journalists gathered at their table. It was well after midnight. He ordered beer and, famished, two plates of spaghetti, sitting at the table until nearly 3:00 A.M., listening to a French journalist predict that his country's army would march in the morning and push the Germans out of the Rhineland.

That's the end of Hitler if the French move, Shirer thought.

*　*　*

> *"Hitler has got away with it!"*
> —William L. Shirer, diary, March 8, 1936

Sunday, March 8, was Heroes' Memorial Day, a national holiday created by Hitler to commemorate the two million German dead of the Great War. Like France, where Shirer had seen the wounded in the streets, Germany's wounded—there were four million of them in 1918—were a large army of the crippled and the limbless and the misshapen. (The combined total of military and civilian dead, plus the wounded, amounted to more than 10 percent of the country's total population the year the war ended.) Shirer went to the Opera House for the celebration of the holiday and saw Hitler, Göring, and Blomberg—"all smiles this noon"—celebrating their bold move into the Rhineland. Hitler wore a "simple brown party uniform, his Iron Cross pinned over the left breast pocket," Shirer wrote.

A government official, unidentified in the diary, told Shirer that afternoon that the German troops were under orders "to beat a hasty retreat if the French army opposed them in any way. They were not prepared or equipped to fight a regular army. That probably explains Blomberg's white face yesterday." Shirer later identified the source as an officer on the general staff of the army.

The correspondent in Cologne had told Shirer that the German troops acted more like a parading army. "The gray-clad Reichswehr troops simply marched in behind blaring bands—there was no battle order whatsoever," Shirer wrote. "God knows I had seen the rot in France during my return to work there in 1934. Frenchmen were more concerned with fighting Frenchmen than Germans. Still. With their army so much more powerful than Hitler's it seemed incomprehensible that they would not march with so much at stake: not only the security of the northeast frontier, over which had come so many German invasions in the past, but perhaps the overthrow of the Nazi regime."

Shirer stayed in the Opera House to hear Blomberg deliver the Memorial Day speech. To Shirer, the general "was surprisingly defiant—even cocky. But then I remembered he was merely uttering words prepared for him by his Master." When the event ended, Shirer walked to Hadel's, a nearby restaurant. He sat alone in a window seat and looked out at the people calmly going about their business on the busy Unter den Linden, the dramatic boulevard he and Tess loved to stroll on warm days. When he had eaten, he returned to his desk and called the Universal News Service office in London to inquire about the British reaction to the German reoccupation of the Rhineland. There was none at all, he was told. The prime minister was away for the weekend. The cabinet was not meeting.

In mid-March, Shirer traveled to Karlsruhe to cover Hitler's speech on the upcoming Reichstag elections, to be held on the twenty-ninth. In his diary on March 13, while in Karlsruhe, Shirer cynically put quotation marks around "election," knowing the event was a fraud. Shirer knew the script by now: Hitler would receive 99 percent of the vote, and the government spokesmen would tell the world how beloved he was and how much he wanted peace. A huge crowd packed under a tent waited for Hitler and his entourage to arrive. Bothered by the crowds, Shirer and a group of correspondents returned to their hotel to drink wine and listen to Hitler's speech on the radio. "Nothing new in it," Shirer wrote in his diary, "though he drummed away nicely about his desire for friendship with France."

On election day, Shirer tried to report on whether there was any dissent anywhere in the country, but he only heard rumors that some election districts in Berlin that had once been communist strongholds delivered a "no" vote that was perhaps as high as 20 percent. But he didn't know, and there was no way to know anything with certainty. The one sure thing was that the Nazis would win all the seats. During the day, Shirer stood in the street outside his office and watched Germany's new zeppelin, the *Hindenburg*, sail over the city. Leaflets urging the populace to vote "yes" in the plebiscite floated down to the street.

* * *

For Bill and Tess, life in Berlin was a whirl of activity that centered on his work for the wire service. When the job could be put aside, they did their best to make a social life for themselves constructed around the things they loved to do. His day as a correspondent typically began in the early afternoon and ended after midnight, most often at his regular table at the Taverne. In March, as he prepared to cover the plebiscite, he wrote to the New York office to ask for a pay raise. He complained that his $60 a week salary was wholly inadequate for the task at hand. Prices in Berlin were 25 to 100 percent higher than in New York, the cost of clothing had skyrocketed, and tobacco for his pipe was absurdly high and the quality poor.

"A tin of miserable weeds costs 60 cents compared to 15 cents for a tin of good pipe tobacco at home," he wrote. "A suit you could buy in NY for 30 costs 80 here. A luncheon that can be had there for 50 to 60 cents costs $1.25 to $1.50 here." He was now the sole correspondent in the office, he added, "And without wishing to overestimate myself I think it can be said that by dint of a 12–14 hour working day I, with the help of one office boy, am giving the opposition, whose staffs are four to five times as large, a fairly good run for their money." A raise was not forthcoming; little did Shirer know that Universal News Service was struggling to pay its bills and maintain its foreign operation.

Bill and Tess's love of music, theater, and the arts was the same as it had been in Vienna, but Berlin under the Nazis was not Vienna. "Now and then we stole off for an evening at the opera, the concert house, the theater," he wrote, adding that the quality of everything had fallen dramatically because of the "idiotic and depressing" banning of works by Jews. Many of the country's Jewish composers and writers had either fled the country for new lives elsewhere or were living lives in the shadows, waiting for more shoes to drop.

Shirer's day was built around a period of hard work from 5:00 P.M. to 9:00 P.M., reporting and then writing a story he would telephone to either Paris or London for transmission to New York. By midnight he would join his colleagues at the Taverne, sometimes, but not often, joined by German journalists who were little more than surrogates of the Nazis and who could not be trusted. "Occasionally they could be helpful in tipping us off to something or in explaining the in-fighting going on around Hitler, [but] we were always suspicious of them and their news," he wrote.

The nights at their long table in the corner were dominated by political talk, with reporters each having their different views. It was one part of the country, one small piece of the capital city—a corner table in a busy Italian restaurant—where speech was free, opinionated, and seditious. One journalist in Shirer's circle who had more neutral views toward the Nazis was Guido Enderis, who ran the *New York Times* bureau in Berlin. Shirer was fond of him, in large part, because he was the experienced elder journalist in the room, "likeable...[and] rather apolitical," Shirer recalled, "and not seeming to mind the Nazis." Enderis had a wealth of knowledge that impressed Shirer, who was easily impressed around journalists who had seen and done a great deal more than he had. Remarkably, Enderis had ridden out the 1914–1918 war in Berlin without being arrested by the Germans, no doubt because he held a Swiss passport. But, to Shirer's eye, he parted ways with his colleagues who loathed the Nazis.

"He had little interest in, and no sympathy at all for, the hatred most of us felt for the Nazis," Shirer wrote. "He thought we were too ideological—as bad as the Nazis in this."

Shirer was in some ways being kind to Enderis, and he may not have been fully aware of his sympathies for the German government. In the *Times'* Berlin bureau, Enderis was seen as someone who papered over his sympathy for the Nazis with demands for fairness and balance in the paper's coverage. Enderis was loath to write about the country's concentration camps and the status of Jews in the country.

Included in Shirer's circle of good friends was Ralph Barnes, who worked for the *New York Herald Tribune*. Bill and Tess, Barnes, his wife, Esther, and their two daughters spent holidays together, particularly the American ones like Thanksgiving. Christmas and New Year's found them together, and he and Ralph frequently collaborated on a story, with Tess often helping with translations.

* * * *

In search of time away from his work he could spend with Tess, Shirer bought a small sailboat from a man he'd met in a bar. The sloop ran eighteen feet in length and had two small beds in a cramped cabin and presented the possibility of getting away on one of the beautiful lakes around the city, where the rich and the party elite also went. Their routine on hot days when Shirer felt confident about escaping the office and the demands of his work was to take a streetcar to the Havel River, where they kept the boat in a marina. They would pack food, beer, and wine and "sail it for eight or nine miles, anchor in a cove, swim off the boat for an hour, have a drink, fix up a dinner, wash it down with a bottle of wine and hit the bunks for a good night's sleep after checking the news on the radio to see that nothing very sensational was breaking."

In June, Bill and Tess left Germany altogether and traveled to Dubrovnik on the Adriatic Sea. They checked into a small hotel overlooking the water where Shirer met Katherine Anne Porter, a Texas-born writer noted for her short stories, who had lived in Germany in the early 1930s. Shirer knew her work and was disappointed that Porter showed no inclination to become better acquainted. They spoke briefly on several occasions, but Porter was there to work and Shirer to vacation, and his effort to sit and speak with her about her writing came to nothing.

Bill and Tess were joined in Dubrovnik by H. R. Knickerbocker, who had won the Pulitzer Prize in 1931 for his coverage of Russia, and his wife, Agnes, who was far along in her pregnancy. In 1933, the year Hitler came to power, Knickerbocker had filed a story with his paper about the Reich's treatment of its Jewish citizens in which he didn't shy away from the truth. "An indeterminate number of Jews...have been killed. Hundreds of Jews have been beaten or tortured. Thousands of Jews have fled. Thousands of Jews have been, or will be, deprived of their livelihood. All of Germany's 600,000 Jews are in terror."

On the morning of June 20 in Dubrovnik, Shirer joined Knick and Agnes on the hotel terrace for breakfast. Tess had gone off by herself to take photographs by the big cathedral. As Shirer sat eating his breakfast, two big cumbersome Yugoslavian bombers appeared overhead, flying low and wildly, as if putting on a show. Suddenly one of the bombers rolled over and went into a dive and in seconds, crashed nose first into the center of the city, followed by a huge explosion. Flames and a column of thick black smoke rose into the sky.

Shirer pushed himself away from the table and made a mad dash for the street, convinced his wife had been killed in the crash. As he got closer to the cathedral, he passed burning houses and, in the small open area in front of the church, saw police carrying away bodies in bloody blankets. He pulled up the blankets to look at faces but stopped himself, growing hysterical and shouting out Tess's name, asking police if they could help him find her. As he stood in a full panic, Tess came up behind him holding her camera and taking photographs of the burning hulk of the airplane.

On another day, Bill and Tess took a steamer up the coastline to visit an ancient chapel filled with sculpture and artwork. For the first time since they left Spain, Shirer felt awed in the presence of great art. He lingered for hours in the chapel examining every painting and sculpture. He couldn't accept the thought that the trip would end soon, that they would board a train back to Berlin and he would pick up his reporting where he had left off. Besides, he was thrilled to be with Tess.

"Tess was twenty-six that summer and I was thirty-two, a wonderful age for married love and much too early for time and circumstance to take their toll," Shirer wrote years later as he looked back on the trip. "We felt lucky to have such a happy, exciting, harmonious marriage."

Bad Writing

By midsummer 1936, Shirer began work on a novel. He had not tried fiction since the year he and Tess had spent on the Spanish coast after his firing by the *Tribune*. It was the kind of writing he wanted most for himself but felt the least equipped to do. It was hard for him to understand why he had such trouble with it. Perhaps he had been a reporter too long, organizing his stories around facts, arranging them in a certain tried and true order. That wasn't fiction. He knew Hemingway had given up being a journalist to concentrate on his fiction and in his mid-twenties while living in Paris had written and published *The Sun Also Rises*.

Shirer's story was set in India. No place moved him like India, and no person he had met had moved him, intellectually and spiritually, more than Gandhi. He saw in the Indian no less than a modern-day Jesus, a giant walking the earth with his lost people. Shirer's hope was that he could translate that passion for the man and the place onto the page and find his voice as a novelist.

But first came his work as an American correspondent. And there was always plenty of that. Escaping his responsibilities in Berlin was nearly impossible. A long afternoon with Tess on their boat lifted his spirits, but the day ended and he was back on the dock making phone calls to see what he might have missed, fearful that a major story had broken while he was out of touch. He'd been fired once; he'd walk over hot coals to keep it from happening again. Still, he managed to find time for the India novel, typing late into the night in the Tempelhof apartment and early in the morning before going to his office. He wrote letters to Mrs. Alfred A. Knopf in New York to introduce himself and to ask her or someone at the publishing house to read chapters.

* * *

"The Lindberghs are here...."

—William L. Shirer, diary, July 23, 1936

Shirer had last seen Charles Lindbergh nine years earlier in Paris on the night he landed the *Spirit of St. Louis* on a grassy airstrip crowded with people. He had followed the news about Lindbergh since then, reading everything he could in the winter of 1932 when Lindbergh's son Charles Jr. was kidnapped out of his second-floor bedroom in the family mansion in New Jersey. The child's body was found in a shallow grave. Three years later Bruno Richard Hauptmann, a German, was arrested and put on trial for the boy's kidnapping and murder. He was convicted and executed. Anyone arrested for *that* crime, for kidnapping and murdering *that* little boy, was going to be convicted and executed.

And now, standing with a beaming, proud Göring was Lindbergh. His being there brought out the joy in Göring, as if he and the Nazis were being validated by Lindbergh's star appearance in the country, and they couldn't have been prouder and happier. Surely, Göring hoped that Lindbergh would go back to the United States and say nice things about the Nazis.

The afternoon of Lindbergh's appearance with Göring, Lufthansa organized a social event for him at the airport at Tempelhof and invited a group of foreign correspondents as guests. As Shirer speculated in his diary, Lindbergh and his wife, Anne, had not been told by their hosts ahead of time about the presence of the journalists and were gun-shy around them—"their phobia about the press being what it is." Lindbergh went aloft in one of the Nazis' major aircraft, the Field Marshal von Hindenburg, and took over the controls, putting the plane into a steep dive to show off his flying skills before landing it gently at the airport and proudly disembarking. "The talk is that the Lindberghs have been favorably impressed by what the Nazis have shown them," Shirer wrote in his diary.

* * *

Across Europe, Shirer watched developments with the eye of someone who knew a storm was brewing. In Spain, a country he loved for its beauty, art, and architecture, fighting between Republicans and Nationalists had erupted in a number of cities, including Barcelona and Madrid. In Berlin, Shirer heard talk that the German government would back the insurgents under Franco. "Tragic land!" Shirer wrote in his diary on July 27.

At the end of the month, Hitler was in Bayreuth to attend the annual Wagner festival. "On the night of the twenty-second an urgent letter from

Franco appealing for German aid was delivered to him after the evening's performance," Shirer wrote. "Hitler called in Göring and General von Blumberg, who happened to be in Bayreuth, and that very evening the decision was taken to give military aid to the Spanish rebels."

In mid-August, the Summer Olympic Games came to Berlin, and as he had done at the winter games, Shirer found himself watching individual events and thoroughly enjoying himself. He recorded in his diary that he brought Mrs. William Randolph Hearst to the press section of the Olympic stadium one day, along with the actor Adolphe Menjou. On the day Hearst and Menjou were in the stadium, Hitler also attended. In his August 16 diary entry, Shirer could not help but conclude that the Nazis had shown a good face to the world. "I'm afraid the Nazis have succeeded with their propaganda," he wrote.

In September, a few weeks after the conclusion of the Olympic Games, Shirer faced another party rally at Nuremberg but this time declined to go. Exhausted from covering events in Berlin during the games, he could not face the enormous crowds and the spectacle that went with them. Besides, his mind was elsewhere. Because of his and Tess's short stay in Spain, Shirer was mesmerized by the fighting in that country. As he noted in his diary, a "dependable source" in the German government told him the Nazis were sending airplanes and bombers to help Franco's Nationalist forces.

The mood of the German government, as it supported Fascism in Spain and Italy, was for war, sometime down the road, when its armaments were ready and the time was right. In a letter to a friend written on September 18 at the conclusion of the rally, Shirer predicted a war would come when the Germans decided they needed the rich lands to the east. He mentioned a visit to Berlin by former British prime minister David Lloyd George, who earlier that year had praised Hitler as a great statesman.

"Lloyd George, after a 10 day visit, may be right in saying that the big boy doesn't want a war, but I don't know a single correspondent, who has been here any time at all, who will agree with him—after Nuremberg," Shirer wrote. "Food already is short; practically impossible to get meat at a butcher shop, and as winter comes butter, eggs, fats, will disappear from the shops as they did last year. And to the east lies plenty of food, or so they think here. Hence a war.... Yesterday over the radio the populace was warned to stop talking to foreign correspondents and keep their voices low in restaurants and public places."

Late in the month, Martha Dodd introduced Shirer to the writer Thomas Wolfe, who was in Berlin, presumably to talk about his novel *Look Homeward, Angel*, which Shirer told him was a great success in the country. They went to Habel's, the street-side restaurant near the Opera House. They sat at a "quiet corner table," he wrote in his diary, and Wolfe ordered a second meal of meat and vegetables when he'd finished with the first one, along with several bottles of Pfälzer wine.

Shirer loved to talk about novels and writers and writing fiction, as he had tried to do without success with Hemingway in Paris. He'd had a bit more luck with Sinclair Lewis, when he was married to Dorothy Thompson and they were staying in Vienna, but Lewis was taciturn and Shirer did not learn much. Wolfe was more talkative. They talked about other American writers—Sinclair Lewis, Theodore Dreiser, and Sherwood Anderson—and how they seemed to abruptly stop writing at certain stages of their lives.

"We parted, promising to meet in New York," Shirer wrote.

Get Out of the Country

Shirer did not detect any new initiatives from Hitler in the winter of 1937. With a sense there were no major developments that would shake up the Continent, Shirer quoted Hitler's January 30 speech to the Reichstag marking his fourth anniversary as chancellor: "The time of so-called surprises has been ended." As spring arrived, Shirer felt that "one could almost relax."

In April, Shirer received an offer for a free ride aboard the huge new Zeppelin, the *Hindenburg*. It was to leave in May and sail across the Atlantic. Shirer had already filed several stories with Universal about the *Hindenburg*, pointing out that it could leave Frankfurt and two and a half days later arrive on the East Coast of the United States. Would Shirer be interested in riding the *Hindenburg* across the Atlantic?

He was, but the Universal office in New York did not see the point. Besides, if he left, the Berlin office would be unmanned. Financial cutbacks in New York had meant that Shirer could not hire an office assistant. He certainly understood the bleakness of the economic situation back in America. His office's insistence that he not hire an assistant only reinforced his worry that the company for which he now worked was also in trouble.

When Shirer said no, the press agent for the *Hindenburg* inquired if Tess might be interested in going in her husband's place. Shirer said no, but, as he wrote years later, he kept the offer to her to himself. Writing then, he could not explain why it just felt right at the time to say no. He forgot about it—until four o'clock on the morning of May 7, when the telephone rang in the Shirer apartment in Berlin. Bill Hillman, the Universal bureau chief in London, excitedly told Shirer that the *Hindenburg* had caught fire as it was landing in

Lakehurst, New Jersey, and had been destroyed. Hillman told Shirer to file a story on the German reaction.

Seated at his desk in the apartment, Shirer called the *Hindenburg*'s designer, Ludwig Duerr, waking him up to tell him the news that his airship had exploded in flames as it was attempting to land. Duerr, stunned, refused to accept the news as genuine. Unable to get anyone else on the phone, Shirer called Hillman back and dictated a few paragraphs about Duerr's shocked disbelief. When he got off the phone, he settled into his own disbelief. "I could not get out of my mind what a narrow escape Tess, and even I, had had. But for a stroke of luck, one of us would have been on that ill-fated airship. I felt better, though, for not having told my wife of the invitation."

Later in the morning, while Shirer was still home, the phone rang again. This time it was Claire Trask, the Berlin representative of the Columbia Broadcasting System, CBS. She asked Shirer to gather German reaction to the *Hindenburg* and to do a live radio broadcast for the network. "I turned her down—the very idea of talking into a microphone frightened me," he wrote. At the Universal office, cables from New York now demanded a more substantive German reaction to the news. Shirer knew more: the *Hindenburg* had exploded into flames as it was nearing the mooring mast at Lakehurst. More than thirty passengers had been killed. A live radio broadcast had captured the moment. There had been wind issues, but the talk was that the hydrogen gas, highly flammable, was the reason for the explosion, although what started the process was not known.

Trask was not to be pushed aside, and Shirer finally agreed to do a fifteen-minute broadcast. Shirer wrote the script while filing his own dispatches with Universal. Then Trask left to take it to the German censors for their approval. A few minutes before he was to go on the air, Shirer arrived at the CBS office in the broadcast center. Trask, still with the censors, was nowhere to be found. When she arrived, minutes before Shirer was to begin, he read over the script and was dumbstruck that the censors had stripped out a reference to German government suspicions that the *Hindenburg* had been sabotaged by anti-Nazis in the United States. Shirer had made that same point in his own story, which he had cabled to New York that afternoon.

In spite of the ticking clock, Shirer got on the phone with the censors to argue his case that the information should be included in the broadcast. They refused to back down. "When I hung up, a radio engineer had already begun to count down the final sixty seconds," he wrote. "I suddenly had a frog in my voice....I swallowed. I tried to clear my throat."

Within a few seconds he calmed down and read the script into a live microphone. That night, when he was back in the apartment, he wrote in his diary: "Fear I will never make a broadcaster."

* * *

In early spring, Shirer, who had been writing in his free time for months, finished his novel of India and put it aside. He was relieved that it was finished, but he was not hopeful about its potential to turn him into a published novelist. Still, he was proud of himself for getting to the end. Then, in late May, the quiet of the previous few months ended with German deaths off the coast of Spain.

Spanish bombers of the Republican government struck the German warship *Deutschland*, killing nearly two dozen sailors. On May 30, Shirer arrived in the German government offices in the Wilhelmstrasse to find officials fuming. "One informant tells me Hitler has been screaming with rage all day and wants to declare war on Spain," Shirer wrote. "The army and navy are trying to restrain him."

The following day, May 31, Shirer wrote in his diary that the Germans had exacted their revenge. At a 10:00 A.M. press conference, Gottfried Aschmann called the foreign correspondents into his office to deliver the news that German ships had shelled the Spanish port of Almeria on the country's southeast coast, setting houses ablaze and killing civilians. "He was very pious about it all," Shirer noted dryly in his diary. While Shirer was too angry to ask questions, two of his colleagues—Guido Enderis of the *New York Times* and Louis Lochner of the Associated Press—did, and Aschmann recited the reasons for the attack and his government's justification.

As disgusted as Shirer was by the behavior of the government he covered, he did not want to lose his job and start all over again, this time in Berlin, looking for work as a foreign correspondent. He wanted to be in the German capital, which he felt was the best place for any serious journalist to be. But the spring was rife with rumors that Universal was about to close, laying off its European employees. Rather than wait for what he feared was the inevitable, Shirer began casting around for another paper. He met with Frank Knox, the owner and publisher of the *Chicago Daily News*, who was visiting Berlin, about working for the paper's foreign desk, and he tried—once again—to get somewhere with the *New York Times*, a paper he had been trying to convince to hire him from his days in Paris working for the *Chicago Tribune*.

Shirer approached Frederick Birchall of the *New York Times*, who had been in Germany since the early 1930s as the paper's chief foreign correspondent. Shirer knew Birchall had covered all the major stories after Hitler came to power, including the Reichstag fire, and they'd crossed paths at the Winter Olympic Games in 1936. Birchall had left an acting managing editor's job in New York to come to Berlin. After several meetings with Birchall, Shirer came away with the optimistic view that a solid offer from the *Times* was imminent, perhaps even an assignment in the paper's Moscow bureau. He would not have to wait for Universal News

Service to fold; he'd get away before the axe fell, and, unlike when he was fired by the *Tribune*, he would be in control of his fate and not at its whim.

June and July, however, were hectic months, with the Hearst service surviving and nothing materializing with the *Times*. In early June, the Nazis beheaded a twenty-year-old Jew named Helmut Hirsch, whose father was an American citizen, after his conviction before a People's Court on charges that he had plotted to bomb government buildings. There was little more than rumor about what Hirsch's actual targets were. On June 4, Shirer wrote that Hirsch was convicted before "a court of inquisition" for planning to murder Julius Streicher, the publisher of the vehemently anti-Semitic newspaper *Der Stürmer.* Official billboards in the city proclaimed Hirsch as working with anti-Nazi traitors outside the country, a reference, the *New York Times* reported in its June 5 edition, to a group led by Otto Strasser, a so-called leftist Nazi with a far different view of National Socialism than Hitler, who had fled the country. Strasser's brother Gregor had been murdered in the *Nacht der langen Messer* purge in June 1934. Shirer had no idea—he never did under these circumstances—what was actually true and what were lies the government wanted the journalists to spread that would serve the Nazis' purposes.

Shirer had heard enough to write in his diary that Hirsch had been betrayed by a Gestapo plant in Strasser's organization. "As far as I can piece the story together, Hirsch was provided with a suitcase full of bombs and a revolver and dispatched to Germany to get someone," Shirer wrote. "The Nazis claim it was Streicher. Hirsch himself never seems to have admitted who.... We shall never know."

The morning of the execution, Shirer had gone to the American embassy to talk to William Dodd, who had tried up to the last minute to get Hirsch's sentence reduced. Dodd told Shirer he'd written Hitler an emotional appeal and had tried to schedule an appointment to speak to him face to face but had been rebuffed. Hirsch was going to the guillotine, and there was nothing Dodd or anyone else could do to stop it.

From Hirsch's attorney, Shirer obtained a copy of a letter Hirsch had written prior to his execution to his sister, Kaete. "I have never read in all my life braver words," Shirer wrote in his diary. "He had just been informed that his final appeal had been rejected and that there was no more hope. 'I am to die then,' he says. 'Please do not be afraid. I do not feel afraid. I feel released, after the agony of not quite knowing.'" Shirer found the letter so emotional it brought him to tears. "He was a braver and more decent man than his killers."

* * *

Through the rumors of Universal Service's imminent demise, Shirer had held out the hope that he would not lose his job, his second in four years, and could ride out the economic hardships his employer was facing. There were also conflicting signals that made him think he would ultimately be fine. In February, Seymour Berkson, at the Universal Service office in New York City, had written Shirer to say he was trying to get him a modest raise, pointing out that a Shirer series on the German four-year economic plan had run in all the Hearst newspapers and in the *New York American*. In mid-March, Bill Hillman at Universal wrote Shirer to inform him he would be receiving an increase in salary and also to write that, at Shirer's request, twenty-five dollars a week would be deducted from his pay and sent to his mother in Cedar Rapids.

If the raise caused Shirer to be more optimistic about his future, he quickly sank into deep pessimism when, on August 14, Hearst informed him that the service was ending. There was no immediate word on his fate. He wrote in his diary: "Universal Service has folded after all. Hearst is cutting his losses. I am to remain here with INS (International News Service), but as second man, which I do not like."

Two days later, the Propaganda Ministry ordered Norman Ebbutt out of the country. Officially, the government's explanation for the expulsion was that the British government had ordered three German correspondents out of the country. Shirer knew that was just an excuse. The Nazis, seeing an opportunity, moved to "get rid of a man they've hated and feared for many years because of his exhaustive knowledge of this country and of what was going on behind the scenes."

Quickly, a group of Ebbutt's colleagues arranged a going-away celebration at the Charlottenburg train station. Several heard whispers from Germans in the Propaganda Ministry that officials there would frown on any of the foreign correspondents going to the send-off. Just before the event, Shirer was approached by Pierre Huss, the INS correspondent in charge of the bureau in Berlin and a man Shirer loathed. With the demise of Universal, Huss was also Shirer's new boss. He regarded him as a favorite of the German bureaucrats who oversaw the foreign press operation.

"Huss came into my office and asked me to stay away from the sendoff for Ebbutt," Shirer wrote years later. "It would embarrass INS, he said, which sold its news service to a chain of Nazi newspapers. It would get him and INS 'in bad' with the authorities."

Shirer did not have to think about his response.

"I can't be that cowardly, Pierre," Shirer told him.

In his diary, Shirer said fifty correspondents from several countries showed up on the platform. Without naming names, he wrote, "Amusing to note the correspondents who were afraid to show up, including two well-known Americans." Along the perimeter of the station, Shirer could see Gestapo men writing down names and taking photographs.

A week later, Shirer was in his office late at night typing a story. An office boy handed him a cable that had just arrived. It ended any illusions Shirer might have had that he would survive. It read: "Shirer deeply regret but necessity consolidating forces requires that we dispense with your services after this week stop management has approved payment of one month's salary as dismissal bonus stop depositing this money your account Paris."

On a small slip of paper, he wrote: "Trying to get a job. 1. after firing from Chicago Tribune. 2. after firing from Universal Service."

Later, he would write, in tiny pencil scratches in a narrow column, inside a 1940 leather-bound diary, on the page for November 6, an account of that night.

> *I was a for. Corr. I was writing a cable, the news from Berlin of that night. The office boy came in. He handed me a brief wire off the ticker. It was from N.Y. It said: "Effective midnight—News services ceases existence and your two weeks extra salary will be forwarded." Like that. Like that I was jobless, broke (except for the 2 weeks salary that would be forwarded). In a few weeks we were expecting a blessed event in our family, our first. I decided not to finish my cable—since it was almost midnight. I went out for a breath of air. When I returned to my office half hr. later there was another wire—from Salzburg—of all places. It was not very exciting. It said: "Can you have dinner with me Friday nite? Murrow. CBS." The name was unfamiliar but I recognized the company. A free dinner in my present circumstances was nothing to sniff at. I wired back—"Delighted dine with you anytime anywhere."*

Drinks at the Adlon

Shirer walked into the handsome lobby of the Adlon Hotel early on the evening of August 27 as a warm summer day in Berlin was coming to a close. Not knowing what to expect, Shirer felt a knot in his stomach. He looked across the lobby, hoping a figure would jump out at him. He was there to meet Edward R. Murrow, the director of European operations for the Columbia Broadcasting System. One man caught his eye: "Black hair. Straight features. Fine chin. Flashing dark eyes. Just what you would expect from radio, I thought. Or even more, from Hollywood. His neat, freshly pressed dark suit, probably cut in London's Savile Row, contrasted with my rumpled gray flannel jacket and unpressed slacks."

The two men made their introductions, and Murrow invited Shirer to dinner in the hotel dining room. For a man out of work counting his pennies, it was a grand invitation. Walking to their table, Shirer thought Murrow wanted "to pump me for material for a radio broadcast" and nothing else. He told himself to be civil. "But as we walked into the bar there was something in his manner that began disarming me. Something in his eyes and especially in his speech that was not Hollywood."

The two sat down and ordered martinis. "We began talking of mutual friends. I was surprised how many there were. Obviously we liked the same kind of people: the more liberal and intelligent of the American foreign correspondents, the Labour party people in England, the New Deal crowd at home. We ordered another round of martinis. He spoke of his interest in getting Jewish and other intellectuals out of Nazi Germany. He had headed some university commission that had already placed several of them in jobs at home."

Murrow began talking about radio. "The important thing, he said, was its potential. It was not living up to it yet, but it might someday."

"Are you tied up this weekend?" he asked.

"Hardly," Shirer said. "I'll probably badger the *Times* people for the job they've apparently promised me. And I'll get in some sailing. Would you like to sail?"

"Very much," he said. He had a very warm smile. "Good place to talk, on a boat."

As Shirer recalled it, Murrow turned toward him, a quizzical look on his face.

"How far are you tied up with the *Times?*" he asked.

"Not far at all," Shirer said. "Birchall's promised me a job for some time now. But it has never quite materialized. He thinks it will be next week. That's where it stands at the moment."

"I'm looking for an experienced foreign correspondent," Murrow said, "to open a CBS office on the Continent. I can't cover all of Europe from London."

Shirer felt suddenly hopeful.

"Are you interested?" Murrow asked.

"Well, yes," Shirer said.

"How much have you been making?"

Shirer told him.

"Good. We can pay you the same—to start with."

Universal had paid Shirer $125 a week, which he and Tess found difficult to live on. Their finances were strained all the time, and she was now pregnant. He was hoping for more, but it was not the time to haggle. Like the offer from the *Chicago Tribune* to stay in Paris in 1925 just as he was packing to return to Iowa, like the offer in 1934 to return to Paris after his sojourn in Spain when he and Tess were down to their last dollar, and, like the offer from Universal to go to Berlin, Murrow's offer came out of nowhere and in the nick of time. Shirer was a believer in luck, and it was blessedly playing out for him again tonight in the handsome restaurant of a first-class Berlin hotel. He thought that it was his fate to remain in Europe while Hitler was in power. He was grateful and relieved.

"Is it a deal?" Murrow asked.

"I...I...guess so," Shirer said. "This is all rather sudden."

"No more for you than for me," Murrow said, smiling, putting Shirer further at ease. "Anyway. Welcome to CBS!"

There was one hitch, Murrow explained. Bill Paley and an office of vice presidents in New York City would want to hear Shirer's voice, to see if it was suitable for radio. "We'll arrange a broadcast for next week," Murrow said. "You give a fifteen-minute talk, say, on the coming Nazi party rally at Nuremberg."

Shirer, worried his voice would fail him, said, "Who's Bill Paley?"

"Bill's the president of CBS. Owns the damned network," Murrow said.

* * *

On Sunday, September 5, 1937, Shirer met Claire Trask at a café near the government buildings. They walked to the Post and Telegraph center, where Shirer was to read a script prepared by Trask. Minutes before they were to begin, however, Trask discovered to her horror that she'd left the script in the café. She ran out to get it, promising she'd be back in time. Shirer felt his nerves begin to fray.

When she returned, the engineer signaled that there were a few minutes to go. His panic rising, Shirer now realized that the microphone he was supposed to speak into towered over his head. It had "apparently been set up for a man at least eight feet tall." He told the engineer to lower it, but it would not come down.

"It is stuck, mein Herr," the engineer said. It would be helpful, the man explained, if Shirer tilted his head toward the ceiling.

As the clock ticked, Shirer tried speaking with his face pointed at the ceiling. His voice, on which the job rested, came out like a squeak. One minute to go, the engineer shouted.

Knowing he could not make his voice acceptable if he were speaking into a microphone far above his head, Shirer climbed up on a mound of packing crates, his face now opposite the microphone. "Quiet," the engineer shouted, and Shirer began reading from the script. A few minutes later, it was over.

That night, his voice test behind him, Shirer left for Nuremberg, where the annual party rally was to begin, with its mix of bold choreography, huge swastika banners bathed in bright lights, enormous crowds, and speeches by top party officials, topped off by the appearance of Hitler before a packed stadium. Two close colleagues who worked for United Press, Webb Miller and Fred Oechsner, both frequent members of the club of foreign correspondents that convened regularly at the Taverne restaurant, had asked Shirer to help them cover the rally.

Having lost his employment, Shirer was thrilled to go along, even though the Nuremberg rally was an event he would have liked to beg off, if only because he could not tolerate the worshipful crowds so adoring of their Führer. He'd seen worshipful crowds around a leader in India when he traveled with Gandhi. But Gandhi was a man of truly simple means, preaching a message of nonviolence. Hitler and the Germans were a far different story. Shirer's three years in the country had begun in many ways big and small to fill him with disgust for the Germans in general and the Nazis in particular. He did not understand how Hitler had transformed the country and turned ordinary Germans into fervent disciples. The people did what they were told. He watched women lined up along parade routes reaching out their hands to touch Hitler, their faces contorted, their eyes rapturous, and it repelled him. Now he was back in Nuremberg to witness it all over again.

A great deal had changed in Germany during Shirer's three years based in Berlin. Like all the foreign correspondents, he chronicled that change, either in the stories he wrote or in his private writings—his diaries, mostly—and in the things he saw and would remember and speak about for the rest of his life and would detail in his memoirs published a half century after the events he witnessed. He was an imperfect witness, as all the correspondents were. They saw only so much. The truth was a luxury well out of their grasp. They knew of the concentration camps, they knew of the roundups of enemies of the Reich, and they knew of the boycott against the Jews in 1933 and the passage of the Nuremberg Laws in 1935. It was all right in front of them, playing out by its own set of rules, manipulated by men they saw frequently, even in social settings. It's not that some stories about these events were not filed with American newspapers—but compared to the vast scale of the story, its scope, was it enough?

A handwritten note jotted down on a scrap of paper is a clue to Shirer's state of mind in those years. He wrote it when he was a white-haired man, and, as he did with so many of his papers, he placed it in a file for safekeeping, probably assuming that someday researchers interested in his work would discover the file in his archive and better understand him. Its few words reveal the balancing act he kept in his head between trying to sell his editors in New York on a story they were probably not that interested in, his own need to write what he knew, and the fear that if he did, if he found an outlet for a story, he would be ordered out of Germany. The note states that the persecution of the Jews "weighed on a foreign correspondent in Berlin more than any other aspect of Hitler's primitive rule, provoking in me a constant depression of spirits and often sickness of heart."

What could he have done? If he found someone who would talk to him, could he protect that person? "A foreign correspondent soon learned that he had to be careful to protect the sources who furnished him with news that Nazi authorities didn't like," Shirer wrote. "The slightest bit of carelessness on your part might result in your informant being arrested and charged with treason, which after the Nazi takeover, meant almost invariably a death sentence. Sometimes the Gestapo would visit my office and question me regarding this suspected informant or that. I never gave them any information whatsoever. After all, I had nothing to lose except expulsion. My informants risked their lives."

He was certain his office was bugged, his phone calls listened to by the Gestapo. "I always assumed my telephone was tapped and that probably a listening device had been hidden in it. When anyone came with sensitive information [to his flat] I would toss a heavy blanket over the phone and adjourn to the bathroom for our talk."

The Nuremberg rally of 1937 came four years and eight months into the Nazi transformation of the country. Germany was a true police state—anyone not fully supportive of the government was suspect. Actual and perceived enemies languished in concentration camps, and Jews continued to leave their country. The effort to force Jews out of the country was pushed along by a constant drumbeat of vitriol and actions by the government and by ordinary Germans. By the end of 1937, historian Richard J. Evans has written, there were about 350,000 Jews still in Germany; there had been approximately 437,000 in 1933. The number of Jews attending schools plummeted because of economic pressures and the hatred heaped on them on school grounds. The Aryanization of Jewish-owned businesses of all kinds moved along without interruption. Renewed anti-Jewish boycotts appeared all over the country. A foreign journalist working for a supportive newspaper could write a story about these efforts every day of the week and never run out of material.

As Shirer covered Hitler's appearance at the rally, he heard the Führer again attack the Jews. He characterized "the Jews as 'inferior through and through,' unscrupulous, subversive, bent upon undermining society from within, exterminating those cleverer than themselves and establishing a Bolshevik reign of terror," Evans wrote. "The speech was followed by anti-Semitic disturbances in Danzig, and then a fresh wave of intimidatory boycotts of Jewish shops during the Christmas season."

At his home, Victor Klemperer wrote every few days in his diary about many aspects of his everyday life, his "political disgust" always prominent. On September 12, a Sunday, he wrote: "Everywhere on my way I see the sign 'Jews Unwelcome!' and now, during the Fifth Party Rally, hatred of Jews is being whipped up again. The Jews are murdering Spain, the Jews are the criminal people, *all* crimes can be traced back to *the Jew*....And the people are so stupid that they believe everything."

Prior to the party rally, the German government had authored a new law that required all Jews to have names immediately recognizable as Jewish. The name "Israel" or "Sara" was to be added to names not clearly Jewish. New policies were approved that required Jews to identify their businesses and carry special identity cards. Soon, Jews were arrested en masse, with the goal of forcing Jews to emigrate. Any Berlin-based foreign correspondent, walking from his or her apartment to an office near the government buildings, would have seen the impact of the government's policies. No doubt many knew Jewish business owners who begged them for help as they passed or frequented their shops.

*   *   *

Shirer was still in Nuremberg when, on September 13, he was greeted with welcome news from Murrow: a firm job offer from CBS. Shirer celebrated with some American diplomats attending the rally and some of his colleagues. Relieved, Shirer went to the stadium to hear Hitler and sat next to Fred Birchall. Shirer told him of his job offer. In disbelief that Shirer would take a job with radio, Birchall told him, as they waited for the speeches to begin, "In two or three years, Bill, I'll wager you'll be wanting to get back to newspaper work."

Grateful to Murrow, Shirer sent him a telegram upon his return to Berlin addressed "Dear Ed." He wrote: "As I told you on the phone I am delighted to accept. I too look forward to our collaboration with great pleasure. You have no idea what a kick I got out of those hours we spent here talking of possible broadcasts all the way from the Khyber Pass to a Tyrolean village. They seemed to me to be the kind of dreams that might and do, sometimes, come true."

Shirer knew the job he had accepted was not, by any means, about journalism. Murrow had explained that it could be, but it wasn't there yet. For the time being, until both men could find a way to do news broadcasts from Europe, they were to arrange radio broadcasts for the CBS network. Some of them seemed to Shirer pretty silly, such as arranging for broadcasts of a children's choir in, say, Nuremberg, or a broadcast from a toy factory, or classical programs to fill certain time slots in New York. Neither man would talk on the radio. In the event someone had to speak about local events, Shirer could not do it himself but was to hire a newspaper correspondent as an expert commentator. He wondered why they needed a voice test if this was all it was, but he was grateful for the job and even happier to be working with Murrow. From the outset, the men got along terrifically, and Shirer found every reason to think of Murrow as something closer to a big brother with a million good ideas than as his boss.

The Shirers packed up the apartment in preparation for a move to Vienna, where Shirer and Murrow had agreed to open the CBS European bureau. "We are glad to be leaving Berlin," Shirer noted in his diary. "To sum up these three years: Personally, they have not been unhappy ones, though the shadow of Nazi fanaticism, sadism, persecution, regimentation, terror, brutality, suppression, militarism, and preparation for war has hung over all our lives, like a dark, brooding cloud that never clears."

As for the Nazis and their intentions—what they were *really* doing—about this Shirer still felt ignorant. "Somehow I feel that, despite our work as reporters, there is little understanding of the Third Reich, what it *is*, what it is up to, where it is going, either at home or elsewhere abroad," he wrote. He conceded that Germany under Hitler was a complex picture, and that he and the others who wrote about it for American newspapers knew next to nothing.

In Vienna, the Shirers found an apartment on the Plösslgasse, adjacent to the palace and grounds owned by the Rothschild family. While it was a handsome apartment in a first-class part of the city, it was on the third floor of the building, which Tess, her baby due in less than two months, found daunting. The city itself, as well as the country, was far different from when they had lived there before. Beggars stood on street corners. Anti-Semitism boiled over, which fed into the growing appeal of the Nazis locally and across the border. Journalists Shirer knew—Walter Duranty and Emil Vadnai of the *New York Times*—explained to Shirer what was going on in Austria with the Nazis. In return, Shirer used Duranty on the air as an expert commentator.

The couple spent Christmas with John Wiley and his wife, Duranty, and others. Wiley helped to manage legal affairs at the American embassy in Vienna.

THE JEWISH DOCTOR

Late in February 1938, with the birth of his baby imminent, Shirer boarded the train in Vienna for the ride to Sofia, Bulgaria, where he was to set up a musical broadcast for CBS. He feared he would miss the birth and wrote in his diary before he boarded the train, "My bad luck to miss the event, but perhaps I shall get back in time." He spent his birthday, February 23, aboard the Orient Express, worrying about Tess.

He was back in Vienna three days later and was greeted at the station by Ed Taylor, who wrote for the *Chicago Tribune*. His face was etched with worry, and Shirer felt his heart sink.

"And Tess?"

"She had a bit of a hard time, I'm afraid," Taylor said. "Caesarean. But she's better now."

Shirer hailed a taxi and rushed to the hospital. After arriving, he realized he had a healthy daughter, but that Tess had been in serious trouble. The birth had nearly killed her. The doctor explained that she would live, but that it had been very close.

* * *

The situation in Austria could not have been more grave. The Austrian chancellor Kurt von Schuschnigg, who was eager to keep the German army out of his country, was a far different sort of Fascist than Hitler; his party was similar in appearance but differed in fundamental ways from the Nazis across the border. When Hitler and Schuschnigg met on February 12, Hitler took charge of the meeting from the moment Schuschnigg walked into the room, referring to himself as a spring storm that would suddenly appear in Vienna without warning.

Over the course of a long and painful day, Schuschnigg was browbeaten and bullied into accepting Hitler's terms for Austria. If he didn't, if more than a few days passed without the Austrian government's endorsing Hitler's demands, then German troops would pour over the frontier. Shirer followed the news as best as he could, spending his days with Tess and baby Eileen at the hospital. He met the doctor who had helped deliver the baby, but immediately after the birth the doctor had fled the hospital and the city. The doctor was Jewish, as were some other key hospital employees, and widespread fear had set in among many on the staff as Austria buckled under Hitler's demands. When a bad bout of phlebitis infected one of Tess's legs, Shirer feared she would lose the leg—if not her life—but could not find the doctor to come to the room and examine her.

As Shirer waited at the hospital, events in the country grew more chaotic. He spoke with Murrow nearly every day and felt keenly frustrated that CBS in New York, for no reason that Shirer could understand, had no interest in a broadcast from Vienna summing up the situation. Instead, they wanted him to leave the city and travel to Yugoslavia to set up "a chorus of school children or something," as he sarcastically noted in his diary.

On March 10, with Tess and the baby still hospitalized, Shirer traveled to Ljubljana, the capital of a province in Yugoslavia, for a broadcast featuring coal miners' children. Upon his return to Vienna a day later, as the taxi brought him from the station to his apartment on the Plösslgasse, Shirer could see the streets filled with blowing sheets of papers that had been dropped from airplanes flying low over the city. The driver explained that they were about an upcoming countrywide plebiscite on the question of the *Anschluss*, or annexation, to Germany.

Shirer knew he was the only American broadcaster in Vienna who could go on the air live and describe what was happening. He was determined to make the most of it. To his disgust, CBS had no interest. He also knew that another American radio journalist, Max Jordan of NBC, would soon arrive and would be the first to send reports back to the United States. Even if given permission to broadcast, Shirer could not get to the Austrian broadcast center, for the streets were jammed with boisterous Nazis who had also taken over the radio stations. At one point, Nazis ushered him out of the radio station with bayonets at his back.

At the apartment, Shirer quickly caught up with the newspapers and then rushed to see Tess and Eileen at the hospital. He found Tess with a high fever; the staff was deeply worried that she had developed a serious blood clot in her leg. After he sat with her for several hours and she fell back to sleep, he jumped into a taxi and headed for a café on the Schwarzenbergplatz, where he found

Marcel Fodor, who wrote for the *Manchester Guardian* and the *New York Post*, along with Taylor and a group of Austrian journalists. Of them, Fodor was the most worried. He was Jewish and knew Austria well and feared for his own safety.

Later in the afternoon, Shirer jumped on a subway train to return to the hospital. When he emerged at the Karlsplatz, he was swept up in an enormous crowd of Nazis and their joyous supporters. In a booming chorus that echoed down the street like thunder they shouted "Heil Hitler!" over and over, along with demands that Schuschnigg be hanged. "And the police! They were looking on, grinning," Shirer wrote in his diary. The crowd swept down fashionable streets, the booming chants bouncing off the buildings like explosions of fireworks, until it arrived at a building draped with a portrait of Hitler.

Pulling himself out of the crowd, Shirer returned to the hospital, where he found Tess better and in remarkably good spirits. A sense of optimism that she would get through this swept over him in a welcome rush. Buoyant, he dashed out again and along with Ed Taylor went to the American consulate to see Wiley, who was hunkered down in his office like a man preparing for a long siege.

Back in the street, Shirer found young Austrian Nazis on the fashionable Kärntnerstrasse throwing paving stones through the windows of Jewish-owned shops to the mob's shouts of approval. Rushing to the Café Louvre, Shirer found Robert Best, a colleague and casual friend who wrote for United Press, at a table surrounded by a number of foreign correspondents. Shirer had seen him at the same table dozens of times; he knew that Best, soon to marry an Austrian woman, used the café as an office. As Best typed his reports at his table, he read them into the phone. Outside, a mob hoisted a huge swastika flag to the top of a building.

Quickly, the café filled up with journalists looking for a refuge. Martha Fodor, Marcel's wife, arrived in tears, scared for what lay ahead as a violent fury raged against Vienna's Jews. Emil Maass, an Austrian who had been Shirer's assistant when he worked for the *Tribune*, stood over the table and pronounced, "It's about time." He turned over his coat lapel to reveal a swastika button, removed it, and, newly emboldened, placed it on the outside of the lapel.

As he did so, several women at the table shouted "Shame!" at Maass, but he was undeterred. A man Shirer identified in his diary as "Major Goldschmidt" stood up from the table and announced, "I will go home and get my revolver."

Across Vienna, as Shirer and the others huddled in the café trying to get a grip on what was happening, mobs set upon the city's Jews. Businesses were smashed across the city, in fashionable as well as less than fashionable neighborhoods. One of those offices struck was no doubt the small photography studio of Helene Katz, the Viennese Jew who had befriended Tess Shirer years

earlier and had probably been her photography teacher. Her studio was at
Stubenring 18, near the fancy hotels and museums.

Large numbers of Jews were summoned by the mob to do street work,
cleaning sidewalks and gutters with toothbrushes. The crowds found the sight
amusing, taunting the Jews, telling them to scrub until everything was spot-
less. Some Jews were made to clean toilets. Shirer made his way through the
crowded streets to the broadcast center, where he hoped to be able to broadcast
a live report to CBS in New York. His efforts to reach Murrow, who was in
Poland, had been unsuccessful all day. Shirer was on his own, and what he
wanted most now was to be able to broadcast.

Outside the broadcast center, uniformed men stood guard with fixed bayonets. Shirer explained who he was and that he needed to get inside, and after
a while one of the guards relented. Once in the building, he found the corri-
dors jammed with men in SS and SA uniforms, some holding their revolvers.
"Two or three stop me, but taking my courage in my hand I bark at them and
make my way into the main hall, around which are the studios," he wrote in
his diary.

Two men Shirer knew well—the general director of the Austrian broadcasting system, and Erich Kunsti, the program director—stood like prisoners
in one of the studios, surrounded by young men in Nazi uniforms.

"How soon can I get on the air?" Shirer asked Kunsti.

"I've ceased to exist around here," he explained, pointing out another man
Shirer did not know as the center's new boss.

Shirer told the man he wanted to broadcast but was met by silence. "Let
me talk to your chiefs in Berlin," Shirer said. "I know them. They'll want me
to broadcast."

"Can't get through to Berlin," the man said.

Several armed men pushed Shirer out of the studio. After a long wait,
he realized that either the man now in charge would not try, or that it was in
fact impossible to reach Berlin. Either way, he could not get on the air, and
he was escorted out of the building. With nothing he could do to improve
his situation—it was now 3:00 A.M. on the morning of March 12—he ran to
his apartment, where he finally reached Murrow in Poland. He explained to
Murrow that he would in all likelihood not be able to gain access to the broadcast studios. And if he did, he would be under strict censorship rules.

Murrow had a thought. "Fly to London, why don't you?" he said. "You
can get there by tomorrow evening and give the first uncensored eyewitness
account." If Shirer could get to London, Murrow would fly to Vienna and
cover for him there.

Shirer was determined to make it work. He called the airport and learned
that there were early morning flights to London and Berlin. After he hung up,
he called Marcel Fodor, who sobbed into the phone, stunned at the anti-Jewish

hysteria in the streets and the shocking sight of elderly Jewish men and women scrubbing gutters with toothbrushes while being taunted by the crowds.

"I'm all right, Bill," Fodor said as he wept. Shirer next called Tess at the hospital and told her he would be away but would be back as soon as he could.

The Vienna airport at 7:00 A.M. on March 12 was filled with panicking Austrians desperate to flee the country. The Gestapo had taken command of the building and the hangars. One of them told Shirer there would be no flights leaving for London but a few minutes later changed his mind and said there would be. Nonetheless, there was no seat for Shirer, so he walked up to strangers, offering to buy their seat for any price they would name. His offer was rejected by all. Shirer soon was able to purchase a ticket on the flight from Vienna to Berlin. It was going the wrong way, but at least he would be going somewhere.

As he waited, troops of the German Eighth Army crossed the frontier into Austria and began, in long motorized columns, to move toward Vienna. Just before Shirer was to board his flight to Berlin, German warplanes landed. His flight took him from Vienna to Prague, to Dresden, and then on to Berlin. There, during a stopover, Shirer bought a stack of the city's newspapers at a kiosk in the terminal. The headline of the *Völkischer Beobachter* read: GERMAN-AUSTRIA SAVED FROM CHAOS. The story went on to describe wild, communist-inspired riots in Vienna, with looting and killings. "It is a complete *lie*," Shirer wrote in his diary.

Soon Shirer was aboard a Dutch flight to Amsterdam and then to London. While in the air, he wrote and rewrote a script, reciting it over and over until he had it memorized. He expected to go on the air as soon as he got to the station in London. There would be no time to rehearse or to read it through—there would be just what he wrote on the airplane and spoke into the microphone.

The idea in London, as outlined by Paul White, CBS's director of public affairs in New York, was for Shirer to host a news roundup, the network's first. "We want you and some member of Parliament from London, Ed Murrow of course from Vienna, and American newspaper correspondents from Berlin, Paris and Rome. A half hour show. Can you and Murrow do it?" Without thinking about it, and knowing that Murrow would agree with him, Shirer said yes.

He needed a great deal to make it work. Both he and Murrow had news-paper friends in the three capitals whom they could ask to speak on the air. Murrow in particular knew the directors of the major European broadcasting systems, and Shirer was friendly with officials at the Reichs-Rundfunk-Gesellschaft, RRG, the government-run system in Berlin. Murrow would set up the Berlin and Vienna end; he informed Shirer that they would need either a short-wave transmitter in each capital or an absolutely reliable telephone line.

"As the evening wore on, the broadcast began to take shape," Shirer wrote in his diary. "New York telephoned again with the exact times scheduled for each capital. New York's brazen serenity, its confidence that the broadcast would come off all right, encouraged me."

Three correspondents were lined up, including Shirer's friend Edgar Mowrer, the Paris correspondent for the *Chicago Daily News*, and exact wavelengths for the short-wave transmitters were relayed to the New York control room. Shirer quickly wrote down notes for his end of the broadcast, which was to address British concerns over the *Anschluss*—the German annexation of Austria. Frank Gervasi, who wrote for Hearst's International News Service from Rome, called Shirer to say the Italian broadcasting system was not up to the task. Shirer offered a backup plan to broadcast Gervasi through a short-wave transmitter in Geneva; if that failed, he told him to phone back in an hour and dictate the story to him, and he would then read it over the air himself.

At precisely 1:00 A.M. London time, Shirer heard the welcome voice of Robert Trout in New York come over his headsets. "To bring you the picture of Europe tonight Columbia now presents a special broadcast with pickups directly from London, from Paris and such other European capitals as have communication channels available.... Columbia begins its radio tour of Europe's capitals with a transoceanic pickup from London. We take you now to London."

It occurred to Shirer—and to Murrow in Vienna—that they were making history on this night with radio's first news roundup. For thirty minutes the show went perfectly, and Shirer signed off. On a scrap of paper years later—and, like so many of his personal papers, one he saved in a carefully preserved file—Shirer summed up the importance of the broadcast: "Radio, as far as news was concerned, had suddenly come of age. This transformation would have a profound influence on our country, our people, our society, our journalism.... This crisis has done one thing for us. I think radio talks by Ed and me are now established. Birth of the radio foreign corrs. [correspondents], so to speak."

Seven days after the *Anschluss*, Shirer flew back to Vienna, where Murrow met him at the airport. They grabbed a cab that took them to Shirer's apartment, where they found armed SS officers standing guard outside the building. Guards stood in front of a number of buildings and surrounded the Rothschild palace next door. When Shirer tried to get into his building, a guard pushed him back.

"I live here," he said angrily.

"Makes no difference," the guard said. "You can't go in."

"I said I *live* here."

"Sorry. Strict orders. No one can enter or leave."

The two men walked over to the palace to find an SS officer they could complain to. As they entered the palace, they encountered German officers carrying out boxes of silver and other valuables. "One had a gold-framed picture under his arm," Shirer wrote in his diary. "One was the commandant. His arms were loaded with silver knives and forks, but he was not embarrassed. I explained my business and our nationality. He chuckled and told the guard to escort us to my door."

After dark, Murrow and Shirer sneaked out of the building and walked to a nearby bar, where Murrow had spent the previous evening. There, as Murrow had watched, a man—Shirer quotes Murrow in his diary as saying the man was "Jewish looking"—had removed a straight razor from his jacket and dragged it across his throat.

Murrow returned to London the next morning, and Shirer went immediately to the hospital, where he found Tess back in critical condition from the phlebitis. His previous optimism that she would be okay abandoned him. Care in the hospital was negligible and chaotic, and Shirer realized that his wife could lose her life if he didn't intercede. On another scrap of paper written years later that he also saved and filed, Shirer wrote: "Atmosphere in hospital. Jews panic. Get in (you left it out of diary) T's doc was a Jew, and disappeared day of Anschluss. Later I located him, he performed in gr secrecy at convent in Wienerwald outside V. He's left some surgical instruments inside T."

On another note, he added details: "New x-rays revealed that metal objects, apparently surgical instruments, had been left inside after her Caesarean operation. They would have to be removed—if possible by the pediatrician who had performed the operation. Being a Jew, he had gone into hiding since the *Anschluss*. I finally located him. He did not want to risk reappearing at the hospital, for which I did not blame him. He agreed however to do it in a safe place. I found a convent hidden in the Wienerwald a mile or two down the Danube."

On the street Shirer watched large groups of Jews, men and women, old and young, cleaning Schuschnigg signs off the sidewalks. He heard reports of suicides by Jews, along with "all sorts of reports of Nazi sadism.... Hundreds of them just picked at random off the streets to clean the toilets of the Nazi boys. The lucky ones get off with merely cleaning cars—the thousands of automobiles which have been stolen from the Jews and 'enemies' of the regime."

Some of Shirer's colleagues had fled Vienna or were threatened with arrest. He was with one colleague near a synagogue that had been taken over by the SS when a Nazi confronted the colleague and accused him of being Jewish. An INS colleague, Alfred Tyrnauer, an Austrian-born Jew, was arrested in his office and held until US officials—presumably John Wiley—got him released and sent to Paris. Marcel Fodor and his wife had also fled.

On April 8, nearly a month after the Germans annexed Austria, Tess and her baby left the hospital, her body free of the surgical equipment. In a note he wrote years later, Shirer said: "Tess and baby home fr hospital. Since she went in Feb. 25, she there 42 days, half of them fighting for life, mostly while I away. She still must have been weak for you say (in the diary): 'I carried her upstairs from the car this morning and it will be some time before she can walk. But the worst is over.'"

CLEARING THE MOUNTAINS

With the birth of his daughter, Shirer's home life and his busy career with CBS became even more challenging. He was a brand-new family man in the middle of a growing storm that threatened to engulf Europe. Like other keen observers, he could guess where it was all leading: all but certain war. But beyond that guess, he could not have imagined what that war would look like in all its many phases or the full scope of the Germans' intentions toward their enemies.

A cataclysmic eruption was certain, he was sure of that, as the Germans under Hitler continued to remake their own country and push outward with the quasi-religious conviction that their "race" was entitled to reimagine and then reshape the very landscape of Europe as well as populate the vast and fertile lands to the east with their own kind. These lands would be for the Germans their *Lebensraum*—their living space, for them only. That millions of other people were in their way was a problem the German government was more than willing to address. These other people were not to be allowed to stand in the way of the German dream. Nazism was the foundation upon which a racial war would be articulated, then fought and won.

The anger that drove Hitler after the German defeat of 1918 continued to boil in 1938, but it was in large part no longer about the terms imposed on Germany by the Treaty of Versailles. Those grievances had been pushed aside by 1938. Even earlier, German anger over the defeat and its bitter aftermath had been overplayed politically as it had also become fully mythologized into a national grievance. It was in some respects a cover story, a smokescreen. Real, yes, but overplayed.

Hitler's anger was a different kind of rage. How else to explain the almost immediate establishment of concentration camps for Germany's new enemies of the state after Hitler's coming to power? Or the Nazis' forcing elderly Jews and women with children in Vienna to clean gutters with small brushes while being taunted and insulted? How else to explain random, violent attacks on Jews and their places of business? These actions amounted to wholesale theft, and before the end of 1938, across Germany and Austria they would intensify to state-sponsored robbery on a vast and organized scale, with bureaucrats keeping record books and tally sheets and setting the foundations for new family fortunes that would last for generations. Hitler talked about other grievances when he wasn't talking about the Jews, but the Jews and what exactly to do with them were on his mind day and night. By this argument, the coming war would be a sideshow; the main event was the Nazi plan, evolving and moving in different and conflicting directions, to rid Germany—and every square mile of land it conquered—of the Jews.

* * *

For Shirer, the trick was to continue to give CBS what it had hired him for—the setting up of musical venues for radio programs played in the United States—but also to stay in touch with his journalist colleagues and look for opportunities to broadcast news. He and Murrow had pulled it off magnificently after the *Anschluss*, and the question had been answered as to whether the two men could broadcast themselves. Shirer knew it would happen again for him as big events piled up. Beyond work, he wanted to spend at least the first few weeks at home with Tess and the baby at their apartment at Plösslgasse 4 in Vienna. Tess had not yet recovered fully from the ordeal she had suffered in the hospital. She needed him at home.

At his desk he kept up with his voluminous correspondence with friends across Europe, with family in the United States, and also with business contacts. Soon after Eileen's birth, an uncle in Humboldt, Iowa, wrote to congratulate Shirer. In his letter, T. G. Ferreby wrote that, when he arrived at home from church that morning, he turned on the radio to catch up on the news and heard an announcer say: "We now turn to Vienna to hear William Shirer's talk." For a family member in a small Iowa farm town, hearing Shirer's voice come across the radio was a profound thrill. In a letter to a friend, Shirer said he had planned to travel but decided to stay in Vienna to cover a speech by "the big boy"—Hitler—and also so that he could stay closer to the apartment. He closed his letter by saying the baby was crying in another room.

Shirer wrote a German couple in Berlin, who had apparently written him in praise of the *Anschluss*. In response, Shirer wrote: "I can understand your joy at the Anschluss and I hope it means better times for the Austrians whom I love. Though I don't like the way it was done. If 99 per cent of the people were for it, why was it necessary to pour in 200,000 troops and thousands of police and threaten war? You see, your German newspapers only told one side of the story. We Americans, being very strange people, like both sides."

Just before his daughter's birth, Shirer had written Gottfried Aschmann, the official in the Propaganda Ministry in Berlin, to request an interview. "Mr. Edward R. Murrow, our European director, and I would like very much to come to Berlin one of these days and have a brief talk with Reichminister Dr. Goebbels on the subject of broadcasts from Europe to America. We will naturally be seeing the officials of the Reichs-Rundfunk-Gesellschaft, with whom we are already in contact, but we should like to talk with Dr. Goebbels if it can be arranged." The request went nowhere.

Shirer's relationship with Paul White in New York City began to fray at this time. It would only grow more difficult over the following two years. While Shirer had been praised by William S. Paley for the historic broadcast from London after the *Anschluss*, White now wrote Shirer to castigate him for leaving Vienna without a backup in place once the state radio system went back on the air and Shirer was still in London and Murrow had left Austria. It was an incredible complaint, bizarre in its allegiance to corporate rules without weighing the reality, from an office manager in a safe and comfortable midtown Manhattan office building to a journalist in the field in Europe. Only a fool ignorant of the hardships of reporting would register such a complaint.

A full month later, White wrote again, this time to apologize for the previous letter, saying he had had no idea that Tess Shirer was in the hospital during the time the network had no one at the station. In response, Shirer wrote White to tell him he had no hard feelings. Reading between the lines of Shirer's response suggests a newfound wariness of Paul White. It's not a leap to think that Shirer wrote him off at that point, putting him down as simply a corporate suit.

Shirer explained that he had tried to line up a replacement for the time he was in London, but "one broke down and sobbed hysterically, a second, with his wife, was already in the jug, and a third was hiding preparatory for making for the Swiss border, which he did the following night." He then added a warning: "The point is that there is now no outlet for us from Central Europe which is not subject to German censorship, as all the landlines even to Geneva now go through Germany."

* * *

In mid-April, Shirer left Vienna for Prague to interview the Czechoslovak president, Edvard Beneš, who like others in his country could look to the west and see the threat building in Berlin. One day before departing from Vienna, Shirer had written in his diary that Czechoslovakia "will certainly be next on Hitler's list. Militarily it is doomed now that Germany has it flanked on the south as well as the north." His goal was to interview Beneš about his country's relationship with Germany and to inquire about the future status of the German-speaking regions along the country's border with Germany.

Hitler had long spoken about his desire to incorporate ethnic Germans into a single empire, often using the pretext that those who lived beyond the borders of Germany were cruelly treated, oppressed, and disadvantaged because they were Germans and beyond his protection. These lands would, of course, include Austria, but also the Polish corridor, Alsace-Lorraine in France, which the Germans had seized after the Franco-Prussian War but lost after the Great War, and also German-speaking regions of a number of countries, including Czechoslovakia and Yugoslavia.

When, in the interview, as Shirer later related in his diary, he asked Beneš about the "German question," Beneš's voice suddenly faded on the radio as if the system had broken down. "I suspect the Germans faded out Beneš on purpose, though Berlin denied it when I spoke with the people there on the phone after the broadcast. They said the fault was here in Prague. The Czechs deny it. I had a long talk with Svoboda, the chief engineer for the Czech Broadcasting System, urging him to rush work on his new short-wave transmitter, explaining that if the Germans got tough, that would be Prague's only outlet....A good-natured fellow, he does not think the Germans will do anything until they've digested Austria, which he thinks will take years."

Shirer was back in Vienna for Easter, but in early May he boarded a train bound for Rome, where he planned to cover an appearance by Hitler. The journey did not go smoothly. Late at night, as the train crossed into Italy, SS guards pushed into Shirer's compartment and rudely looked through his belongings. One of the guards confiscated all of Shirer's money, and he understood them to say he was under arrest. But he wasn't, and after a long conversation they returned the money and withdrew from his compartment, leaving a nervous Shirer to fall back to sleep as the train sped south across Italy.

In Rome, Shirer set up his microphone on the roof of a stable overlooking the grand Quirinal Palace, which had been built in the sixteenth century as a residence for Pope Gregory XIII. Hitler was to arrive in a horse-drawn carriage on a lovely spring evening, and Shirer would broadcast live as the sights and sounds—clomping horse hooves on cobblestones, the marching of gaily decorated guards—unfolded before him and his microphone. A listener in a farmhouse in the American Midwest could sit in his living room and hear William L. Shirer speak off the cuff from Rome while Hitler paraded by in a gilded carriage and imagine what it all looked like in such a far-off country.

*   *   *

Late May found Shirer able to spend long days with Tess and Eileen in Vienna. They ate in outdoor restaurants and walked through magnificent gardens and palace grounds and listened to music, always a favorite activity for the couple. Shirer, like his mother back in Cedar Rapids, who spent her Sundays seated in front of her radio listening to the Metropolitan Opera broadcast from New York City, adored classical music. There were few things that made him happier than to sit in auditoriums and concert halls and outdoors under starry skies and be entertained by an orchestra.

On the evening of May 20, Shirer and Tess met two friends at a Hungarian restaurant near the Opera House in Vienna. On the street outside the restaurant, uniformed Nazis enjoyed the evening, too. The Shirers' friends were Charles Dimont, a correspondent who wrote for Reuters, and his wife, whom Shirer does not identify in his diary. Halfway through dinner, Dimont was called away to a phone. When he returned, he announced that his editor in London had informed him that the Germans were sending large numbers of troops toward Czechoslovakia. Dimont immediately left the table and made arrangements to drive to the Czech border. Shirer decided to work the phones and see if he could find out if the Germans were in fact preparing to move militarily into the German-speaking regions of Czechoslovakia.

Within a day, Shirer had learned enough to convince him that he should leave for Prague. He wrote in his diary on May 21: "The story is that Hitler has mobilized ten divisions along the Czech frontier.... Had hoped to remain here a few days since Tess must have another operation day after tomorrow." Shirer also planned to move his family to Geneva, and he wanted to accomplish that by mid-June since Tess had applied for a Swiss visa that would shortly expire. The point of the move was simple, he explained: "Have picked Geneva because it's no longer possible to do my job from here, what with the currency restrictions, the Nazi censorship and snooping, and all."

On June 10, the Shirers packed up their Vienna apartment under the watchful eye of the Gestapo, who went through Shirer's belongings looking for anything he should not be allowed to take to Geneva. Tess was weak and in poor condition from her recent operation. At the airport, more Gestapo went through all the belongings again, as well as wallets and pockets, looking for currency violations. In his diary, Shirer said a "Nazi spy" he identified as "X" greeted him at the offices of a shipping company and that for a moment Shirer feared he was about to be arrested.

In the airport terminal, Shirer helped a very weak Tess to a bench, where she lay down while a nurse held the baby. Another Gestapo officer demanded that she sit up so she could answer his questions. "I tried to hold her up," Shirer wrote in his diary.

Then a police official led me away....In a little room two police officials went through my pocketbook and my pockets. Everything was in order. They led me into a side room. "Wait here," they said. I said I wanted to go back to help with the baggage inspection, that my wife was in a critical state; but they shut the door. I heard the lock turn. I was locked in. Five, then, fifteen minutes. Pacing the floor. Time for the airplane to leave. Past time. Then I heard Tess shout: "Bill, they're taking me away to strip me!" I had spoken with the Gestapo chief about that, explained that she was heavily bandaged, the danger of infection....I pounded on the door. No result.

Through the window I could hear and see the Swiss racing the two motors of their Douglas plane, impatient to get away. After a half-hour I was led out to a corridor connecting the waiting room with the airfield. I tried to get into the waiting room, but the door was locked. Finally Tess came, the nurse supporting her with one arm and holding the baby in the other.

"Hurry, there," snapped an official. "You've kept the plane waiting a half hour." I held my tongue and grabbed Tess.

She was gritting her teeth, as angry as I've ever seen her. "They stripped me." she kept saying....We hurried across the runway to the plane. I wondered what could happen in the next seconds before we were in the plane and safe. Maybe X would come running out and demand my arrest. Then we were in the plane and it was racing across the field.

The airplane rose sharply to clear the mountains and was lost in storm clouds. Airsick passengers heaved into bags. "Then there was Zurich down there, Switzerland, sanity, civilization again."

Shirer summed up the horrors of the trip out of Vienna in a letter written to Valerie Fuhrmann, who owned the apartment the Shirers rented in Vienna. "We had a very bad time at the airport the day we left. They locked me in the waiting room while they took all the clothes off my wife and searched her....Even though we had a very stormy flight in the fog most of the way to Zurich, we felt very good at setting our feet on free soil again."

Fuhrmann wrote back, reminding Shirer that he owed her money. She then referred to "abuse and lawlessness everywhere," an obvious reference to what the Nazis had wrought in her country in just a few short weeks. In a second letter, she told Shirer: "You will understand how worried I am, if I tell you that my son has been called to military service yesterday and I could not even say goodbye to him and do not know where he is. Where is this going to lead to?"

* * *

The Shirers found in Switzerland everything they needed and wanted—great beauty all around them, in the lakes and mountains, and peace and quiet. Being away from the Nazis suited them both. The fear that somehow either one of them would do something seen as criminal by the Gestapo and be arrested now abated. To Bill in particular, not being in Vienna or Berlin meant breathing easier, and he was grateful for it and to Murrow for agreeing to let him move his family to a neutral country.

In Geneva, they rented an apartment at 29 Avenue de Miremont. When Shirer wasn't working, they enjoyed the city and all that it offered. They looked for places to hear classical music and for small restaurants and cafés where they could sample the food and wine and still live within the confines of a very tight budget. For the Shirers, money was—and always would be—a neverending source of worry and tension.

On a warm day in June, the Shirers and Ed Murrow boarded a paddleboat on Lake Geneva for a day on the water. Shirer found the lake fantastically beautiful—a huge body of blue water surrounded by the tall snow-covered Alps. "It was almost overwhelming," he wrote in his diary. He and Murrow were together to attend a conference of the International Broadcasting Union, a group of European broadcasters who gave lip service to cooperation on technical matters. Both found the proceedings boring, which allowed them to enjoy the lake and stay outdoors.

What did draw both men's attention was the political talk that dominated the conference. The London *Times*, which to Shirer's eye tilted toward the Nazis and was the paper Norman Ebbutt had complained about in his and Shirer's nightly gatherings at the Taverne, published an editorial calling on the Czechoslovakian government under Edvard Beneš to allow the Sudeten Germans—German-speaking Czechs living in a broad rim along the country's border with Germany—to vote on whether they wanted to split off and join the Reich. As an editorial in a major European newspaper, it was remarkable for its wide-open embrace of the German cause. Shirer found it deeply offensive, writing in his diary, "The *Times* argues that if this is done, Germany would lose any claim to interfere in the affairs of Czechoslovakia." Shirer found the argument specious and naïve.

"This Old Lady [the *Times*] simply won't learn," he wrote. "Ed and Dick Marriot of BBC, an intelligent and courageous young man, very pessimistic about the strength and designs of the 'appeasement' crowd in London."

If Shirer had any doubts about Ebbutt's complaints that his paper would not print his stories, they were erased now.

In July, Shirer traveled to Evian on Lake Geneva to sit in on a conference meant to deal with European refugees. "I doubt if much will be done," Shirer wrote. "The British, French and Americans seem too anxious not to do anything to offend Hitler. It's an absurd situation."

He found it upsetting that CBS had not asked him to do a broadcast from the conference. The refugee issue, and perhaps the far larger issue of the growing peril surrounding Germany's Jews, evidently held no interest for the network.

"I guess I was a little hasty thinking the 'radio foreign correspondent' had been born at the time of the *Anschluss*," he wrote. "We are not really covering it at all."

Lovers of the outdoors and the mountains, Shirer and his wife Tess, who was Austrian, skiing in her native country.

To whom it may concern.

This is to certify that

WILLIAM SHIRER

Correspondent of

CHICAGO TRIBUNE

whose autographed photograph appears opposite, is a member of The Anglo-American Press Association of Vienna and as such is entitled to the usual press courtesies.

All authorities and others to whom these credentials may be presented are respectfully requested to render to this correspondent all possible facilities and assistance in the fulfillment of his duties.

President

Secretary.

Anglo-American
PRESS·ASSOCIATION
of Vienna

The press pass that Shirer received soon after moving to Vienna in the late 1920s to work as a correspondent for the *Chicago Tribune*.

Shirer in Vienna in 1930, while working as a correspondent for the *Chicago Tribune*.

Tess Stiberitz, who later married Shirer, circa 1930.

William L. Shirer attending one of the elegant balls in the Adlon Hotel in Berlin that the German government held for foreign correspondents.

After the signing of the Munich Accord in late September 1938 that allowed the Germans to occupy the Sudentenland regions of Czechoslovakia, Shirer broadcast the news from the Friedrichstrasse in Berlin.

Shirer broadcasting live for CBS from Rome in 1939.

A frequent activity—Shirer checking in with Berlin police.

Shirer in Geneva playing with his daughter Eileen Inga circa 1939–1940. Shirer frequently flew to Geneva, where his family stayed while he was based in Berlin.

William L. Shirer standing by his office in Berlin.

084 Telegramm **Deutsche Reichspost**

aus 2784 GENEVE TEL 3742 26 30/8 1815 =

Aufgenommen
Tag Monat Jahr Uhr
30 VIII 38   41

SHIRER HOTEL ADLON BERLIN =

Übermittelt

von: Zürich   durch:

Haupttelegraphenamt
Berlin

SO SWEET OF YOU REMEMBER BIRTHDAY THANKS SO MUCH ROSES JUST
GOT STOP APPRECIATE IT DEEPLY YOU THOUGHT OF IT SUCH TIME +

A cable Tess Shirer sent from Geneva to her husband, living at the Adlon
Hotel in Berlin, thanking him for sending roses to her on her birthday.

Shirer arriving at the Berlin broadcasting center sometime in 1939, the year
before the Germans invaded Poland.

Shirer walking by the Brandenbung Gate in Berlin sometime in 1940. In May of that year the Germans invaded the Low Countries and France.

His finest moment as a correspondent, Shirer typing his story of the French surrender in June 1940 in Compiègne, north of Paris. He broadcast the surrender live on CBS radio.

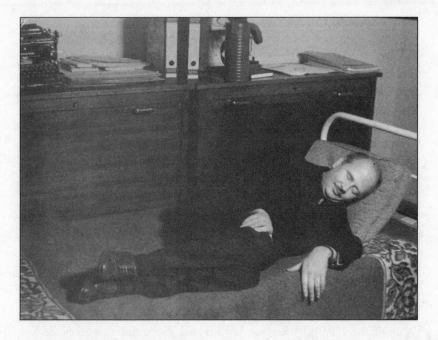

Due to the British bombings of Berlin, Shirer often could not leave the broadcast center. Here he is shown sleeping in his studio.

Shirer was very close with his CBS boss, Edward R. Murrow. While Shirer was based in Berlin, Murrow broadcast from London. The two later had a horrific falling out.

THE PHOTOGRAPHER

One of the 170,000 Viennese Jews trying desperately to extricate herself from the country in the summer of 1938 was Helene Katz. Since the *Anschluss* in March, the hatred in her country toward her and the country's other Jews had boiled over. Tens of thousands of Jewish-owned businesses and apartments across Vienna were confiscated, their inhabitants forced out on short notice. Assets held by the country's Jews were confiscated, often after severe beatings and killings. In the countryside, Jews were pushed into Vienna, where they could be kept under watch until the government devised the next plan of action. Those Jews with the means and the courage left at the first opportunity, by any means available. Many desperate Jews committed suicide.

To better organize the forced emigration, a new office was set up in Vienna. It was the Central Agency for Jewish Emigration, and it opened its doors the third week of August 1938. Its head was Adolf Eichmann, a bland, narrow-faced, and thoroughly unattractive man. He was also a bureaucrat who cared about doing a good job, who worked hard at it, who showed initiative, zeal, and excessive loyalty, and who was anything but the banal desk-bound numbers counter some would later call him. His office, with its staff workers and secretaries and filing cabinets filled with names and numbers and statistics, would now fully organize and bureaucratize the theft that was underway.

What a researcher or interested party can learn about Katz's life today, what scant details can be gathered to fill in her biography, would not fill a 3×5 card. Born in Lemberg, Poland (today the city of Lviv in Ukraine) on

September 20, 1899, she moved to Austria with her family in 1915. It is likely that the Katz family left Lemberg that year because of general unrest, the deeply rooted anti-Semitism, and of course the landscape-altering turmoil of the Great War. Her father's name was Joachim Katz; her mother's name seems to have been lost to history. Her mother died while Katz was still a young woman, perhaps a teenager; her father was dead by 1925, when his daughter was in her mid-twenties and just beginning to come into her own as a Vienna portrait photographer.

That summer of 1938, as Eichmann was organizing his new office, Katz was a month shy of her thirty-ninth birthday—single, worldly, a woman of the arts, no doubt very well read, and the owner of a photography studio at Stubenring 18, in the heart of Vienna's tourist and hotel area. She also had an apartment in Vienna, at Zinckgasse 18. Katz signed her letters and her striking gelatin silver portrait photographs "Hella." Some examples of her photography can still be found for sale at Vienna-based art galleries— their provenance is something of a mystery. Her work centered on portraits of men and women in the rarefied worlds of theater and music, such as Thea von Uyy, a ballet and cabaret dancer who performed in Vienna and Berlin, and the composer Franz Lehar, who wrote the popular operetta *Die lustige Witwe*, The Merry Widow. Both portraits were taken in the late 1920s.

The name "Helene Katz" was found in a series of letters in a box in the Shirer collection at Coe College in Cedar Rapids, Iowa. Like so much of Shirer's personal papers—from manuscripts to newspaper clippings to thoughts jotted down on scraps of paper—he saved his correspondence with Katz. In doing so, in his very small way, he kept her name alive for someone going through his papers decades later. They stand out in a large archive—a few letters in just one box, stacked carefully on a shelf containing dozens of other boxes of Shirer's personal records—because of all the questions they do not answer. There are just a few of them—short, pleading letters, to Bill and Tess Shirer; from Shirer back to Hella; from Shirer to his friends John and Frances Gunther; and from the Gunthers to Hella.

Hella's first letter is addressed, "With great regard, Mr. Shirer and dear Mrs. Shirer." It is dated August 18, 1938, the week Eichmann opened his office in Vienna to facilitate the robbing and forced emigration of Jews out of Austria. The letter is written on her stationery, the top of which reads: "Helene Katz, *photographisches Atelier*, Wien 1, Stubenring 18, Tel. R-21-8-40." In fountain pen ink, she wrote, in German:

> *Please don't be angry if my letter bothers you. However, these doubtful times have given me the courage to ask. I must leave Germany in 4 weeks at the latest. I'm being kicked out of my flat and I have no idea where on earth I can go. It may*

be inappropriate for me to turn to you, but maybe you could help me immigrate
somewhere.

Pardon me, but when someone is in distress, it is difficult to know what is
appropriate to do. Please dear Mr. Shirer perhaps you know something. I am very
hardworking and good at my work. I could find success anywhere.

Perhaps my S.O.S. will reach you. Please call and there is still help for me.

With sincere greetings for you both,

Hella Katz

How did the Shirers know her? An easy guess is that she crossed paths
with Bill Shirer when he lived and worked in Vienna. He and Tess loved music
and theater, so perhaps he met her at a concert or an opening. All three moved
in the same arty circles. Tess was an amateur photographer, and it is clear from
records in Vienna that Hella taught photography and had students of her own.
Tess might have been one of them.

A second letter in the Coe College file shows Shirer writing to Frances
Gunther. It is dated August 13, 1938, which suggests that Katz had written a
letter *before* the one she dated August 18, or perhaps Shirer typed the wrong
date on his letter and the "3" in "13" is really an "8." In the letter, addressed
"Dear Frances," Shirer says:

> *You will not have forgotten Hella Katz, who taught you and Tess some of the tricks*
> *of photography in Vienna once. As you may well imagine she is now in a bad way and*
> *would like to come to America. When I saw her the other day in Vienna she wondered*
> *if you could help. What she would like to do is to go into business with some American*
> *in America. Could you find someone who is interested? She thinks the Nazis will let*
> *her take her cameras and paraphanalia [sic] with her to N.Y. though I think she is*
> *kidding herself.*

This letter suggests that Hella had met Tess before she met Bill when she
taught Tess and Frances Gunther how to take photographs. That could have
been years earlier when the Shirers and Gunthers were both living in Vienna.
The letter also shows that Shirer had run into her in Vienna in mid-August
1938 and that she had asked him for his help—more likely *begged* him for
help—mentioning the name of Frances Gunther as a possible sponsor, which
Hella would need in order to get a visa to travel and remain in the United
States. Hella's mind would have been racing, groping for any lead that might
get her out of the country. While he surely had a great deal of empathy for
Hella, Shirer could in no way have fully imagined what lay ahead for her and
for Austria's Jews if they remained in the country.

In the Coe file is a letter from Frances Gunther to Bill. It is not dated, but
it must have been sent right after she received his letter. The return address is

Chestnut Hill, Norwalk, Connecticut. She addresses it "Dear Bill":

> *Certainly I remember Hella Katz and her picture of Johnny is always up front. We are moving into New York next month (after Oct. 1 at 300 Central Park West), and I will see what can be done about interesting someone in getting her over and will write you again. How is Tessie?*

She goes on to ask about the baby, Eileen, and to inquire why Tess has not written her back. "Why doesn't Tessie answer my letters? Doesn't she love me anymore? Well, it doesn't matter, I love her just the same....John's working on his next book—as usual. Yours, Frances."

John Gunther died in 1970. His papers are in the library of the University of Chicago and contain two letters that he wrote to Hella. The first was written October 17, 1938, in which Gunther opens by saying, "My wife and I were heartbroken to get your terribly tragic letter. Believe me we will do everything we can for you." He tells her he has written the US consulate in Vienna and provided an affidavit on her behalf that she would have an American sponsor. He suggests that if she can't get a visa, she should apply for a visitor's visa. "I am sure you can get this type of visa at once," Gunther tells her. In the second letter, written November 14, days after the rampages of *Kristallnacht* (the Night of Broken Glass), he tells her he has cabled the consulate with an urgent appeal on her behalf that she be given a visa to emigrate to the United States. He closes by saying, "I know how particularly awful things must be following this last week of turmoil. Please keep in touch and we will do everything we can."

Shirer's letters show that he was as involved in helping Hella as John Gunther. Shirer, though, traveled extensively, while Gunther wrote from home. Shirer had less time to put into the effort to help her but wrote when he could. On September 1, 1938, two weeks after seeing Hella in Vienna and after receiving her letter to him, Shirer wrote back to her. "Dear Miss Katz:"

> *Excuse me for not writing sooner but I have been away in Czechoslovakia and Germany and only found your letter on my return here this week. Last month I learned that the Gunthers had returned to New York from China and on August 13 I wrote Mrs. Gunther asking if she could find somebody there who would be interested in going into business with you in America. I expect a reply from Mrs. Gunther very soon....Have you been in to see the American Consular General, Mr. Wiley, about your American visa? I wrote Mrs. Wiley about you. As they are good friends of mine and are leaving in a few days for a new appointment in Riga, I would urge you to see him at once. Just mention my name. I do hope something comes out of this and don't fail to let me know.*

Six weeks later, on October 18, Shirer again wrote Frances Gunther. He refers to "Gauleiter Chamberlain," a reference to British Prime Minister Neville Chamberlain and "shameful" events that had recently unfolded in Germany and Czechoslovakia. He begins his letter:

> Here is another pitiful letter from Hella Katz which I found on my return this week from covering Czecho and Germany during the recent sad and shameful mess. I do wish we could do something for the poor girl. The only practical thing is to get her name advanced on the quota list and I am trying to get John Wiley, who is now in Riga, to see if he can swing that. If you know anyone in Washington—you know Messersmith, don't you?—it might help to work from that end. Unless we can get her name put up towards the front of the list, she will have to wait years for an American visa.

The rest of the correspondence related to Katz amounts to four letters that, collectively, beg the question: What happened to her? On October 19, Shirer, from his home in Geneva, wrote two letters. The first was to Hella, the second to John Wiley in Latvia. In that letter, Shirer tells his friend he has been playing golf on "two lovely courses" in Geneva. He speaks of Czechoslovakia and doing 151 broadcasts for CBS, "an all time record." He ends the letter with a personal plea for Hella:

> Is there any way that you know of by which we can advance that Viennese photographer lady, Hella Katz, about whom I wrote you and Irene, on the list for an American visa? I'd like to help her. The Gunthers are providing her with an affidavit.

In the letter to Hella, Shirer informed her of his letter to Wiley, and he wondered if perhaps she could get to Latvia. It was a letter meant to allay her fears, and he closed it by saying, "In the meantime, don't despair, Cordially yours, William Shirer."

Hella's letter to Shirer, written in her best but poor English, is also dated October 19. She tells him that the Gunthers have provided an affidavit of support so that she could apply in Vienna for an American visa.

> I take the liberty to give many thanks to you who has helped me in such a fine manner. Now I see still yet one difficulty and this is a protection to come to the consul of Vienna for getting the permission to start to America outside the quotation. Could you help me with your influence to this? I am already very obliged to you and I hope that I shall find occasion once in my life to proof my thankfulness. I hope that Mrs. Shirer and the baby are in the best healthness which I wish with my whole heart.

John Wiley wrote to Shirer on October 27 and says he was "utterly delighted" to get Shirer's "cheerful" letter in which he referred to playing golf in Geneva. Before he closes his letter, Wiley writes: "I am writing to the Consul General in Vienna with regard to Hella Katz. I am sure that he will do anything that is possible and proper."

A month later, on November 22, Shirer wrote to "Miss Katz:"

> *Mr. Wiley writes that he has written the Consul General in Vienna about you. I therefore suggest that you go and see the Consul General as soon as possible. Mrs. Shirer is now in America, and I hope that you will be able to get there fairly soon.*

As much as had happened in Hella's life since March, November brought more terror on a far wider, more organized scale. Her panic level by the time she opened Shirer's letter must have been overwhelming, her need for some kind of answer to her plight having reached the point of desperation. Earlier that month, over the course of two nights, November 9 and 10, the state had turned its violent hand on the Jews of Germany and Austria in what became known as *Kristallnacht*, or the Night of Crystal—the Night of Broken Glass. The thin veneer of an excuse that the Nazi leaders in Berlin needed to unleash a wave of violence against the Jews came when Ernst von Rath, a secretary in the German Embassy in Paris, was shot dead by Herschel Grynszpan, a Polish Jew then still in his teens. The death in Paris coincided with a major event in the Nazi calendar—November 9, 1923, when the so-called Beer Hall Putsch to topple the government came to an ignominious end in the streets of Munich with the shooting deaths of Nazi punks. Those who had been in the streets that night met each anniversary with Hitler to remember their martyrs. Now, fifteen years later, they had the death in Paris to talk about. Throughout Germany and in Austria, mobs looted synagogues and shops and set them ablaze.

Where was Hella at this time? Her studio would not have survived; any photography equipment she might have left in her studio would likely have been stolen, the premises ransacked. She escaped arrest, even as thousands of other Jews in Vienna were picked up by the Gestapo and sent to camps. It is not difficult to imagine how she felt when she saw the November 22 letter from Shirer telling her to venture out into the open and make her way through the city's streets to the American embassy to meet the consul general.

Shirer's published diaries for the month of November—and the voluminous correspondence that he saved over the years—shed no light on Hella's fate. In fact, his diary entries for November do not mention *Kristallnacht* at all. His entry for November 6 shows he was in Geneva enjoying terrific fall weather, playing golf, and battling what he called "the worst mental and spiritual depression of my life." He also writes of starting a play he called

"Foreign Correspondent." On November 11, he was in Warsaw for a broadcast commemorating the twentieth anniversary of the establishment of the Polish Republic; on November 20, he was in Brussels for a radio conference; on November 26 Belgrade; and on November 29 in Rome to set up coverage of the pope's critical illness.

* * *

What happened to Hella Katz?

The Central Database of Shoah Victims' Names maintained by Yad Vashem, the museum and research facility in Jerusalem, shows that a woman named Helene Katz was deported from Vienna on March 5, 1941. Records in Vienna kept by the Documentation Center of Austrian Resistance show that the March 5 transport left from Vienna's Aspang Station with 999 Jews crammed into cars. On that day, nearly one thousand men, women, and children stood on a train platform in a major European city clutching whatever belongings they could carry, leaving behind their lives, and waiting on the orders of armed and uniformed men who now controlled their fate. There was nothing secret being done in Vienna on that winter day. Jews weren't mysteriously disappearing, their neighbors wondering in the morning what happened to them. They were being removed as government policy and, in this case, shipped into German-occupied Poland. Prior to being deported, the Jews still in Austria had been moved into severely cramped housing in Vienna's second district in preparation for deportation.

Another of the 999 was a man with the same address as Helene Katz. His name was Daniel Katz; they might have been brother and sister as no marriage records exist for them. The information collected by Yad Vashem reads: "Helene Katz was born in 1885. During the war was in Wien [Vienna], Austria. Deported with transport from Wien to Modliborzyce. Helene perished in the Shoah."

1885? This Helene Katz was not the photographer who had begged Shirer and the Gunthers for help. This was a different Viennese woman of the same name—one of millions lost to history except for a few lines in an archive.

The last correspondence exchanged between the photographer Helene Katz and Shirer came on November 22, 1938. After that, there is nothing in the Shirer files. It may be that he believed he had done all he could—writing his American government friend Wiley hoping to get her a visa to the United States, asking the Gunthers in New York if they could find a sponsor for her, urging Hella not to give up and to keep trying. He may have been told, and never written it down anywhere—certainly odd for a man who wrote down so much—that Hella was safe. What more could he have done? What were his responsibilities as an American journalist to a person who desperately needed his help?

A researcher in Vienna, Katja Maria Chladek, found a reference in the city's archives stating that Hella Katz, the photographer, had emigrated in March 1939. She got away. More of her slim biography began to come out, through Chladek's work and the research of others, including the Austrian journalist Anton Holzer. According to Holzer's research, Hella became a well-known photography teacher and drew students such as Hans Popper and Elly Niebuhr, whom Holzer interviewed for a biography he wrote of her. Holzer wrote: "Only a bit later, in March 1939, Hella Katz, Elly's master teacher, left Vienna. Under the oppression of anti-Semitism, the photographer closed her studio, deregistered on March 20, 1939 from her home address, Zinckgasse 13, and shortly thereafter left the country in the direction of England. Here all trace of her disappears."

The state archives in Austria shows that a Nazi bureaucrat named Franz Jungwirth, in charge of disposing of Jewish-owned property, had inventoried Hella's belongings and written a report on them, dated July 1, 1939. The report starts: "Report on wealth, liquidation plan, and simultaneously Final Report No. 12. Regarding: KATZ Helene, Photo Studio, Vienna 1, Stubenring 18 1V." The English translation reads:

> Helene Katz long after November 1938 possessed approval from a party office to distribute photographs and related items to emigrating Jews. For this reason she was free from surveillance and was also able to dispose freely of her possessions. She terminated her lease as primary tenant for her studio on April 30, 1939, and cleaned it out according to the rules. She turned it over to the landlord without arrears. Fraulein Katz owned one or two cameras, accessories, and only the most necessary furnishings of minimal worth.

* * *

Hella Katz did reach England. In April 1939 she registered with the Jewish Refugee Committee in London. A short file contains this information:

Name—Helene Katz
Born—20 September 1899, Lemberg, Poland
Arrival in Britain—21 March 1939
Nationality—Austrian
Home address—Vienna 5, Zinckgasse 18
British address—c/o: Mrs. Lloyd, Oaksend, Oxshott, Surrey
Profession—Photographer

The committee's records further state that Hella held an affidavit for America and on May 3, 1939, soon after arriving in England, asked the Committee for help finding a company that would forward her luggage—to where exactly, the records don't state.

SIGRID WAKES HIM UP

September 1938 brought the party faithful back to Nuremberg for the annual rally. Shirer was grateful to skip it and instead took the train from Berlin to Prague to cover the crisis between Germany and Czechoslovakia that had been building all summer. In German-speaking regions inside Czechoslovakia, Nazi leaders agitated against their country and in favor of joining the German Reich. In some areas, demonstrations were held and violence erupted.

In the Czechoslovakian capital, Shirer covered a speech by Edvard Beneš, the country's beleaguered president. "I have never been afraid in my life," Beneš said in his broadcast. While he prepared his notes, Shirer picked up a Reuters dispatch of Göring's speech at the party rally in Nuremberg. Referring to the Czechs as a "miserable pygmy race without culture," Göring said the Czechs were oppressing the Germans—"a cultured people"—and behind the Czechs, as with all the Nazis' enemies, was "the eternal mask of the Jew devil."

On the evening of September 12, Shirer and a number of foreign correspondents crowded into an apartment in Prague and listened to Hitler's speech at the party rally in which he hurled threats against Czechoslovakia. "Prague on this day when war and peace have apparently hung in the balance has been dark and dismal, with a cold, biting, soaking rain," Shirer wrote in his diary. He walked the streets of the city looking at people's faces, wondering if they fully understood their plight.

A week later, Shirer took the train back to Berlin and that night went on the air with his CBS broadcast. "Hello America. This is Berlin calling," he began. He went on to discuss Prague and the crisis and remarked that Neville

Chamberlain, the British prime minister, would be meeting with Hitler at the Hotel Dreesen in Bad Godesberg on September 22. "The hotel lounge was refurbished this afternoon and decorated with bowls of flowers and German and British flags," Shirer said in his broadcast. "Chancellor Hitler will occupy the little suite which is reserved for him the year around. And probably the meeting will be held there.... One thing is certain: Mr. Chamberlain will certainly get a warm welcome."

Shirer spent the middle of September with a group of English and American correspondents in the Ambassador Hotel in Prague. They all expected German bombers to appear over the city, but none came. In the Sudetenland he heard reports of rioting and plundering of Jewish-owned businesses. The hotel lobby was chaos; with one outside phone line, it was nearly impossible for the correspondents to phone in their stories. Rumors piled on rumors: the Germans would bomb the city at midnight; they might use poison gas; anyone fearful of the Germans was fleeing the city on any flight or train they could book. To Shirer, it was Vienna the previous March all over again.

For several days in a row, Shirer received cables from Paul White in New York telling him that his broadcast had not gotten through. "Murrow called from London and suggested I get off immediately to Berchtesgaden," Shirer wrote in his diary. "Don't know whether I can. Czech trains have stopped running across the border and I can't find a Czech driver who will take his car across the frontier."

Because he could not get his broadcasts through to New York, Shirer decided to write out his stories and cable them to New York, where someone would read them on the radio. Everywhere, Czechs stopped to tell him that Chamberlain was going to sell their country down the river, as the Germans demanded a plebiscite so that Sudeten Germans could vote to break away and join the Reich. Murrow called again, strongly suggesting that Shirer find a way to return to Germany and cover Chamberlain's meeting with Hitler.

On September 20, Shirer boarded a train to Berlin and then went on to Bad Godesberg, where Chamberlain and Hitler were to meet. At the big Friedrichstrasse train station in Berlin, the Reichs-Rundfunk-Gesellschaft, RRG, the state radio system, set up a microphone so that Shirer could interview foreign correspondents about the prospects for a new European war over Czechoslovakia. He put on Sigrid Schultz, Webb Miller, and his good friend Ralph Barnes.

As Shirer went back and forth between Germany and Czechoslovakia, doing broadcasts from Bad Godesberg, Berlin, and Munich, William S. Paley in New York sent him a telegram, dated September 26, in the midst of the crisis. "Columbia's coverage of the European crisis is superior to its competitors and is probably the best job of its kind ever done in radio broadcasting stop you have contributed very largely to the establishment of this opining by the superb job you have done both in your broadcasts and the arrangements you have made stop I want you to know how genuinely pleased I am."

In a telegram Shirer sent to Paul White, he wrote about what lay ahead with a level of certainty. "A week in Berlin gave me the impression that Hitler will invade Czechoslovakia between September 15 and October 15, if he can make sure that France and England will stay quiet." Meanwhile, Tess and Eileen left Europe for New York for a visit with Shirer's family, arriving at a berth on the Hudson River on the morning of October 3.

In Berlin, Shirer listened to Hitler's speech in the Sportpalast on the night of September 26. Hitler boasted he would have the Sudetenland by no later than October 1. "The old man full of more venom than even he has ever shown, hurling personal insults at Benes [sic]," Shirer wrote in his diary. "Twice Hitler screamed that this is absolutely his last territorial demand in Europe." Seated in the balcony directly above Hitler, watching his every move, Shirer thought that the German chancellor had lost control.

* * *

Shirer went to Munich for Chamberlain's final meeting with Hitler, which was also attended by Benito Mussolini of Italy and Édouard Daladier of France. The Czechs had not been invited. "It's all over," Shirer wrote in his diary. The Munich Agreement, signed on September 29, gave Hitler the Sudetenland. Chamberlain told Hitler in a formal declaration that his country and Germany would never go to war again. It was this declaration that Chamberlain famously waved over his head upon his return to London. "I believe it is peace for our time," Chamberlain proclaimed.

In Munich, Shirer stood in the lobby of the Führerhaus as Hitler, Göring, Goebbels, Rudolf Hess, and the German foreign minister, Joachim von Ribbentrop, walked past him. Hitler looked the "conqueror," Shirer noted in his diary, a man full of swagger. For Shirer, though, the day was a great personal defeat, as Max Jordan, the radio correspondent for NBC, went on the air a full hour ahead of Shirer and read from the complete text of the Munich Agreement. No matter that Paley had congratulated him on his work just days earlier, Shirer now felt himself the source of criticism in New York.

The meeting between Hitler and Chamberlain over, and with Shirer feeling badly defeated because of Jordan's beating him with the text of the agreement, he boarded the Munich-to-Berlin train. On board was a group of German reporters and newspaper editors and Karl Boehmer, the foreign press chief from the Propaganda Ministry. The German journalists could not have been more elated at Hitler's great victory. They downed champagne bought by

Boehmer as the train rushed to Berlin—"gloating, boasting, bragging," Shirer wrote in his diary.

* * *

Exhausted, Shirer took a few days off and flew to Paris to meet Murrow, who came in from London to spend time with his colleague. What began as a business partnership, each helping the other to grow a European news franchise, had blossomed into genuine friendship. Each enjoyed the other's company, and each respected the other's talents and limitations. Theirs was a partnership of equals. Shirer relished the thought of spending a few nights in Paris with Murrow, as good a companion in a bar as he could find. Besides, he had little desire to be in Geneva, since Tess and Eileen were in the United States—he loathed the empty house when they were away. Shirer missed his wife and daughter acutely, and he had found the pace of recent weeks overwhelming and thoroughly exhausting.

Beyond the work level, the continued success of the German enterprise had depressed him. It had become a mammoth effort for him to have regular dealings with the government, to talk to the bureaucrats in the Propaganda Ministry, and to ask for their permission to go after a certain story. His contempt for the censors threatened his ability to work in Berlin at all. While he had good friends in the foreign press corps who he respected, there were many others he had come to loathe. He saw some of them as collaborators who went along because they would be favored in the future.

Once in Paris, Shirer's disgust grew. The mood of people he encountered was euphoric—war had been avoided. Just twenty years after the horror of the Great War, they saw it as a blessing that another war had been averted and that Hitler would go no further. Shirer found their optimism contemptible. "The French Socialists, shot through with pacifism; the French Right, with the exception of a few...[are] either fascists or defeatists. France makes no sense to me any more," he wrote in his diary.

Murrow was as gloomy as Shirer. They drank until early in the morning in different bars and walked the streets, talking about the state of Europe and their belief that another great war "is now more probable than ever, that it is likely to come after the next harvest, that Poland is obviously next on Hitler's list." After a few days, unable to bear the mood in Paris, Shirer returned to Geneva.

In December, Tess and Eileen returned to Switzerland from the United States, where Tess had filed papers to become an American citizen. To celebrate the end of a horrific year, the family traveled to Gstaad, the chic ski resort high in the Swiss Alps, for the Christmas holiday. Snow was plentiful, and Shirer was glad to be back skiing for the first time since the accident in Austria six years earlier had nearly gouged out his eye. He was also thrilled to escape the gloomy mood of the previous year, noting in his diary that he'd gone through the Austrian *Anschluss*, the birth of his daughter, Tess's brush with death, the Czech crisis, and the extraordinary British capitulation at Munich.

At a Christmas ball held at one of the hotels, hundreds of wealthy, socially prominent guests crowded into a ballroom to celebrate the holiday, drinking champagne and singing hymns, as if Europe were the same old place it had always been, their lives unchanged. "I found the merry-makers so nauseating that we left early," Shirer wrote in his diary.

As was their custom after nearly eight years of marriage, Tess and Bill sat up New Year's Eve after they put the baby to sleep to look ahead to the coming year, wondering what it could possibly bring that would be more eventful than 1938.

* * *

Spring 1939

A few days into the new year, one of the officials in the Propaganda Ministry cornered Shirer and told him that officials were displeased with the work of H. V. Kaltenborn, the Wisconsin-born radio commentator who worked for CBS in New York. They were particularly displeased over his work during the Czech crisis. Shirer could not have been happier.

"I consider that a great compliment," he wrote in a letter to Kaltenborn.

The censors' constant demands and threats had by now pushed Shirer to a new low point. He wondered, as he had many times during the previous year, if he could go on working in Berlin if all he was allowed to do was broadcast propaganda. He shared his pessimism with Murrow in London, who faced no restrictions, and with Paul White in New York. Of the two of them, Murrow was more in agreement with Shirer's views. Shirer liked White but did not trust him, whereas he trusted Murrow to look out for him. He saw in White a man too quick to criticize and judge others who worked far away and under far more difficult conditions than he had ever faced. He viewed White as a man who looked out for the interests of the corporation first and foremost.

By contrast, Murrow knew from near daily contact with Shirer how hard the work was, what it meant to be a reporter in the field, and how excruciatingly difficult it was to put together an honest story and come away at the end of the day with any feeling of self-respect. Shirer thought all the time: *I am not going to do their bidding for them.* In New York—sitting in his office and enjoying life in the city, his secretary typing his letters for him, going to corporate events and looking out for anything that might trip up the company—White could only pretend to understand.

In a letter to a friend in Rome, Father Delaney, who had helped Shirer with CBS's coverage in February of the death of Pope Pius XI, Shirer said, "I feel low, low tonight because of Hitler's latest steal. It seems to me the light is going out for European civilization. And that decency and truthfulness are becoming extinct. I'm flying to London Saturday as that is the only spot in Europe from where I can tell the American people the truth—or as much of it as I can see."

Early in the spring, Shirer flew to Berlin to cover one of Hitler's speeches and to broadcast it live back to New York. He went to the short-wave control room at the RRG to set up and prepare for Hitler's speech. A German Shirer had not met before came into the room and demanded that the American relay be cut off. Furious, Shirer confronted the man's boss who, just as Hitler began his speech, gave orders for the relay to the United States to go ahead. Satisfied, Shirer went into a sound booth to listen to the speech. Twenty minutes later, the same man who had approved the relay now cut it off.

After several minutes of silence—the Germans "put on some silly record," Shirer wrote in his diary—New York called demanding to know why Hitler had been cut off. Had Hitler been assassinated? Kaltenborn, in the CBS office in New York, got on the line with Shirer and wanted to know what had happened. Shirer, surrounded by a dozen German officials, tried to be circumspect. He assured Kaltenborn that Hitler was alive and giving his speech, which Shirer could hear over another line. For the next ninety minutes, Shirer and the censors argued loudly over whether Shirer should be allowed to read from the notes he had made of Hitler's speech. Finally, the censors relented.

*   *   *

In late June, Shirer boarded an ocean liner for the voyage to the United States, where Tess had returned to complete the citizenship process. In New York and Washington, Shirer's dark view of the situation in Europe and Hitler's intentions were greeted with blank stares. At one point, Tess took him aside and told him he was making himself unpopular by talking so pessimistically. "The trouble is everyone here knows all the answers," he wrote in his diary. "They *know* there will be no war. I wish I *knew* it.... Oh well, it's pleasant to be here with the family and loaf and relax for a few fleeting days."

By mid-July, Shirer was back in Europe. On July 14, he met in London with Murrow and Paul White to talk about news coverage if war broke out in the coming weeks. He played golf with Murrow before going on to Geneva, where John Gunther had arrived to spend a few days. They sat up all night drinking wine, with Gunther arguing that peace was more likely than war.

August came, and Shirer spent much of the first part of the month in Berlin, where he could read in the German newspapers that the Nazis were preparing for war with Poland. Germans he had used as news sources before were now hostile to any criticism of Hitler. "A discussion with Captain D," Shirer wrote in his diary. "A World War officer of proven patriotism, he was against war during the Munich crisis, but changed, I noticed, after April 28, when Hitler denounced the Polish and British treaties. He became violent today at the very mention of the Poles and British. He thundered: 'Why do the English butt in on Danzig and threaten war over the return of a German city? Why do the Poles provoke us? Haven't we the right to a German city like Danzig?'"

"Have you a right to a Czech city like Prague?" Shirer asked. Captain D. had no answer to the question.

By the middle of the month, Shirer was in the city of Danzig on the Baltic Sea, where ethnic Germans had been agitating to join the Reich. He found his hotel filled with German army officers. Several Poles told him that the roads into the city were blocked with tank traps. He tried to broadcast from a German facility but was refused, so he hired a driver to take him to a Polish radio station inside a post office twelve miles away.

"Spoke from a floor mike while leaning on a piano," Shirer wrote in his diary. "Don't know if the broadcast actually got through." Wandering through Danzig's streets, he ran into John Gunther. The two men taxied to a casino on the Baltic and spent the night playing roulette "and talking a blue streak, settling the world's problems."

Several days later, when Shirer got to Warsaw, he met the American ambassador to Poland for lunch and did another broadcast at four in the morning. In his diary, as he prepared to board a train to return to Berlin, he wrote: "I think Poles will fight. I know I said that wrongly about the Czechs a year ago."

*   *   *

By the third week of August the talk of war had heated to the boiling point. The government-controlled press portrayed the Germans in Danzig as aggrieved and oppressed and the Poles as foul aggressors. Shirer found the government's lies to be so over the top that he could not fathom how the German people could possibly accept them as truths. On top of that, his view of the Germans as a people had hardened and grown more cynical. He saw them as cows. They wanted to be led around by a strong leader who lied to them every time he opened his mouth. They did what they were told and did not debate moral issues. They *never* debated moral issues when self-interests were involved. He thought the women were ugly, "the least attractive in

Europe. They have no ankles. They walk badly. They dress worse than English women."

Shirer was in Berlin when Kaltenborn arrived in the city. Minutes after his plane from London landed at Tempelhof, the Gestapo picked him up and held him until he could be forced onto a return flight to London. The Reich did not want him. Infuriated, Shirer felt personally to blame for Kaltenborn's situation. He had spoken to officials in the German government weeks before about Kaltenborn's visit and had been told there would be no problem. "We have been nicely double-crossed by the Nazis," Shirer bitterly wrote in his diary. Shirer waited impatiently for Kaltenborn to clear customs. When he saw all the other passengers free to leave, he knew something was wrong. With Shirer were Kaltenborn's wife and several of her German relatives. The airport steamed with the August heat, and as the hours went by, the air inside the terminal grew more and more oppressive. Finally, Shirer confronted a Gestapo official, and after a loud argument, Kaltenborn was allowed out of custody as long as he stayed in the building. Shirer took him and Kaltenborn's family to the airport café.

Soon after they sat down with a round of beer, another Gestapo agent came to the café to tell Kaltenborn he would be taking the 6:00 P.M. flight back to London. Shirer grew indignant.

"Why? He's just come from there," Shirer said.

"And he's returning there now," the agent said.

"May I ask why?" Kaltenborn asked.

The agent had a quick response. "Looking at his notebook, he said with tremendous seriousness: 'Herr Kaltenborn, on such and such a date in Oklahoma City you made a speech insulting the Führer.'"

Well after midnight, more than six hours after Kaltenborn had been kicked out of Germany, Shirer, bitter and fuming at the arrogance of the Gestapo at the airport, arrived at the Taverne. The room was packed with American, British, and French correspondents, and a number of Germans as well. He found his colleagues talking excitedly about news that had been reported on German radio. Germany and the Soviet Union had agreed to sign an extraordinary nonaggression pact. That day, Wednesday, August 23, the German foreign minister, Joachim von Ribbentrop, had traveled to Moscow to sign the accord.

Shirer went on the air in the broadcast center when word broke that the accord had been agreed upon but not yet signed. "Hello, America! This is Berlin," he began. "Nazi Germany and Bolshevik Russia getting together! Well, even in Berlin where as a foreign correspondent I've seen many surprises since Adolf Hitler came to power in 1933—even here in Berlin people are still rubbing their eyes....I rode around Berlin today on buses, street cars, the elevated and subway. Everyone had their heads buried in a newspaper....I mean, you all know that before yesterday Bolshevik Russia was not exactly the idol of the Nazi press. But look today. I have the *Angriff*, always the most fiery of the Nazi afternoon papers here. It rejoices that the old traditional friendship between the Russian and German peoples has at last been revived."

After 2:00 A.M. at the Taverne, Shirer spoke with Joe Barnes, who had worked in Moscow for the *Herald Tribune* and spoke fluent Russian. Barnes was devastated. He was too shocked to comprehend that the Soviet government had climbed into bed with the Nazis. Barnes had hoped the Russians would sign a pact with the French and British that would force the Germans to reconsider attacking Poland. The German journalists, who for the previous six years since Hitler came to power had accepted as an article of faith the party position that Communism was a great evil, now had a complete about-face and toasted the pact. Shirer found their dishonesty and hypocrisy sickening, as he did that of the American correspondents who played up to them. When Mrs. Kaltenborn appeared at the Taverne after 3:00 A.M., she accused Shirer of not having tried hard enough to keep her husband from being expelled. Disgusted, Shirer announced that he was leaving, and he and Barnes left the restaurant to walk through the Tiergarten back to his room at the Adlon Hotel as the sun was beginning to come over the eastern horizon.

* * *

The next day, Thursday, August 24, Shirer awoke in the middle of the afternoon and thought of everything he had to do that day and in the coming days to prepare. He wondered how he would know when the war had started. Would there be some sort of official announcement on German radio after the troops had crossed the frontier into Poland? He had people who could tell him, but he did not know if they would risk it.

All afternoon he thought of Tess and Eileen, and at 7:00 P.M. he reached them on a phone call from the Adlon to Geneva. Tess said hello and then put their daughter, now a year-and-a-half old and jabbering "Papa, Papa, Papa," on the phone. He could not have been happier. When he was away from them, he missed them keenly, and now, with war approaching and all that it would mean for him, he worried about their safety and well-being, even if they rode out the fighting in Geneva.

"It looks like war tonight," Shirer told his wife when she got back on the phone. "Across the street they're installing an anti-aircraft gun on the roof of the I. G. Farben office. The German bombers have been flying over all day. Hitler may go into Poland tonight." As for Shirer's colleagues among the British correspondents, the last of them had left Berlin that evening for Denmark on orders from their country's embassy in anticipation of their country declaring war on Germany in the wake of an invasion of Poland.

* * *

Monday, August 28, 1939, 2:00 A.M.

The German government released to the correspondents the text of a French statement. Shirer was struck by one line in it: "If French and German blood is now to be spilled, as it was 25 years ago, in an even longer and more murderous war, then each of the two peoples will fight, confident in their own victory. But surely Destruction and Barbarism will be the real victors."

At 4:00 A.M., Shirer went on the air in the broadcast center and described last-minute meetings between the Germans and the British. "In the meantime, as the night wore on, troops thundered through the streets, eastward bound towards Poland," he said.

Wednesday, August 30, 1939, 3:00 A.M.

Shirer borrowed a car from a friend, but when he went to fill it up, he was told he was entitled to only ten liters of gas a day. He met Sigrid Schultz, the *Chicago Tribune* correspondent, and after seeing her, he found a station that would sell him more gas in spite of the restrictions. He knew he needed to be prepared to travel. In the early morning hours he went to the Taverne to meet up with his colleagues.

Thursday, August 31, 1939

The three-piece orchestra that played night and day in the lobby of the Adlon—he had to walk by it to get to the elevator to go to his room—had gotten on his nerves. He wanted them to stop playing and to recognize the reality of the moment. "It does not go well with the tension," he wrote in his diary when he reached his room. Another thing bothered him: "the bespectacled automaton who plays the piano every night at the Taverne non-stop should be mobilized. We sit there nightly going hot and cold on the prospects for War and Peace, but he, the pianist, drums on with his stale jazz and light operetta pieces."

Friday, September 1, 6:00 A.M.

"Sig woke me up at 6 this morning—after two hours sleep—with news that the war was on." Surely, he believed, the British and French would soon follow with war declarations of their own.

Shirer rushed to the RRG and went on the air, the first American correspondent to do so. "Herr Hitler has at last decided to resort to force against Poland. The decision came in the early morning hours of today, Friday. In a proclamation to the army dated this morning Herr Hitler says: 'Poland has refused my offer for a friendly settlement of our relations as neighbors. Instead she has taken up arms.'

" 'The Germans in Poland have been victims of bloody terror, hunted from house to house. A series of frontier violations that a Great Power cannot accept proves that Poland is not willing to respect Reich frontiers. To put an end to this foolhardy situation, I am left with no other means than from now on opposing force to force. The German army will lead the struggle for the honor and vital rights of resurrected Germany with hard determination.' "

As he sat in his small studio in the broadcast center, the morning's Berlin newspapers spread out in front of him with their bold headlines, he pictured German troops pouring across the Polish frontier. He was grateful to Sigrid for the phone call, and he wondered who had awakened her with the news. Had Göring phoned her this morning to tell her that his country had invaded Poland?

He continued speaking into the microphone: "It's a gray day here with overhanging clouds. So far absolutely nothing unusual about the picture in Berlin except that the radio is going full blast alternating with martial music and announcements."

At 1:15 A.M. the next day, Shirer went on the air again. Berlin was preparing for war and British bombers.

> Hello. This is William L. Shirer in Berlin. It's a little bit strange at first, and takes some getting used to. You grope around the pitch-black streets and pretty soon your eyes get used to it, and you can make out the white-washed curbstones—and there's a blue light here and there to guide you—and somehow you get along. Every window in Berlin tonight is curtained with heavy black paper. Behind the darkened windows the people sit in their homes and listen to the radio, which plays martial band music, or a stirring symphony from Beethoven or Brahms, and every once in a while you get a news announcement....
>
> One curious thing about Berlin tonight. The cafés, restaurants and beer halls are full. I went out a couple of hours ago to get a bite to eat. My restaurant looked so dark outside I thought it had shut down. But once I got through the double set of curtained doors, I found the restaurant very light and full of people. I had no trouble getting a good meal, a glass of Pilsner beer and a cup of coffee. It was a vegetarian day, but I got plenty of vegetables and eggs.

An air raid alarm broke Berlin's calm early in the evening, but nothing came of it. "A word about Americans here," Shirer said as he closed his broadcast. "Our Embassy today gave Americans a last chance to get out by a special train which will take them to the Danish border tomorrow morning.... All wives and children of Embassy and Consulate staff members will be evacuated on that train tomorrow. The Embassy tonight distributed gas masks to the staff."

"So there we are. And as long as radio keeps going, I hope to be on the air again tomorrow to tell you what I see from Berlin."

After his broadcast, Shirer walked out into the dark Berlin morning. He and Max Jordan, the NBC radio correspondent, talked for a few minutes. Both men were exhausted and worried about what would come next for them now that war had been declared. Surely the British—who would declare war against Germany on September 3—would soon begin nightly bombings of the city. Standing on the street waiting for a taxi to take him to the Adlon, Shirer felt an uneasiness and an overwhelming sense of isolation, cut off from the world and his family. At the Adlon, in spite of the time, he got through on the phone to Tess in Geneva. She was worried. As he wrote in his diary, "I felt numbed at this interspersing of a little sweetness in a completely mad world."

Lies as Thick as Grass

In late September 1939, nearly a month after Germany's invasion of Poland, and after England and France had declared war on Germany in response, Shirer received a letter at his Geneva address from Blanche Knopf, the cofounder (along with her husband, Alfred A. Knopf) of the publishing firm that bore the Knopf name. He was thrilled to receive it, seeing in it a ratification of his place in the world, even though he barely had time to ponder its significance in his life or to think through what it might mean to the direction of his career as a journalist.

Blanche Knopf, who followed events in Europe closely, if only to keep her eye out for writers of talent she might bring into her publishing house, had a suggestion for Shirer. She saw in him someone who could possibly write an "important" book about Germany. "The only thing I suggest you do now, if you haven't been doing it, is to keep a very careful diary...of everything that has happened because it will be of human interest as well. You would, of course, include in this a broadcaster's experiences and what he has to go through to get the news."

As grateful as he was for the suggestion, Shirer did not need Knopf's advice to get him started. He had been keeping a diary for years, his earliest being entries he made in a pocket-sized notebook while an ROTC student at an army camp in Kansas when he was still in high school in Cedar Rapids. Since his arrival in Germany in August 1934, he had faithfully maintained regular entries, writing in notebooks, on typed sheets of paper, and on pocket calendars. He wrote on what was in front of him. He was now more than five years into his "Berlin diary." As onerous and as time consuming as it sometimes was, particularly when he was exhausted, he kept at it, adding entries every few days.

He saved important German newspapers critical to understanding events at a certain moment. Backing that up, he saved clippings of the articles he had written for the *Chicago Tribune* and also copies of New York newspapers that picked up his stories from the Hearst wire service. He carefully maintained files and moved them whenever he moved, an informal archive of everything related to his life. He saved carbons of outgoing letters, as well as those letters that came to him. Because it was a diary, and because he lived in a police state, he was careful with names, concealing important contacts with an "X," made-up initials, or nothing at all.

* * *

September brought the first wave of British bombers over Germany. Shirer noted in his diary of September 7 that bombs were dropped on two German coastal towns, Wilhelmshaven and Cuxhaven. The Berlin papers dismissed the attacks as meaningless. They also dismissed British charges that on the night of September 2, a German U-boat had sunk the SS *Athenia* en route from Scotland to Canada, carrying 1,103 passengers, including more than 300 Americans. "The war of propaganda is on," he wrote in his diary. "Lies as thick as grass everywhere. Germans conducting terrific press campaign to convince their own people Britain alone is responsible for the crime of war. Mystery here about why no action on the Western Front.... Last night for first time moon was hidden by clouds and getting about in blacked-out Berlin difficult. You couldn't see people in the streets. Lucky ones with flashlights used them to keep from bumping into one another. But no more flashlights to be had in the stores. J. and I met at 1 A.M. this morning in my room to talk things over. We have an idea Britain and France will not shed much blood on the Western Front."

In spite of events going on around him, Shirer did everything he could to stay in touch with Tess and their daughter in Geneva. He called Tess during his free time or early in the morning when he returned to his room at the Adlon Hotel, often waking her up. He longed for mail from his wife and was thrilled when she sent photographs of Eileen. He could not look at them enough, could not miss them more than he did every night when he finished work in the broadcast center and returned to his room or stopped for a drink at the Taverne.

On warm afternoons he walked by himself or with a colleague through the vast Tiergarten, lost in thought, wondering how it could be so calm, so peaceful, in Berlin, while fierce fighting raged in Poland. He would sit on a bench and look up at the sky and wonder how long it would be before British bombers appeared overhead in great numbers, bombing the government buildings and setting the city ablaze. Some nights, unwilling to go upstairs to an empty hotel room, he would stand at the bar in the Adlon and have a drink and talk to perfect strangers until the conversation went dead and there was nothing to do but go to bed.

The third week of September, Shirer drove along roads clogged with German troops and armor from Berlin to Danzig. He was surprised to see troops marching toward home rather than toward the front, a sure sign that a war not yet a month old was going well for the invaders. In a thick stand of woods he smelled mountains of dead Polish cavalry horses. A division of Polish cavalry had charged German tanks and been slaughtered. The Germans with their new tanks were in Poland to fight a modern war, with modern tactics and modern weapons; the Polish were fully prepared to fight a war that had ended in 1918. Dead Polish troops lay in the woods, abandoned where they fell.

In a diary entry made in Berlin on September 9, Shirer wrote of the monstrosity of the German machine attacking Poland: "Not a word in the press about the heroic resistance of the Poles, no talk amongst the Germans of the righteousness of a country defending itself against a gigantic military force which has attacked it. People here absolutely unmoved by that spectacle."

It was yet another rap against the German character, which Shirer thought little of even without a military campaign like the one the Germans were waging in Poland. "P. H...told me this noon he'd seen some of the horribly mutilated bodies of G's killed by Poles, but also how G's were rounding up civilians, men, women, boys, marching them into a building for a summary court martial then out the backyard against a wall, where disposed of by firing squads."

Two days later, on September 11, a German naval officer he knew well told Shirer that Germany was fighting an honorable war in Poland. Shirer was sickened. "Not a word from him about the women and children their bombers have killed....F. O. told me when he was up at the front, he noticed how the blackcoated boys came in to take care of things behind the lines. Tough faced babies, he said. Of four Polish boys in their hands...he said he bet they didn't live very long." Three days later, on September 14, Shirer wrote: "The boys also tell me how the Polish Jews are being put to work on road gangs."

In the same diary entry, Shirer fumed bitterly about the Germans as a people. Germans he encountered on the subway were "rather smug about their country's actions." Recounting a conversation he had with the maid who cleaned his room at the Adlon, he wrote: "For a people who like it both ways, these people are unbeatable....I haven't heard one German who gave a second thought to the lot of the Czechs. Here they scream to heaven about how foreign countries treat their own *Volk*, but they have absolutely no feeling for other racial or national groups which they are terrorizing far worse than G's ever were....The number of sincere, intelligent G's who take in every lie they're told is appalling."

As he drove toward Danzig, Shirer could see the backwash of the fighting—bodies in fields, rotting carcasses of horses alongside dirt roads, destroyed houses in rural villages, the inhabitants gone. Near the city of Gdynia on the Baltic Sea where Shirer and John Gunther had spent a night gambling just five weeks before, Shirer and a group of foreign correspondents were allowed to stand on a hilltop and watch fighting being carried out miles away. In his diary he wrote that it was "tragic and grotesque. We stood there and watched the lives being snuffed out as though we were spectators at a football match. About 15,000 Poles surrounded on three sides by Germans and the sea on the fourth side were making a last desperate stand.... We were only 2 miles away, and our hilltop was being used as an observation point by the General Staff."

Shirer's trip to the Polish front was not sponsored by the military but by the Propaganda Ministry. The journalists were to be shown only what the ministry's officials wanted them to see, told only what they wanted them to be told. Shirer chafed under the restrictions and grew angry at himself for going along with it. It was crap, all of it. A number of the ministry's bureaucrats were along to mind the correspondents and to reinforce the German narrative that the Poles were the aggressors and the Germans were defending their people. They lied as they looked at him. He had been able to deal with it a year or two before at press briefings in Berlin, but now it had reached a new level of arrogance and shamelessness. Before he had been able to smile and nod and pretend to be listening; now he could barely contain his anger and cynicism. His contemptuous feelings toward the bureaucrats, and the Germans in general, threatened to boil over. He held his tongue.

Making matters worse on this trip to Poland, the ministry had paired him off with an odd American named Philip Johnson, who was described to Shirer not as a visiting journalist but as a Fascist on a fact-finding mission. The two would be sharing rooms on the trip. Johnson was in his early twenties and told Shirer he was a representative of the Catholic priest Father Coughlin, whose radio broadcasts in the United States Shirer knew to be anti-Semitic diatribes. And here was one of his acolytes come to watch the country he admired pushing its army into Poland. Like the journalists, British and American, who played up to the Germans, Johnson was to Shirer a loathsome wretch. It was all he could do to hide his contempt for him and keep his distance. Shirer and some of the other American correspondents agreed to stay away from Johnson out of concern that he was there to spy on them. Alone in a hotel room with Johnson, Shirer wrote in his diary that the visiting American posed as an anti-Nazi and engaged Shirer in a conversation about his political views.

"I have given him no more than a few bored grunts," Shirer wrote.

* * *

Physically and emotionally exhausted, Shirer made it to Geneva on October 11, six weeks after the invasion of Poland. He felt drained, as if his body and mind had given up on him. Tess met him at the train station—"pretty and fresh as ever." He had not seen his wife in two months and felt great love for her as she drove back to their home, where, to his disappointment, he found Eileen asleep. Geneva was a city aglow, and Shirer found the change enormously welcome. The streetlamps burned, homes and storefronts were brightly lit with welcoming warmth, and cars ran with their headlights on. Six weeks of blackouts in Berlin had taken a grim toll, suffocating him with cold dreariness and wrapping him in fear. He'd walked into streetlamps in the dark of night and banged up his face as everyone waited nervously for British bombers to appear. He had not gotten used to it, the gloom of a city that turned itself off to conceal itself until sunup, laden with the weight of official oppression.

The next afternoon, he and Tess went out to dinner. Everything unavailable in Berlin could be found written happily on a Swiss menu—butter, steak, eggs, snails, fresh vegetables, cheese, coffee, red wine, and cognac. He was stunned by how normal life was in Switzerland, even with a war underway in Poland and conflict—but not yet open warfare—in the West. It was coming, he knew that. On the train to Switzerland, he had seen the Germans hauling supplies to the western front. "Queer kind of war," he wrote in his diary.

He was sad and overcome with emotion when on October 15 he boarded the train for the long overnight ride back to Berlin. Tess stood on the platform, weeping. Of his wife, he wrote in his diary, "We dined and danced and talked and loved." He played with his daughter, whom he found "perky and bright and growing every day, physically, mentally and especially the latter." He read to her from picture books. He hoped above all his hopes that whatever happened in the West would not involve Switzerland, that the Germans would simply let it be.

The journey back into Germany was like going from day into night, from bright light and happy people and glorious music to a dark underground world, grim and burdened with the fear and day-to-day concerns of life in a robust police state. It was a world filled with informers, officious bullies, and beaten-down inhabitants. When the train arrived in Frankfurt, he found the station shrouded in complete darkness. Soldiers bumped into each other on the platform and tripped over their bags. Exhausted, miserable at leaving Geneva, Shirer switched platforms in search of the overnight train to Berlin, but it was so dark he got lost looking for his sleeper car. To his horror, he discovered he had boarded the wrong train, but it was too late to flee back onto the platform. All the berths were taken, and there was no place for him to sleep, so he sat up all night, the train's aisles packed with scared people who had nowhere to go. He sat on the floor, squeezed in between other people, no one acknowledging the other person, and closed his eyes and tried to sleep.

The hardships were piling up, from the concerns that full-scale war would come to Berlin, to the daily hardships of just getting by, to dealing with the censors and their demands that he say only what they wanted him to say. There were more and more *Eintopf* days—one-pot meals, usually a poor stew—at Berlin's restaurants. He had heard that clothing rationing was to be imposed, that shoe sales and even shoe repairs were to be severely restricted. On top of these impositions was the matter of just dealing with the government and its actions. A typical diary entry, this one in late October, reads: "The secret police announced that two men were shot for 'resisting arrest' yesterday. One of them, it is stated, was trying to induce some German workers to lay down their tools in an important armament factory. Himmler now has power to shoot anyone he likes without trial."

That the mass of the German people believed the newspapers and government pronouncements strained Shirer's ability to look at these people as anything but intellectual and moral failures. "The people are very patriotic and being fed a terrific barrage of propaganda....I have still to find a German, even among those who don't like the regime, who sees anything wrong in the destruction of Poland," he wrote in his diary. "All the moral attitudes of the outside world...find little echo among the people here. People from all classes, women and men, have gathered in front of windows in Berlin and approvingly gazed at maps in which little red pins showed the victorious advance of the German troops in Poland."

His clock was ticking. He was not sure he could tolerate all the hardships and indignities much longer or handle emotionally the long separations from his family as he continued his broadcasts for CBS. It made him wonder, as he had for so many years now, if he could support himself as a book writer and live wherever he wanted. His and Tess's year on the Spanish coast now seemed like the most idyllic time in his life; the financial hardships and worry about the future that had consumed them that year had faded and been replaced by the picture of a writer at work. He had the letter from Blanche Knopf in his files, and he could only hope he could hand her a manuscript one day that she would be happy to publish.

* * *

The indignities and horror piled up for Shirer as 1939 came to a close. At a November reception in the Soviet embassy in Berlin, Shirer spoke with Göring, who lectured him on America's lack of production of airplanes.

Shirer recounted the conversation with Göring when he later wrote in his diary:

"What do you think of the general situation?"

"Very favorable to Germany."

"So far your air force has only attacked British warships. Why?"

"Warships are very important objects. They give us good practice."

"Are you going to begin bombing enemy ports?"

"We're humane.... You shouldn't laugh. I'm serious. I *am* humane."

He noted later in the month a German press report that nine young Czech students at the University of Prague had been executed before a firing squad. One of the press spokesmen for the Propaganda Ministry, when asked at a press conference about the executions, said the students had staged anti-German demonstrations. Three more Czechs were executed later in the day. In Germany, three students were executed for "treason," the press reported.

To Shirer's disgust, a journalist with the *New York Herald Tribune*, Beach Conger, who had only recently arrived in Berlin, was forced to leave the city after he refused to retract a story the Nazis complained about. As they had done when Norman Ebbutt left Berlin, Shirer and a small group of his colleagues, in defiance of the government, escorted Conger to the train station and wished him well on his return to New York.

Shirer reflected on Conger's fate in his diary. "Though the Nazis don't like me, I suppose I shall never get kicked out of here. The trouble is my radio scripts are censored in advance, so that whatever I say over the air cannot be held against me. The newspaper correspondents can telephone out what they please, subject to the risk of getting what Conger got. This is almost a worse form of censorship than we have, since the New York offices of the press associations and New York newspapers do not like their correspondents to be kicked out."

While Shirer had no way of knowing exactly what the Germans were doing in Poland, he picked up tips here and there, all of them horrifying. In a late November diary entry, he wrote that Hans Frank, the German governor-general of Poland, had decreed that the Jewish ghetto in Warsaw would be walled off as the Jews were "carriers of disease and germs." Shirer learned more from an "American friend" who had been in Warsaw, who was almost certainly an official of the US embassy in Berlin. This friend made it clear that the German policy was to exterminate the Polish Jews. The years of official policies against the German Jews, harassment, stealing their property, and forcing them to leave the country, had, if this report was true, now come down to extermination.

"They are being herded into eastern Poland and forced to live in unheated shacks and robbed of any opportunity of earning bread and butter. Several thousand Jews from the Reich have also been sent to eastern Poland to die, he says."

* * *

In December, Shirer was pleased to see Christmas trees for sale on street corners, and Berliners buying them up, no matter their own hardships. In visiting different stores looking for Christmas gifts, Shirer could see there was little to buy, and everything except books was rationed. He wanted to buy some gramophone records but could not find any. Music, he concluded, was too much to ask for these days. He tried to avoid reading the papers for a few days, as more and more death notices for soldiers killed in Poland appeared in the city's newspapers. More executions were reported in the newspapers, and Germans were told they would be shown no mercy if they listened to foreign news broadcasts like the BBC.

Without his family for Christmas, Shirer stayed around his broadcast office at the RRG to attend an official party complete with champagne and music. He was at least glad for the company but disgusted when he saw William Joyce, who was born in New York and raised in England, arrive to celebrate with the Germans. Joyce broadcast Nazi propaganda, as did an English actor, Jack Trevor, who also showed up at the party. To his relief, Shirer's friend Fred Oechsner, who covered Germany for United Press, invited Shirer to his studio apartment for a Christmas dinner complete with turkey, trimmings, and a pumpkin pie. He spent New Year's Eve with a group of American correspondents at Sigrid Schultz's apartment.

* * *

At their home near Dresden, Victor Klemperer and his wife, Eva, endured. Each day he wrote, each time he expressed himself, his diary took on added importance to him. It would only grow more important, but like any diarist, he could not see far enough down the road to know that. There was, to Victor and Eva, the here and now in the new Germany. The diary was his way of expressing the bitterness he lived with daily and his way of committing treason against the government he loathed by expressing his personal thoughts in these pages.

Like the Germans Shirer saw sacrificing by buying a Christmas tree and decorating it with candles in a corner of their homes, the Klemperers found a tree and did the same. As comforting a ritual as it was to them, it brought no happiness. "We are simply, so to speak, in extremis," Klemperer wrote, adding on a positive note that he was now certain the West would finally go to war against Hitler. He welcomed that.

To celebrate the holiday, a former student of Klemperer's showed up at the house with extraordinary Christmas gifts purchased with ration cards: "two big scallops of veal, an egg, a tin of ersatz honey, a bar of chocolate, two gingerbreads, a pair of socks, two tins of milk and half a liter of opened skimmed milk." As happy as Klemperer was at the abundance of the gifts, he saw nothing ahead but trouble. "Either this is our last bad Christmas or our last Christmas altogether."

Of the gifts from his former student, one stood out enough for Klemperer to comment on it in the last line of his diary for 1939. "I believe the pogroms of November '38 made less impression on the nation than cutting the bar of chocolate for Christmas."

The Germans Are Out of Their Minds

Spring 1940

Warm weather finally arrived, and with it Shirer's mood brightened. After all it had been a very cold winter, with the rivers and canals in Berlin frozen solid. Ice skaters on sunny days had crowded the ponds in the Tiergarten. Meals in the Adlon Hotel's restaurant had been little more than old potatoes and canned vegetables. Now, with the arrival of spring, he did his best to spend part of each day outdoors, walking along the grand boulevard Unter den Linden or in the Tiergarten. He was grateful that the winter was finally over, and he could sit in the sun and smoke his pipe and warm his face. Winter heightened his isolation in Berlin; the warm sun brightened his spirits. The family had met in the Swiss Alps in late February for a ski trip to celebrate his thirty-sixth birthday, but the holiday had gone by too fast and soon he was back in the German capital.

The darkness of the blackouts continued to overwhelm him. He had not found a way to get accustomed to them. Riding a dark train through a dark city unnerved him. Plus there was the waiting for British bombers. He knew they would come soon, and he pictured himself trapped on a dark train as bombs blew it to pieces. Still, he could not predict the next few weeks or months. Nearly nine months into the war and nothing had changed in the West. French troops sat at their posts along the frontier. British bombers stayed away from Berlin. It wouldn't last, he knew. The signs were everywhere. On several occasions, he had seen trains packed with German troops heading west or waiting on sidetracks at rail junctions, along with trains loaded with tanks shrouded in tarps.

He did his best to get along with his minders in Berlin. More than once, a censor in the Propaganda Ministry or the military or the Foreign Office had warned him to watch his step. He knew they were watching him, wanting him to trip up so they could put him on a train and send him away. The worry that the government would one day come for him ate away at him. Shirer's office in the broadcast center was two doors from that of William Joyce. Shirer could sit at his desk typing a broadcast and hear Joyce preparing to broadcast his Nazi propaganda to Britain. It was not possible for Shirer to loathe the man any more than he did, but he found it nearly impossible to escape him. Almost every day they passed in the hallway or sat near each other at press conferences.

Outside the broadcast center, Shirer had to watch himself. He'd gone by himself to Habel's restaurant one night for dinner and argued with an old man about the war; as the argument got louder, two Gestapo men had walked over to his table. He left, but he convinced himself they had followed him all the way back to the Adlon.

* * *

The phone in Shirer's room at the Adlon rang early on the morning of May 10, startling him out of a deep sleep. He had broadcast at 12:45 that morning and gone from there to the Taverne and had only recently fallen into his bed. When he picked up the phone, he heard the voice of one of the women he knew at the RRG. German troops were at that moment marching into Belgium, Holland, and Luxembourg. The war in the West had finally begun.

She asked when he wanted to broadcast, and Shirer shouted, "As soon as I can get there." She informed Shirer that Ribbentrop, the foreign minister, had scheduled a press conference at 8:00 A.M. He told her he would skip it, and he asked her to alert New York that he would be at the broadcast center in an hour and would be ready to broadcast.

When he arrived, Shirer went to his office and began typing out a script. Eager for information, he went to different offices of German broadcasters in search of official communiqués from the government, piecing together what had already transpired. The government's Order of the Day quoted Hitler as saying, "The hour of the decisive battle for the future of the German nation has come." When Shirer showed the censors what he had written, they demanded he take out the word "invasion" in the first paragraph to describe what the Germans were doing in Holland and Belgium. It's not an invasion, they said. He lost his temper and wanted so badly to tell them all to go screw themselves, but, eager to get on the air, he said he would change it to "march in" instead.

"I didn't like the compromise," Shirer wrote in his diary. "It was a question of sacrificing the whole important story for one word."

Shortly after 2:00 P.M., Shirer sat in front of his microphone in his tiny studio, a portrait of Hitler on the wall over his head, a gas mask in a case next to him, and began his broadcast. "Good morning," he began. "This is William L. Shirer in Berlin. The blow in the West has fallen. After a week of accusations in the German press that the Allies intended to make an aggressive move, the Germans themselves took the initiative today and at dawn their army, supported by a great air armada, moved against Holland, Belgium and Luxembourg. As German troops moved over the three borders into these three small neutral states, German airplanes bombed airbases, according to the first report of the German High Command."

Hitler had gone to the western front, Shirer told his listeners, and at the 8:00 A.M. press conference, Ribbentrop had demanded that no country resist the Germans. If they did, the governments themselves would be held accountable for all the horror and bloodshed that resulted. Shirer, in his private thoughts in his diary, wrote that Ribbentrop's comments were "nonsensical hypocrisy," and that the comments in the German press that Allied troops were about to invade Belgium and Holland en route to a full-scale assault on Germany were the biggest lie of the day.

When he reached his room at the Adlon at the end of a very long day, Shirer wrote in his diary: "The Germans are out of their minds. Tired, after broadcasting all this day, and sick in the pit of my stomach."

As Shirer observed the incredible speed of the German advance from Berlin, he grew increasingly worried about Tess and Eileen. Every hour seemed to bring alarming news that the Germans were unstoppable. Reports of bombardments of cities and towns and the deaths of large numbers of civilians panicked Shirer. Worried, he and Tess talked every night, mulling her options. He feared that the Germans, who respected no country's borders, might bomb Geneva or send troops across the border. She was Austrian born and not Jewish—two things certainly in her favor—but he had no idea if that would matter to the Germans. "Tess said on telephone last night the Swiss had tried to confiscate her car for the army. She got out of it somehow. What should I advise Tess to do now?"

As Holland approached a total collapse and surrender, Dutch and Belgian journalists in Berlin were rounded up by the Nazis. Some were friends of Shirer's, and this pushed him further into despair and anger. He could only fear for his own future. As the days progressed, his diary entries grew more breathless in their tone. The Belgian city of Liège had held out for twelve days in 1914; it fell in mid-May after just four days, he wrote in a tone of disbelief. "A G officer told me today that even the high command was astounded at the progress made," Shirer wrote.

"T. phoned this morning...," he wrote on May 15. "Again I urged her to leave with the child and at least she seems willing. She said she was packing.

She and Mrs. V. with her two kids will strike out across France for Spain. From Lisbon, they can get a clipper for NY. Worried all day about this and hugged the radio for news of Italy. Going across southern France to Spain if Italy attacks France would be bad. Will feel better when Tess and Eileen are out."

The next day his worries about his family fully preoccupied him. "T. taking it all in good spirits. Feel she's hiding real unease. If Italy goes into the war in the next day or two, as some think, escape in that direction is out. Today there are more reports of more German activity along the Swiss border. The Nazis may break out there any moment now." He summed up his feelings: "How fast the dark age envelops us."

Tess called her husband at 10:00 P.M. on May 16 when he returned to his room at the Adlon. Through arm twisting and cajoling, Shirer had managed to get her a French visa so she could make her way from Geneva through France and on to Portugal. She was relieved, but Shirer was certain she was concealing a great deal of worry. "I thought she was keeping back the tears with difficulty. She called again at midnight and seemed more buoyed up. But now, as in the past crisis of our lives, she's being very brave and outwardly cool....It will be difficult with a 2-year-old baby getting across Fr. Some in Geneva urge her to stay and go to a mountain village. But I feel if there is time to get out, she should play safe and go."

The next morning, the German communiqués Shirer picked up in the broadcast center spoke of a furious westward advance. "The news gets worse and worse," he wrote. "We're all dazed....Everything looks very bad for the allies. Any help from the US will come too late. BBC admits nothing has slowed the G advance. All indications are of a French rout."

Shirer went on the air in Berlin early on the afternoon of May 17—up and down the East Coast, Americans were sitting down to breakfast—to tell his listeners that the Germans had breached the fabled Maginot Line in northern France. He had done eleven broadcasts in just a week, each day bringing surprising news of the German aggression. His voice and his choice of language reflected a profound horror at what he was reading, as if even he found it hard to believe. As he opened his broadcast on this afternoon, a warm spring day in the German capital, he spoke of the Maginot Line giving way on a broad front of sixty-five miles, and said, "This would bring the German army to within 100 miles of Paris."

It was almost too shocking to be believed, but he continued to read. And for a moment, perhaps, Shirer seemed to remember the boy he once was seated on the living room floor of the family home in Cedar Rapids, entranced as he looked over the battlefield maps printed in the *Chicago Tribune* of a great battle being waged in France. "And if you look at your map, you'll see that Maubeuge, itself a strong fortress, just south of which the Germans say they've broken through, is at least forty miles to the west of the Meuse River line running south from Dinant and Givet to Sedan," he read into the microphone. "The news I've just given you has just been announced on the German radio to the accompaniment of fanfare and patriotic songs. Extras are just coming out on the streets."

Where for several days he had urged Tess to gather together her belongings and head for France en route to Portugal, he now feared he had given her bad advice. "Now hope she hasn't done it, especially as she would have had to go over Paris,... The G's may beat her there. Couldn't get through to her on the phone, which made me think she might already have left for Fr."

He found the situation in Berlin, where people continued to go about their business, jarring and bizarre. A huge war was underway, a continuation of the war that had ended in 1918, and, on his walks through the city and in the Tiergarten, he passed people who acted as though they did not have a care in the world. "People sit nonchalantly in the warm sun in the Tiergarten. No air raid sirens have gone off. High Command tells correspondents G troops entered Brussels at sundown. In 1914 it took 16 days for the G's to reach Brussels. This time, 8 days."

On May 18, officials in the Propaganda Ministry organized a trip to the front for foreign correspondents. When Shirer received the offer, he was badly torn. He wanted to see for himself what the Germans were doing, and how, but he feared that there would be some developments concerning France and that the announcement would come in Berlin and he would miss it. He also worried, as he always did, about being used—that the trip would be an "arranged dud." But he decided he would go, and at 10:00 A.M. on May 19, he joined a party of four Americans, three Italians, a Spaniard, and a Japanese correspondent.

Before the group left Berlin for the city of Aachen, the Belgian city of Antwerp fell to the Germans. He wrote in his diary: "A piece in the well informed *Boersen-Zeitung* tonight hints that the German armies now converging on Paris from the north-east may not try and take Paris immediately...but strike north-west for the channel ports in an effort to cut off England from France."

* * *

Near midnight on May 19, a weary Shirer and his group checked into the Hotel International in the western German city of Aachen, a short car ride from both the Belgian and Dutch borders. En route Shirer saw no signs of British bombings. Bridges and factories were all standing. "All rail lines intact," he wrote in his diary shortly after checking into his hotel room. "Factories smoking away as usual."

On the trip from Berlin to Aachen, they had passed the remains of a British bomber lying in a field east of Hanover. "Crew of 5 escaped in parachutes," he wrote. "4 gave themselves in. One is still at large and the peasants and gendarmes were scouring the countryside for him." The caravan of cars stopped, and the correspondents examined the wreckage. Hundreds of Germans stood around gawking. By nightfall the sky filled up with the bright light of a full moon, and as the line of cars moved southwest toward Aachen, Shirer found the countryside strikingly beautiful. The light illuminated long sections of roads clogged with German troops, in trucks and marching on foot, "moving along happily, many singing."

Shirer's room in the hotel was little more than a corner of a cramped attic. German officers and government officials filled the hotel and the small restaurant and coffee shop in the lobby. At 1:00 A.M., unable to sleep out of worry that the bombers would appear overhead at any moment, he sat in front of a small window under the eaves and scanned the sky. The hotel and the buildings around it were pitch-black, bathed in the glow from the moon. Exhausted, he stretched out on a makeshift cot and quickly fell asleep. At 2:50 A.M. he awoke to the explosion of antiaircraft guns on the roof of a nearby building, the noise so loud and ferocious that it threatened to destroy the hotel all by itself.

Peering out the narrow window, he could see that the British were bombing the Aachen railroad station one hundred yards from the hotel. Curious to see what was happening, he walked into the hallway and encountered groups of frightened men and women rushing down the stairs to the basement. A number of German officers went with them, but Shirer and his party of journalists stayed in the attic until the bombing stopped, twenty-five minutes after it had begun.

RIDING IN STAFF CARS

This has been a day in my life. To have seen the destruction of war, what guns and bombs do to houses and people in them, to towns, bridges, railroad stations and tracks and trains, to universities and ancient, noble buildings, to enemy soldiers, trucks, tanks, horses caught along the way. It is not pretty. No, it is not beautiful.
—William L. Shirer, diary, midnight, May 20, 1940

At dawn, with the sun beginning to brighten the eastern sky, the journalists and their minders crossed into Holland. It had been five days since the Dutch surrender. Shirer saw no sign of the Dutch resistance to the Germans and wondered what had been done to slow up the advance other than the destruction of a single bridge over the Maas River. As the car caravan proceeded, German trucks heavy with supplies rolled past them in long lines. Shirer was awed by what he saw. It was as if he and the others were following a massive piece of machinery, with all its components working in sync. The Germans were audacious; they moved boldly, and they brought with them everything they needed, including makeshift spans to throw across rivers and canals if bridges had been destroyed. They seemed to want for nothing, the troops well-equipped and well-trained and highly motivated. From the leadership in the field down to the troops, they all acted as though they had a well-conceived plan and were in the process of carrying it out to the letter.

Shirer, as he noted in the diary that he updated every few minutes as the morning proceeded, asked a German officer about Dutch efforts to blow up bridges and halt the invasion. "We were too quick for them," the officer calmly told Shirer, loudly warning him and the other journalists not to wander off on their own for fear of land mines. Along the side of the road, freshly dug graves marked with Belgian steel helmets mounted on sticks protruded from the earth. The Germans went wherever they wanted at a breathtaking pace, and Shirer could calculate the number of days it would take for them to reach their goal, Paris.

They passed through small villages and medium-sized towns, from Holland into Belgium, that had been destroyed. At 7:45 A.M. he wrote:

> *Real devastation....The town is destroyed. Smashed to pieces. Stuka dive bombers and artillery, the officer explained. Railroad station in shambles. Cars and locomotives derailed. Town deserted. Hungry dogs poke through the rubble.*
>
> *8:10: houses smashed, shambles, bitter faces Belgian civilians...they just starting to return...women sobbing...their men folk? Where?...Here houses destroyed at random...Stukas careless?...on purpose?...war or roads...the G. army on wheels...germans just went up the roads...with tanks, planes, artillery, anti-tank stuff, everything...all morning roads massed supplies, troops going up, curious. Not a single allied plane yet...And those endless columns of troops, guns, supplies, stretching all the way from the German border...what a target!...Refugees streaming back along the roads...Tears your heart out to see them...I stopped looking at them after a while...Hollow feeling in my stomach. Then remembered I was a reporter. Remembered, as a man, I must see it all and register it in my heart and mind...*
>
> *The refugees trudged up the road, old women lugging a baby or two in their old arms, the mothers lugging the family belongings. Lucky ones had theirs balanced on bicycles; luckiest had a car. Their faces—dazed, horrified, lined with sorrow, but full of dignity. Dignity and courage still.*

At 9:15 A.M. they reached the town of Louvain in Belgium. For several days in August 1914, the Germans had sacked the town, destroying a library and a church, and setting ablaze other buildings that they had already looted. Now, as Shirer and the others entered the town with a contingent of German officials, they could see it had been destroyed again.

"Block upon block upon block of houses gone and still smouldering. Another university library, burned in 1914 and rebuilt by Americans, destroyed again." Shirer approached a German officer and asked, "What happened to the library?"

The officer, rather smugly, attempted an answer. "You will see in a minute. There was a sharp battle in the town itself. Heavy street fighting. Town changed hands several times. We would come in and they would drive us out. There was bound to be damage, *mein Herr.*"

The library had been gutted, the tower the only part of the building still standing. Against the instructions of the officer, Shirer walked to a collapsed wall where there was a plaque he could read listing the institutions in the United States that had helped pay for the rebuilding of the library after the

Great War had ended: THE FINCH SCHOOL, UNIVERSITY OF ROCHESTER, PHILLIPS ACADEMY, ANDOVER, UNIVERSITY OF ILLINOIS, AMERICAN ASSOCIATION OF UNIVERSITY WOMEN, PUBLIC SCHOOLS OF THE CITY OF PHILADELPHIA.

"And the books?" Shirer asked the officer.

"Burnt, all of them."

Before leaving Berlin a few days before, Shirer had attended a press conference where an officer from the High Command announced that the British had destroyed Louvain. "The British have plundered that fine old town," the officer announced with great solemnity, as if reading the first count of an indictment charging the British with war crimes. "Plundered it in the most shameful manner." Now, standing by the destroyed library, another German official walked over to Shirer and repeated the message. "The British did it. Set it afire before they left. Typical, isn't it?"

"Balls!" Shirer muttered when the official was far enough away not to hear him. He did not need another reminder that the Germans were liars.

Under tight supervision, the officer took the journalists to see that the town's city hall and a cathedral were still standing. He used this to lecture them on the accuracy of German bombs. "See how the Rathaus and cathedral have been spared. Ordinary bombers attacking the town probably would have hit them, too. Not our Stukas. They hit their targets."

Shirer and the others walked into the government building, which had been the headquarters of the British expeditionary forces. The British had arrived on the Continent in the wake of the declaration of war the previous September, until they fled west. The room smelled of stale air and cigarette smoke. On a large table were maps, notebooks, and liquor bottles, along with empty tins of English biscuits. The floor was stained with blood. A large bronze plaque lay smashed against a wall. It commemorated the citizens of Louvain who had been executed as hostages by the Germans in 1914. The officer casually dismissed it as all lies and went on about German honor. Not wanting to hear a word of it, Shirer turned away in disgust. The Germans had their story to tell the world. There was no German barbarity in a village in Belgium. The officer's going on about how the Belgian story of executions was an affront to German honor only served to remind Shirer that he could not last much longer in Berlin. He did not know how or when his time there would end, but the end was coming.

As the group moved through the rubble, groups of refugees passed them. They were women and children and very old men. Shirer went up to one group and asked what had happened, but one of the Germans stayed too close and, fearing reprisals, no one spoke up. He saw a German nun standing nearby and walked over to talk to her. In a low whisper she said there had been no warning, just a sudden onslaught. Her candor abruptly ended when she saw German officers nearby. Now she raised her voice and said, "Of course, as a German, I was glad when it was all over and the German troops arrived."

Near Brussels the group passed a castle with its roof blown off and its windows shattered. Its inhabitants had left in a great rush of panic as they learned the Germans were fast approaching. Clothes littered the floor, beds were unmade. In a bedroom a gramophone and a stack of records sat on a table alongside a set of golf clubs. In the kitchen, china lay scattered on the floor. It was as if a tide had suddenly risen up out of a calm ocean and drowned the residents of an unsuspecting village, carrying them away to anonymous deaths. History repeating itself is history's oldest story. A man who had been thirty in 1914 when the German army surged into his Belgian town was now just fifty-six. The memories of 1914–1918 were fresh in so many minds, and now the Germans had arrived again. *My God! The Germans! Again!*

All around him, Shirer watched happy German officers and bureaucrats grabbing souvenirs. Some of the journalists began to do the same. They acted as if they could do what they wanted since they were traveling with the victors, and to the victors went the spoils. An officer handed Shirer a fancy cap with the expectation that he would be grateful and would keep it. Outside the castle, the road was so jammed with German army trucks, motorized guns, and troops moving westward that the journalists had to wait for an opening. Germany as a whole seemed to be throwing itself toward the English Channel and on toward Britain. On the far side of the road, long columns of weary refugees walked through the heat and clouds of dust kicked up by the trucks.

When they reached Brussels, Shirer found the streets busy with people. The German officer in charge of the journalists, like a tourist in search of a good meal, asked a Belgian where he might take the correspondents for a grand dinner, and the man suggested the Hotel Metropole, pointing out how to get there. Shirer had eaten in the hotel's tavern years before, and as he walked in late on a hot, dusty day, he felt acutely ashamed to be showing up again with a knot of uniformed Germans. He felt fortunate when no one recognized him.

The hotel had been commandeered by the German Foreign Office and the Propaganda Ministry. Its lobby was packed with officials, some carrying rolled-up maps and suitcases and briefcases. They were moving in. There was no shortage of quality food in the hotel, and Shirer and the other journalists loaded up on supplies—coffee, tea, shoes, and clothing. Shirer bought three packs of Lucky Strikes.

After a meal, Shirer and another American journalist walked to a nearby shop that Shirer had visited on a prior trip to Brussels. "It came so suddenly," the owner said. "I can't get it straight yet. First the attack. Then the government fled. We didn't know what was happening. Then about eight in the evening the Germans marched in."

"Where's your husband?" Shirer asked.

"I don't know," she said. "He was mobilized. He went to the front. I've heard nothing. I only keep hoping he's alive."

Two German soldiers walked into the shop to buy American cigarettes, and the owner stopped talking until they left. "I will keep the shop open," she said. "But for how long? Our stocks come from England and America. And my child—what about milk? I've got canned milk for about two months. How will it end? I mean, do you think Belgium will ever be like before? Independent and with a king?"

"If the Allies win," Shirer said.

"But why do they retreat so fast? With the British and French we had more than a million men in Belgium. And they didn't hold out as long as the few Belgian troops in 1914. I don't understand it."

Walking back to the hotel, Shirer was struck by the scene in the street. The streetcars were running. The movie houses, their posters still advertising American and French cinema, were closed. Signs tacked to poles and on buildings told Belgians to respect German troops. The foreign journalists, their arms full of booty, walked about as if what they were doing was perfectly proper. Shirer went to his room and typed out a radio report. It was an exercise in frustration, as he had to give it to the censors in the Foreign Office, the Propaganda Ministry, and the High Command. It was a loathsome, tedious process, one he likened to ass kissing or boot licking, and he had no patience for it. He knew the censors on a first-name basis, but that did not bring him any benefits. They were scared of letting anything get by, so they overreacted with excessive caution. Fueled by anger, Shirer argued loudly with them, but they merely turned their backs on him and walked away without allowing him to say what he wanted. In addition to these censors, Shirer was forced to read his report into the phone to a voice on the line in an office in Berlin.

At 1:00 A.M. Shirer hired a driver and a car to take him to Cologne, where he could broadcast, hoping they would not encounter British fighter planes that would swoop down and strafe them. At 4:32 on the morning of May 21, Shirer sat in front of a microphone in a small radio studio that his driver had had a difficult time finding in the blackout.

"Good evening. This is William L. Shirer in Cologne, Germany." He went on to describe the German onslaught into Belgium and how little British fighters had done to disrupt the offensive. Of the long columns of refugees, he said: "I saw them filtering back, dazed and bitter and sad from their experience, but trudging along in the hot sun with their belongings on their back or on a bicycle or if they were lucky a cart. Tomorrow, we hope to get to the actual front and I hope to be back tomorrow night or the next day with a report on that."

* * *

Later that day, Shirer and his entourage arrived in the Belgian town of Enghien, a short distance from the front. They were driven to a château outside of town that had been confiscated and transformed into the field headquarters of General Walter von Reichenau, commander of the German Sixth Army. The general knew the terrain, having served on the western front during the Great War. Shirer had met Reichenau in Berlin, and now the general came out of the château and greeted Shirer and the others. He was handsome and fit, his face weathered by the hot spring sun, his monocle planted firmly over his right eye.

They talked informally, and Reichenau spoke in broad terms about the operations underway. Several correspondents asked questions that the general attempted to answer. Later in the day, Shirer sent a cable to CBS in New York: "Despite the G. successes to date, Reichenau emphasized to us that the fighting so far had been only an enveloping movement and that the decisive battle had yet to take place."

"When and where?" Shirer asked.

"Where?" the general asked. He explained that it depended on what the enemy did now. "Remember, the preliminary fighting at Waterloo lasted several days. The decisive battle at Waterloo was decided in eight hours."

Without citing hard numbers, Reichenau said German casualties had been light. His forces had captured more than 100,000 prisoners. The general was in a jovial mood, not worried about the days ahead. Finally he turned the correspondents over to his adjutant, who opened a bottle of Bordeaux from the chateau's wine cellar. In his diary, Shirer wrote: "A few miles down the road two million men are slaughtering each other."

After a brief respite, the caravan proceeded down a dirt road closer to the fighting. Only a few hundred yards ahead, the French army was putting up strong resistance. The air smelled of dead horses rotting in the sun. Bloated cows with stiff limbs littered fields alongside the road. Their escort was a first lieutenant, whom Shirer considered a "conceited ass who acts like Napoleon, standing in the front seat of the car trying to give signals as to where to turn, stop, etc."

A deep *woof* rattled the air, followed by another and another, as artillery thudded against the earth in the distance. The remains of a French armored column lay down a narrow road. "All this left of a small French column after G. air attack," he scribbled in his diary. "Along the narrow road are a dozen dead horses stinking to heaven in the hot sun, two French tanks, their armor pierced like tissue paper, an abandoned six-inch gun and a 75; a few trucks abandoned in haste; scattered about are utensils, coats, shirts, overcoats, helmets, tins of food—and letters to wives, girlfriends and mothers back home."

Hastily dug graves lined the edge of the road. Some graves had sticks protruding from freshly turned earth, on top of which a French army helmet hung like the symbol of a defeated army. Walking among the ruins, Shirer picked up some of the letters, thinking he could find a post office and mail them. But there were no addresses or envelopes, just letters someone had started and intended to mail but never got there. One began "Ma chère Jacqueline," another "Chère Maman."

Heavy guns erupted in the distance, the noise building into a crescendo and then falling back again. Long columns, thousands of German soldiers, marched down the road toward the fighting. The village of Leuze was so packed with German heavy equipment waiting to be deployed that nothing could move forward. Blocks of houses had been destroyed, blown up by artillery barrages or crushed by tanks. The stalled caravan of journalists stopped, and Shirer got out and walked to a nearby school that had been converted into a hospital.

"Dying everywhere," he wrote in his diary.

Unable to move forward, the group stopped for a brief meal—canned fish spread over thick brown bread. A German officer yelled at the group: "You must follow my orders to a 'T.' There is danger ahead. Look out for bombers."

They moved forward and into the Belgian town of Ronse (Renaix), where heavy German guns planted on hillsides fired over their heads and into a stand of woods in the far distance. A German officer told Shirer they were hitting the roads behind the French troops. Another officer yelled that the group was exposed, so they moved higher up a hill into a forest, the guns firing directly over their heads, the noise so deafening it felt as though the earth had cracked open.

Ju-87 bombers—the Stukas—appeared overhead and began to bomb positions in front of the German troops. Huge clouds of smoke and dust rose into the sky. More artillery guns erupted behind a long row of tanks. The Germans were advancing so quickly that they did not hold a position for more than a few minutes.

"We have a last look at the Schelde Valley, at the smoke from the bursting shells on the other side of the river," Shirer wrote. "It all has meaning to these German officers all around us. Each whistling shell has a certain errand. Each gun and truck running down the road is going to some place assigned to it. The whole chaos of the battlefield is in reality a picture of a well-oiled machine of destruction."

* * *

On May 23, Shirer returned to Berlin for two broadcasts. "Good evening," he began his first broadcast. "This is William L. Shirer in Berlin." He wanted his listeners to understand the speed and ferocity of the German advance through Belgium.

"And one of the things that impressed me most was the picture of the German army bringing up men, guns and supplies, jamming the roads with them for miles and miles behind the front, without hindrance from the Allied air forces," he said. "I'm convinced that the ease with which the German Command has been able to bring up reinforcements and guns and ammunition, and at an unbelievable speed, is one of the reasons for the German success so far."

For the next seven days, Shirer broadcast almost daily—twice on May 23, once on May 24 and May 25, twice on May 27, and again on May 28, 29, 30, and 31. Each broadcast brought another breathless update on the German advance. "The German steamroller pushes on," Shirer broadcast on May 24. Anyone following Shirer with a map spread out before him could follow the big arrows showing the army's progress down the French coast and the tightening encirclement of Allied troops—with the arrows pointing to Paris in the center of the map.

May 25: "In the opinion of German military circles, the fate of the great Allied army bottled up in Flanders is sealed."

May 27: "Calais has fallen.... Its capture by the Germans practically completes the cutting off of Great Britain from its ally on the continent."

May 28: "The surrender of the Belgians certainly puts the encircled British and French forces in a terrible hole."

May 29: "Lille, Bruges, Ostende captured! Ypres stormed! Dunkirk bombarded! Fate of encircled Allied armies sealed!"

There was so much to tell his listeners that Shirer went on the air twice on June 1. Trying to capture the euphoric mood in Berlin, Shirer read the headlines on the front page of one of the city's newspapers: "Catastrophe before the doors of Paris and London. Five armies cut off and destroyed. England's expeditionary corps no longer exists. France's first, seventh and ninth armies annihilated."

The following day, Shirer departed from his usual military news of the hour and talked about the German people. "How do Germans at home feel about the tremendous victory?" he said in his broadcast. "As a whole, the German people, I think you can say, are feeling pretty elated at the victory. For one thing, they believe they cannot now lose the war—hence the nightmare of another defeat, which their leaders have told them would be worse than Versailles, is removed. They also believe that the decisive battle has been won and that the war will certainly be over by the end of the summer. Many Germans I've talked with have an idea that a sort of united Europe—under German leadership, to be sure—will come out of the war, and that will be a good thing."

As for Berlin, Shirer expressed surprise at how calm it was.

> Last evening just before dark, I strolled down Berlin's main street, the Kurfürstendamm. It was jammed with people, strolling along pleasantly. The great sidewalk cafes on this avenue were filled with thousands, chatting quietly over their ersatz coffee or their ice cream. Most of the women you saw were smartly dressed. Life goes on here so peacefully. Every theater in town is open and playing to packed houses. Today, being Sunday, you could observe tens of thousands of people, mostly in family groups, going out to the woods or the lakes which line the outskirts of the capital. The Tiergarten—Berlin's Central Park, where I took my walk this morning—was filled with folk. They all had that sort of lazy, happy-go-lucky Sunday morning feeling.

In his diary entries, Shirer did not hide his contempt for everything he had witnessed while on the front, heard in press conferences, or seen on the newsreels he watched in Berlin's movie houses. "G's are bringing this war back to the standards of the Middle Ages," he wrote. After watching a newsreel put together by the Propaganda Ministry showing the destruction of French towns, Shirer wrote: "The German commentator's enthusiasm for the destruction seemed to grow as one burning town after another was shown. He had a cruel, rasping voice, and by the end he seemed to be talking in a whirl of sadism....Is Europe soon to be ruled by such a people, by such sadism?"

* * *

Shirer did everything he could to keep in touch with Tess, who remained in Geneva. The Germans' swift advance into Holland, Belgium, and northern France had wrecked any hope that Tess and Eileen could reach Portugal. She had also discarded an alternate plan of getting to Bordeaux, where she had hoped to board a US ocean liner for New York. For the time being, at least as long as there was still fighting, Tess and Eileen had to remain in Switzerland and Shirer in Berlin.

As he worked in Berlin and worried about his family, Shirer presented one image to the German bureaucrats he dealt with on a daily basis and another in his private diaries. A photograph shows Shirer standing in his studio next to one of the censors who pored over his broadcasts before he was given permission to go on the air. The man, whose face features a narrow mustache, is wearing a dark suit and holding a pencil over Shirer's pages, as if sternly pointing out what he could not say. Shirer looks on, irritated, fully realizing he has few options other than to complain loudly at cuts he considers unfair.

In a diary entry dated June 4, he let his own feelings be known, writing that he hoped British bombers would soon appear over the city and exact revenge on the German government. The next day, he wrote again of his contempt for the German people. "There is nothing more arrogant in this world than a G when he's on top, or dealing death and destruction on others—especially when they can't retaliate." He made a similarly bitter entry a few days later when he wrote that he had watched another propaganda film about the fighting in France. "Most Gs seem to get a sadistic pleasure from these pictures of death and destruction. A few still react like human beings."

On June 7, as he continued to read military communiqués announcing the latest victories on the battlefield, Shirer took the day off. He traveled to the vast Grunewald, a forest on the outskirts of the city center, hiked along beautiful trails for hours, and swam in the Havel River. "Found a neat little restaurant in the woods with surprising good beef steaks," he wrote. "After lunch, walked, sun-bathed, swam some more. Felt good today."

His bitterness overflowed when he attended a press conference at the Foreign Office. While they waited for Ribbentrop to appear, a radio played a shrieking speech by Mussolini. "The combination of this tin can racket and the foul, hot air, and the fotogs scrapping and most of the newspapermen standing there like obedient cows and the Nazi officials swinging their shoulders and prancing about as if they were lords of the earth was enough for me." He grabbed his colleague Sigrid Schultz by the arm and the two of them left the room.

* * *

Nearly every day something happened that reminded him how perilous the situation was for Tess and their daughter. After a post-midnight broadcast on June 11—the day on which the High Command announced German troops were thirty-eight miles from Paris—Shirer sat in a colleague's studio at the RRG listening to a broadcast from New York. The US liner *Washington*, en route from Lisbon to Ireland, with 1,020 passengers on board, most of them refugees, had been stopped in the darkness by a submarine whose captain said that the boat would be sunk in ten minutes.

"One can imagine the panic onboard," Shirer wrote in his diary. "While boats were being hastily lowered, Washington kept signaling: 'American boat! American boat!' But this didn't appear to make any difference to this submarine. Finally, at the zero hour, the U-boat commander signaled: 'Sorry. Mistake. Proceed.'"

Listening to the broadcast was a German naval captain, along with officials from the Propaganda Ministry. All, as Shirer wrote, went into a rage, accusing the British of being behind the incident. When Shirer suggested it was a U-boat, the captain shouted, "Impossible!" (The next day the Germans announced it was their U-boat.)

The following day, Shirer was listening to the 3:15 P.M. BBC broadcast when it was announced that bombs had fallen in a suburb of Geneva and that there were casualties. "For a moment I was floored," he wrote. "Out of 150,000 people, I calculated Tess and the baby would have a pretty good mathematical chance of not being among the dead. But the announcer said the bombs fell in a suburb. That's where our home in Geneva is."

For the next five hours, Shirer tried unsuccessfully to reach his wife. Finally, at 8:00 P.M., she picked up the phone. Neither she nor Eileen was hurt, but bombs had in fact fallen in their neighborhood and shaken their house. If Geneva was no longer safe, Shirer suggested Tess and Eileen come to Berlin and stay with him. "It's safest now and she's cut off anyway from any possibility of getting home," he wrote. "Wish she'd gotten out when there was still time—the last of many reservations was on a plane this week to Lisbon."

On the afternoon of June 14, Shirer sat at a small table in the courtyard of the Adlon Hotel eating his lunch. Suddenly, the Germans at the other tables rushed into the bar to hear an announcement on the radio. He later wrote: "Paris has fallen. This morning G. troops entered the city. The hooked-cross flag of Hitler's flutters from the Eiffel tower there by the Seine in that Paris which I knew so intimately, and loved. Poor Paris! I weep for her. For so many years it was my home—and I loved it like I loved a woman. And already the spirit of German revenge and sadism is rising. Said the VP [*Völkischer Beobachter*] editorially this morning, to paraphrase it: 'Paris was a city of frivolity and corruption, of democracy and capitalism, where Jews had entry to the court and niggers to the salons. That Paris will never rise from its fall.'

"Tomorrow, probably, I will leave for Paris. I do so with the saddest of hearts."

War of the Worlds

First shock. The streets were utterly deserted, the stores closed, the shutters down tight on all the windows. It was the emptiness which got you.
—William L. Shirer, diary, June 17, 1940

Early on the morning of June 15, the day after German troops marched into Paris, Shirer set out from Berlin for the long trip over the new autobahn to France. He hoped to reach Paris as quickly as the car could travel and as his stamina would allow. He was exhausted, worn down to the marrow, angry, and frightened, but he was eager to push on and get there and to see for himself what the city looked and felt like under German occupation. As hard as he tried, he could not imagine it.

He knew that what he was seeing was extraordinary history. He had no idea at all how it would end. But in the late spring of 1940, he and almost everyone else in Europe could have concluded that the Hitler government had won everything. There was no more dramatic proof of that than the swastika flying over the Eiffel Tower and government buildings in Paris.

"Leaving for Paris today. I do not want to see the heavy-heeled German boots tramping down the streets I loved," he wrote.

Near the city of Magdeburg on the Elbe River, he found a room in a small hotel that hugged the autobahn. The car had been trouble since he left Berlin, and now, as he pulled off the highway, it quit. Pounding the steering wheel in frustration did nothing to make it better. It was useless to try to repair it, so he set out to find a replacement as quickly as he could. He cursed his bad luck. Just when he needed to make great progress in getting to Paris, his car had failed him.

In the hotel's small restaurant, Shirer found a table and ordered red wine and sank down in his seat, tired and hungry. He would get another car, but it would take hours and delay his arrival in Paris. He overheard Germans in the restaurant talking about Verdun falling this time around; in 1916 more than 300,000 Germans had been killed on that same ground. History, it seemed to Shirer, was a great circle that came back to the beginning time and time again. The Germans had a history at Verdun, and now they had rewritten it, changed the ending, giving them everything they had wanted the first time around but had failed to achieve.

Shirer rose early the next morning and, joined by a number of other foreign correspondents who were all trying to get to Paris, drove to Aachen on the border, then crossed into Belgium, where they stopped in the city of Charleroi before proceeding into occupied France. In Maubeuge, German communiqués were handed out advising the town's citizens to turn off lights at night and to do what they were told. Doctors were ordered to report to the German military commander. A German official with the group of journalists told them, without a hint of regret or sadness, that five hundred civilians lay buried under the debris of a church. The group went on to the commander's residence, confiscated just days before, where red wine and biscuits were distributed.

The commander talked about first closing and then reopening the local whorehouse, as if he were confused by what he was supposed to be doing in the town. The commander, who Shirer in his diary described as a "very human" fellow, complained privately that he was homesick and hoped with all his heart that the war was finally over because he wanted desperately to return to his family. The man explained that he had been in the same area during the Great War, but that the damage was worse now. Unlike the Germans traveling with the journalists, the commander was not hesitant about expressing regret for the damage to civilian structures and the loss of life.

After a decent dinner, an orderly took Shirer and the journalists to a nearby home that the army had also confiscated. From the papers he found in the house, Shirer concluded that it had been the residence of a local banker. The house was big enough for several correspondents to have their own bedrooms, and in his Shirer found the banker's clothes, including a long-tailed black coat, hanging in an ornate armoire.

"Obviously he has left in a great hurry," Shirer wrote. "On the dining room table are the breakfast dishes." He wondered where the banker and his family were now and imagined them walking along a dirt road, hungry and thirsty.

The next morning three soldiers escorted the journalists through the rubble of the town, past the church where the civilians lay buried. They encountered an old woman digging through a pile of bricks, and they shouted at her to move on. When she didn't, one of the soldiers approached her while holding his rifle. Shirer heard her say to the soldier, *"Voulez-vous coucher avec moi ce soir?"* He felt a keen embarrassment and pity for the woman, as he translated her words—"Would you like to sleep with me tonight?" He could imagine her remembering life in the town during the 1914–1918 war; now it was repeating itself.

* * *

Paris, June 17

"We came in about noon and it was one of those lovely June days which Paris has in this month and which, if there had been peace, would have been spent by the people going to the races at Longchamps or the tennis at Roland Garros or idling along the boulevards under the trees, or the cool terrace of a café."

Shirer slipped into a numbed silence when the cars arrived in Paris. It was a beautiful afternoon, a few days from the start of summer, and the streets were "utterly deserted." Looking around the great wide streets he knew so well, Shirer could not believe his own eyes. German cars and trucks moved about the empty city, which looked like a theater set for a story about the end of the world. Swastika flags fluttered in the breeze atop the great buildings.

As he had on so many occasions in Berlin, he found the German journalists' behavior reprehensible. They were giddy with joy to be in Paris, unable to hide their emotions. They were here and they were going to enjoy it, and because they rode in with the victors, they had a sheen of invincibility about them, as if the city was theirs to do with whatever they wanted. Shirer found his own role in the drama confusing and troubling. He was, after all, *with* the Germans. Surely he was an observer, but what did that mean? He could not affect anything—could not stop their momentum, their cruelty, or their arrogance, certainly could not come to the defense of the old woman picking through the rubble. He could not intervene, but only watch and take notes and try to say something that met his own personal standards when he sat in front of the microphone to talk to America across the CBS radio network.

Shirer sat in stunned disbelief as his car moved down the Rue Lafayette, past German army cars and other official vehicles, the happy driver leaning on the horn as if celebrating a great sports victory until Shirer had had enough and told him to stop. Everything around him was so familiar. He recognized a number of cafés where he had sat years before; now their tables had been taken inside, the buildings locked tight, their owners and employees gone into the countryside or heading south in long lines of refugees. They passed the *Journal* building where Shirer had worked for the *Chicago Tribune* soon after his arrival in Paris in the summer of 1925, an idealistic, naïve twenty-one-year-old fresh out of college in Iowa. The two cars of correspondents turned down another great boulevard and then another, past the Opera House, where sandbags had been piled up on the street. At another café he watched some Frenchmen putting out their tables as German soldiers walking in pairs and in long columns passed by. Some of the soldiers sat at the tables to be waited on like tourists who were enjoying the city's beauty.

The cars arrived at the Place de la Concorde at the end of the Champs-Élysées. In the distance alongside the Seine River, a giant swastika fluttered over the Chamber of Deputies, a sight that pulled Shirer up short. All he could do was stare. German tanks, their crews sticking their heads up out of the hatches like sightseers, sat in menacing clumps. The journalists' cars pulled to a stop in front of the lavishly ornate Hôtel de Crillon, where President Woodrow Wilson had stayed during the peace conference after the Great War. It was now German army headquarters. One of the officers accompanying Shirer and the others went inside to book rooms while Shirer walked to the nearby American embassy, where he hoped to find contacts and old friends. But they were all gone, the building deserted.

Every room in the hotel had been taken by the Germans, so the caravan went on to the Hôtel Scribe, where they were able to book rooms. Shirer knew the hotel and the porter who had worked there for years. As Shirer's group came in with its German minders, the porter tried his best to be gracious and greeted them in German. *"Willkommen! Willkommen! Kommen Sie herein, meine Herren! Bitte. Bitte."*

In the lobby, thick with German military and civilian officials, Shirer ran into two journalists he knew, Demaree Bess, who wrote for the *Saturday Evening Post*, and Walter Kerr of the *New York Herald Tribune*. Both had stayed in Paris to watch millions of the city's residents flee in panic and, after the city had become empty and quiet, to witness the arrival of the first German troops. Shirer asked them about other journalists and friends he knew had been in the city, but all had fled in advance of the Germans.

Bess talked about the panic and the packed cars leaving the city on every available road, while others—old people, young couples with babies, and hundreds of thousands of others—simply walked south. Shirer could hardly imagine it. Like so much that had happened in the previous six weeks, the image of hundreds of thousands of refugees fleeing Paris sounded like a scene in a science fiction story, perhaps *The War of the Worlds*. Bess was almost too excited to talk, seeing in Shirer someone to whom he could relay the incredible sights he had witnessed.

The bitterness of the Parisians at their government was extraordinary, Bess tried to explain, unable to find the right words to convey the depth of the anger. They had been betrayed; their leaders were incompetents and traitors; their army had collapsed completely, like a boxer paid to throw a fight who goes down in the fifth round with a minor blow to the head and a cut above the eye. To Shirer, it was as if French society, not just the government and the leadership of the army, had completely broken down. It was too tremendous to believe, he wrote in his diary.

That first night, Shirer walked into the bar at the Hôtel Scribe. The room was crowded, and as he looked around, he saw, standing at the bar and wearing the uniform of a German lieutenant, a former colleague from Hearst's wire service, Carl Flick-Steger. Shirer, who had worked with Flick-Steger in Universal's office in Berlin and Vienna, believed he was an American citizen; he knew he had gone to college in the United States. Shirer was so shocked to see a former journalist who worked for an American wire service in a German uniform that he convinced himself it could not be true. When their eyes met, Flick-Steger turned red with embarrassment. Walking over to Shirer, Flick-Steger explained that he had been hired by the Germans to do short-wave broadcasts to the United States.

"Perhaps you didn't expect to see me in this attire," Flick-Steger said.

"I certainly did not," Shirer said.

* * *

Across Paris on June 18, word spread that Marshal Henri-Philippe Pétain had asked the Germans for an armistice. Pétain, the mythical figure of the Great War who days earlier had been named the French premier, was eighty-four years of age and a figure of great standing in the country. It was a profound blow that it should be Pétain, of all Frenchmen, who stepped up to ask the Germans for an armistice. The rumor spread from street corner to street corner, building to building, house to house. Some just shook it off—it couldn't be true. Others resigned themselves to the fact that, in a city where the Nazi flag now flew over the Eiffel Tower, it most certainly was true. Pétain, whom the French had hailed as their savior at the Battle of Verdun in 1916, would now be the one to seek terms from the Germans. To make sure the city's residents heard it, the Germans set up loudspeakers so that people in the street could listen to Pétain making his announcement that the fighting would cease. There would be no escaping it.

"Everyone is completely against it and thought the government would flee to Africa and set itself up," Shirer wrote in his diary. "I stood in a throng of French women and men on the Place de la Concorde when the news first came. They were almost struck dead.... There was a tremendous bustle of German troops and officers all around the French, but they did not notice, the news was so staggering."

After their first day in the city, the Germans had imposed a 9:00 P.M. curfew. Anyone caught outside after that hour would be arrested. All streets would remain dark and deserted. Shirer used his diary to freely express his thoughts, and some entries read as if he could not convince himself that anything he wrote could possibly be true.

> *So far as we can learn, there has been little friction between the German troops and the inhabitants. On some occasions I've seen open fraternizing! On the squares and boulevards you can see them speaking with each other; the Germans asking directions or some other information, asking it politely and receiving polite answers. Most of the German troops on the street act like naïve tourists and this has proved a pleasant surprise to the Parisians. It seems funny, but every German carries a camera. I saw them by the thousands today, photographing Notre Dame, the Arc de Triomphe, the Invalides. Thousands of German soldiers congregate all day long at the tomb of the Unknown Soldier where the flame still burns under the Arc. They bare their blond heads and stand there gazing.*

Two newspapers soon began publishing, *Le Matin* and *La Victoire*, tailoring their coverage so as not to offend the occupiers. Shirer saw the publisher of *Le Matin* at an event he covered and wrote in his diary: "A worm of a man. I'm told he is anxious to please the Germans and see that his paper gets off to a favorable start. It has already begun to attack England for France's predicament!" He said the second paper was run by a "crank" who insisted that Parisians show respect to the Germans.

Shirer stayed in Paris waiting for word on when the armistice would be signed. Several other correspondents ventured south to talk to refugees and when they returned told Shirer they had seen more than 200,000 French, rich and poor, lying along roads or in and around towns and villages. There was very little food or water to go around. "Had a long talk with X this morning," Shirer wrote in his diary. "He estimates there are seven million refugees between here and Bordeaux. Almost all face starvation, unless something is done at once. The French government in Bordeaux—criminally belatedly—now advises all refugees to remain where they are. The German army is helping a little, but not much."

An official Shirer later described as a "friend" in the German High Command, whom Shirer spoke with at the Hôtel de Crillon, told him the Germans would insist on a French surrender at the little village of Compiègne north of Paris. The surrender would take place on the very same ground, and in the very same railroad dining car, where the Germans had surrendered on November 11, 1918. Hitler insisted on it, and his presence would bring the lines of history together.

Through the services of his friend in the High Command, Shirer drove out to Compiègne to see for himself what preparations were underway and also to make his own plans for a broadcast. He would need all kinds of approvals, along with phone lines to Berlin so that he could make a live broadcast to New York and meet the requirements of the censors. Arriving at Compiègne, Shirer was greeted by the incredible sight of German engineers destroying a small museum that the French had built to house the railroad car in which the Germans had signed the surrender.

A German colonel showed Shirer through the railroad car. Someone had gone to the trouble of putting down small cards showing precisely where the French and the Germans had sat at 5:00 A.M. on November 11 to sign the surrender. One card marked where Marshal Ferdinand Foch, the commander of all Allied forces, had sat. If Hitler did in fact come for the signing of the armistice, as Shirer had been told he would, he would no doubt sit in the same seat from which Foch had presided.

Shirer and several military officials drove back to Paris at dusk, the sky to the west slowly losing its light as they passed through the village of Senlis. The roadside was a scattered monument to the French defeat. Dead horses partially covered with dirt rotted in the sun, and graves of French soldiers hastily buried on the spot bracketed the road. In various piles were guns, ammunition, backpacks, blankets, shoes, and an abandoned cannon left over from the Great War that had been pressed into service in a failed attempt to stop the Germans from entering Paris.

* * *

If a person's entire life can be summed up in a day, or a single scene, or even a moment, it would be for William L. Shirer the warm afternoon of June 21 in a clearing at Compiègne, France. Years later, Shirer described the scene that day: "It was a perfectly lovely summer day. A warm June sun beat down on the stately trees, elms, oaks, cypresses and pines, casting pleasant shadows on the wooded avenues that led out from the little circular clearing." At 3:15—Shirer looked at his watch at this very moment—Hitler arrived with his entourage in a caravan of black Mercedeses. Hitler stepped out of the big sedan, wearing a gray military uniform decorated with the Iron Cross, awarded to him during the Great War, hanging from his left breast pocket. Next to him were those he had brought along to witness the undoing of 1918: Hermann Göring, resplendent in a blue Luftwaffe uniform and holding a baton; Generals Wilhelm Keitel and Walther von Brauchitsch; Admiral Erich Raeder, in his naval uniform; Hitler's deputy, Rudolf Hess; and the foreign minister, Joachim von Ribbentrop.

Shirer knew Göring, whom he had met at the monthly beer parties at the Adlon Hotel and also in Göring's office, sitting across his desk where they chatted about Göring's writing a column for the Hearst wire service. He had also met Ribbentrop, whom he considered a profoundly stupid man but loyal as a dog to Hitler. The group walked by a monument put up by the French to commemorate their great victory in 1918 to within a few hundred yards of where Shirer and William C. Kerker, an American freelance journalist who worked for NBC, were watching and about to do a joint broadcast to America. Shirer had brought a pair of binoculars and, holding them to his eyes, trained them on Hitler.

"I observed his face," Shirer wrote. "It was grave, solemn, yet brimming with revenge. There was also in it, as in his springy step, a note of the triumphant conqueror, the defier of the world. There was something else, difficult to describe, in his expression, a sort of scornful, inner joy at being present at this great reversal of fate—a reversal he himself had wrought. Now he reaches the little opening in the woods. He pauses and looks slowly around. The clearing is in the form of a circle some two hundred yards in diameter and laid out like a park.... This has been one of France's national shrines for twenty-two years."

Hitler paused to read the inscription on a granite block: HERE ON THE ELEVENTH OF NOVEMBER 1918 SUCCUMBED THE CRIMINAL PRIDE OF THE GERMAN EMPIRE VANQUISHED BY THE FREE PEOPLES WHICH IT TRIED TO ENSLAVE.

"I look for the expression on Hitler's face. I am but fifty yards from him and see him through my glasses as though he were directly in front of me. I have seen that face many times at the great moments of his life. But today! It is afire with scorn, anger, hate, revenge, triumph....He slowly glances around the clearing, and now, as his eyes meet ours, you grasp the depth of his hatred....It is now three twenty-three P.M. and the Germans stride over to the armistice car."

Standing in a makeshift half-circle of chairs and tables, surrounded by uniformed Germans, Shirer spoke into the microphone in the voice of a man who knew that he was making history and that countless Americans were seated in their living rooms across the land anxious to hear what he was about to say.

Hello America. Hello NBC. Hello CBS. This is William L. Shirer of CBS and William C. Kerker of NBC is also here. We're broadcasting to you from a little clearing in the forest of Compiègne, four miles to the north of the town of Compiègne, itself some forty-five miles north of Paris.

Here a few feet from where we're standing, in the very same old *wagon-lit* railroad coach where the Armistice was signed on that chilly morning at 5 A.M. on November 11, 1918, negotiations for another armistice, the one to end the present war between France and Germany, began at 3:30 P.M. German summer time this afternoon.

What a turning back of the clock, what a reversing of history we've been watching here in this beautiful Compiègne forest this afternoon! What a contrast to that drama of twenty-two years ago! Yes, even the weather, for we've had one of those lovely, warm June days which you get in this part of France close to Paris at this time of year. The railroad coach—it was Marshal Foch's private car—stands a few feet away from us here, at exactly the same spot where it stood on that gray morning twenty-two years ago.

Only—and what an "only" it is, too—Adolf Hitler sat in the seat occupied that day by Marshal Foch—Hitler who, at that time, was only an unknown corporal in the German army. And in the quaint old wartime *wagon-lit* car, another armistice is being drawn up as I speak to you. An armistice designed, like the other that was signed on this spot, to bring armed hostilities to a halt between the ancient enemies, Germany and France. Only everything— *everything* that we've been seeing here this afternoon in Compiègne forest— has been so reversed. The last time the representatives of France sat in that car dictating the terms of the Armistice. This afternoon we peered through the windows of the car and saw Adolf Hitler laying down the terms. Thus does history reverse itself, but seldom has it done so as today, on the very same spot.

Twelve minutes after French officials arrived in the railroad car, Hitler stood up and walked out. He was through. The French, their faces the picture of defeat and humiliation, remained at the table facing Keitel, who began reading the terms of their surrender. Hitler and his entourage walked back to their caravan of Mercedes sedans as a German band played "Deutschland über Alles" and the "Horst Wessel Lied."

Telling his listeners that the French and the Germans were now negotiating in the railroad car over the exact terms of the surrender, Shirer said, "That's all for the moment. And William C. Kerker and William L. Shirer return you now to America."

* * *

The next day, June 22, back in Paris, Shirer went early to the dining room at the Hôtel Scribe. Over coffee he learned to his great dismay that Hitler had demanded that all correspondents in France, including Germans, be sent to Berlin. The signing of the new armistice, which allowed for nearly three-fifths of the country, including Paris, to be occupied, was to be announced in Berlin to great fanfare. All the reporters were to be in the same room at the same time to hear it.

All the Americans Shirer talked to in the hotel dining room said they were going to follow the instructions and board a military plane for the flight back to Berlin. Shirer, while keeping his plans to himself, would have none of it. Kerker felt the same way. Adding to Shirer's resolve, his friend in the German High Command said the armistice would be signed that day in the railroad car in Compiègne. Whoever this "friend" in uniform was, it is tempting to see him in the context of the "good German," the label given to those Germans who opposed Hitler and the policies and plans of the Nazis. Other high-ranking German officers were to fall under this fabled, somewhat mythical label, but only after staggering military defeats and when it was obvious that the end was near. In this case, it was June 1940, and an officer in the High Command was sharing private information with a foreign correspondent. When Shirer told him he would leave immediately for Compiègne and ignore the order to return to Berlin, the officer "was pleased that I was defying Hitler, whom he despised," Shirer wrote.

But there were technical issues that would prevent Shirer from broadcasting, the officer told him. "He warned me that the Führer had ordered that all broadcasts this day from Compiègne be automatically recorded in Berlin. They could be retransmitted to America when Hitler himself gave the word."

Determined to leave Paris for Compiègne immediately, Shirer felt he could live with the technical restrictions. "At least, unlike the newspaper correspondents, I would have an eyewitness story, and it would get out of Berlin at the same time as the newspaper dispatches," he wrote. "And being instantaneous it would beat them by hours before their stories could appear in print."

As his colleagues waited in the lobby of the Hôtel Scribe for their rides to a waiting military plane, Shirer and Kerker climbed into a car with Harold Diettrich, the German who ran his country's short-wave transmitting program, and Shirer's friend in the High Command. They drove out of Paris and proceeded to Compiègne. Neither Diettrich nor the officer acted as if they were worried that they were helping Shirer violate Hitler's personal order that all correspondents, foreign and German, be returned to Berlin to cover the news from there. Diettrich's view of the order, however nonsensical, was that it applied only to newspaper correspondents. Shirer and Kerker worked for American radio, so they were exempt.

At Compiègne, Shirer found that as a correspondent he pretty much had the run of the area, perhaps because he was a familiar face from the day before. He walked around and talked to officials, French and German alike, and no one confronted him about being there. Dozens of French army and government officials stood off by themselves, a stunned, sad knot of men in uniform and suits who looked as though the humiliation of their six-week rout by the Germans would at any moment strike them dead. Their country, their beautiful Paris, were now *occupied*, a reality that these men found impossible to grasp. No doubt all of them, while standing in the sunlight outside the railroad car watching the day unfold, pondered all the questions this collapse raised about French society. And beyond the questions about the collapse itself were those still waiting to be addressed about what lay ahead. They found it impossible to interact with the Germans who were there to read them the terms of their surrender; some of the French delegation would not look a German in the eye. Most, if not all, of them were veterans in one form or another of the Great War; they had defeated the Germans and pushed through the Treaty of Versailles with what the Germans saw as its humiliating terms. The small group of Frenchmen inside the railroad car with the Germans were now hearing surrender terms forced on them. As Shirer had said in his broadcast the day before, history had been turned upside down.

For Shirer the goal was to learn everything he could about the surrender, type out a story on his lap, and read it into a phone line to Berlin, where it would later be transmitted to CBS in New York. If all went well, his would be an extraordinary achievement, and he knew it from the moment he arrived. By positioning himself near a communications truck set up by a German army captain, complete with telephone lines connecting Berlin to Bordeaux, where the French government had temporarily set itself up after fleeing Paris, Shirer could listen in on the conversations inside the railroad car.

What he heard was "a good deal of bickering between the two sides" but mostly over relatively minor points. Present in the railroad car for the French was General Charles Huntziger, who spoke over an open telephone line to Bordeaux with Maxime Weygand, who was, like Huntziger, a veteran of the Great War. It had been General Weygand who, in 1918, read the terms of the surrender to the Germans in the same rail car. Huntziger, thoroughly embittered sitting with the Germans in the car and unwilling to grasp the terms of France's surrender, told Weygand over the phone line—with Shirer listening from the communications truck—that he would have to be ordered to sign the armistice. When General Keitel told Huntziger that the French must accept the German terms by 6:30 that afternoon, and Huntziger relayed that demand to Weygand, the order was given that the French delegation sign the agreement. The depths of French defeatism in the government in Bordeaux were now fully apparent to Shirer.

Looking at his watch—it was 6:42 P.M.—Shirer saw the French and the Germans reassemble in the rail car for the signing. Standing where he could see through the car's windows, Shirer watched Huntziger, who was fighting back tears. Shirer wrote down what Huntziger then told the Germans: "I declare that the French government has ordered me to sign these terms of armistice." He then heard "the scratching of pens as the armistice agreement was signed. It was 6:50 P.M." At Keitel's demand, everyone in the car stood for a moment of silence for the dead, an act the French might have found distasteful, as if suddenly Keitel and the Germans wanted the French to believe they cared about the French dead. When the moment had passed, the French departed for Paris.

Shirer now had to write out a story. A photograph taken at the time by a German photographer named Otto Kropf shows him seated on a wooden plank in an open glade typing out a story, his pipe clenched between his teeth, uniformed Germans around him. To his relief, everything he needed to broadcast his story fell into place when German army officials, along with civilian broadcasting personnel from the RRG, including Diettrich, gave Shirer the great gift of an open phone line to Berlin. As Shirer wrote years later, the army insisted that he broadcast with Kerker.

"Diettrich and my OKW (the army High Command) friend assured me that I would speak first, since NBC had sent only a stringer...without much journalistic experience. I spoke first, as I recall, for about twenty minutes and Kerker, using mostly my unused notes, for the last ten minutes."

Shirer set up his microphone a few yards from the armistice car. The sky overhead had turned gray, and the smell of approaching rain descended on the forest clearing. He hoped it would hold off until he and Kerker had finished their broadcast, but he was determined to continue reading even if it did not. At 8:15 P.M. Shirer spoke his first words into the microphone as if he were live and not transmitting to Berlin, where he would be recorded for later transmission to CBS in New York.

Hello America. Hello NBC. Hello CBS. William C. Kerker and William L. Shirer calling NBC and CBS. This is William L. Shirer speaking to you from the forest of Compiègne in France. The armistice has been signed. The armistice between France and Germany was signed exactly at 6:50 P.M. German summer time, that is, one hour and twenty minutes ago....

The skies were slightly overcast, but the sun occasionally came out, transforming this beautiful forest of Compiègne into a sort of fairy land. A mile down the road, through one of the wooded avenues, you could see the refugees, slowly, tiredly filing by—on weary feet, on bicycles, on carts, a few on trucks. They were very tired and footsore and dazed, and they did not know yet that an armistice had been signed and that the fighting would soon be over. But judging from their tragic, weary half-starved faces, they all wanted it to be.

When he finished, Shirer turned the microphone over to Kerker. As he did so, a drop of rain landed on his forehead. The sky darkened as the rain approached.

He hoped Kerker could get through his broadcast before the heavy rains began. He walked away from the microphone, feeling relieved that he had gotten through his broadcast without problems. A short distance from where he stood, a line of refugees made their way along a dirt road. As he watched, a group of German engineers prepared the railroad car for a long trip to a new site where it would serve as a museum to Germany's triumph.

"Where to?" Shirer asked one of the engineers.

"To Berlin," he said.

* * *

The rain was falling harder when Shirer climbed into a car and headed back to Paris. The next morning he was awakened in his room at the Hôtel Scribe by Walter Kerr, who told him that his broadcast had not been relayed to Berlin for recording and then later transmitted to New York, but instead had gone out directly on short-wave.

"You scooped the world yesterday," Kerr said as a weary Shirer opened the door. "Congratulations!"

Because he had no credentials to travel with the Germans, Kerr had stayed behind in Paris and listened to the live CBS broadcast on a short-wave radio in the *Herald Tribune* office. He also picked up a CBS announcer in New York talking about Shirer's broadcast. In London, Ed Murrow had also heard Shirer's broadcast. Stunned at the news of the French signing, Murrow called Winston Churchill at his country estate to tell him that the French had signed the armistice. Churchill told Murrow that he was certain the news was wrong.

A day later, in Cedar Rapids, Iowa, Shirer's mother picked up the *Gazette* and read a United Press dispatch that quoted CBS and NBC reporting that the armistice had been signed. The story noted that Shirer had been the first to broadcast the news to America—"a pinnacle in his career as a radio correspondent"—and under his photograph reminded readers that he had grown up in Cedar Rapids and had graduated from Coe College.

Shirer lingered in Paris for a few days, enjoying the weather and walking the city's streets with Joe Harsch, a writer for the *Christian Science Monitor*. One afternoon Shirer, Harsch, and Kerr had a late breakfast at the Café de la Paix, watching the German officers strolling the streets and spending their money. Before heading back to Berlin, Shirer showed Harsch the sights in Paris, taking him to the places where he had lived and worked after arriving in the city in 1925. In Montparnasse on the Left Bank of the Seine, they stopped for drinks at an outdoor café and overheard middle-aged French women complaining that younger women were fraternizing with German soldiers.

On the morning of June 26, Shirer and an entourage of journalists and German officials left Paris in a caravan of cars for the drive to the German border. The Germans were not going home empty-handed. They had loaded up the cars with suits, wool, silk stockings, perfumes, and trunkloads of other goods purchased in Paris. They passed through a customs post without problems, and in the German city of Aachen, Shirer caught the last night train to Berlin.

A Long Train Ride to Tess

Here for a week's rest. The excited cries of Eileen when I take her in swimming for the first time in her life, the soft voice of Tess reading a fairy tale to Eileen before she goes to bed—these become realities again and are good. Everyone full of talk of the "new Europe." The Swiss are resigned to it and have no military position, as they are now surrounded. Mt. Blanc from the quai today was magnificent, its snow pink in the afternoon sun. We had dinner along the lake, on the Alpine side. Lights sparkled across the lake.

—William L. Shirer, diary, Geneva, July 4, 1940

Two weeks after visiting his family in Geneva, Shirer mingled with a huge crowd at the Brandenburg Gate in Berlin for a victory parade. Long columns of German troops paraded in front of cheering crowds, including thousands of school children in their uniforms, let out of their classes for the day. Businesses and government offices closed in honor of the country's great victory over France.

"Hitler to speak in the Reichstag tomorrow, we hear," Shirer wrote. "But we're threatened with expulsion if we say it to America. My hotel filled with big generals arriving for the show."

Shirer watched the speech with Joe Harsch. Hitler spoke of "peace" with Britain in a tone that made it clear it was all up to the British. "Of course it is peace with Hitler sitting astride the continent as its conqueror," he wrote in his diary. It was Harsch's first time witnessing Hitler, and he was mesmerized. "Said he couldn't keep his eyes off his hands; thought the hand work brilliant," Shirer wrote. The two sat near Göring, now the Reichsmarschall, who to Shirer's eye "acted like a happy child playing with his toys on Christmas morning."

In mid-August, Tess took the train to Berlin to spend a few days with her husband. At 2:00 A.M., soon after Shirer returned to the Adlon Hotel from his broadcast, the air-raid alarms across the city sounded. Tess was to leave the next morning, and neither of them wanted to stay in the cellar of the hotel until the alarms went off hours later. Under orders from the air-raid wardens to go to the cellar, they at first said they would and then abruptly changed their minds and stayed in their room, watching the sky over the city light up with antiaircraft fire.

The next day, Shirer flew to the French coast aboard a German army transport to watch the air war against Britain. "Germans are claiming 80 to 100 British planes shot down daily against 18 to 25 of their own," he wrote. "Doubt I will get to the truth."

There were fourteen correspondents on the flight, and because there were no seats, they all squatted on the floor of the transport, flying low the entire way, bouncing and holding on to anything they could to avoid being tossed about. When they neared an airstrip in Ghent, a German fighter escorted them to the ground. When they reached Ostend on the Belgian coast, Shirer left his group and walked on the beach, smelling the salt air. Just back from the beach, hundreds of destroyed houses lined city streets. He was reluctant to proceed with his group, which included officials from the Propaganda Ministry. But he was curious to see if the Germans were preparing for a massive invasion of England, so he went on to Calais on the French coast.

While he was eating lunch at a seaside restaurant, someone shouted that bombers were overhead. Shirer looked up to see twenty-three German aircraft surrounded by fighters. "It's going to be a nice day—for death in the air," he wrote in his diary. Later in the day they watched a wave of Heinkel bombers "limp back from the direction of Dover, gliding down over our heads. One was in difficulty and just managed to make the first field on the mainland. Messerschmitt 109s and 110s dash about at 350 mph like a lot of hens protecting their young. They remain in the air until all of the bombers are safely down, then climb and make off for England. We have stopped our cars to watch."

*   *   *

On this trip, Shirer and a number of the correspondents came to the conclusion that the Germans wanted them to see their preparations along the French coastline and to hear the talk of an invasion of England across the Channel. German pilots flying missions over London were brought around to talk freely with him. One of them told Shirer: "It's a matter of a couple of weeks, you know, until we finish the RAF.... The British are through."

Shirer did not believe it, in large part, because an American official in Berlin had told him prior to his trip that if he did not see large numbers of barges and other transports being readied to bring troops and tanks across the Channel, it could not happen. And Shirer, so far on the trip, had seen very little evidence that the Germans were assembling transports for such a massive undertaking. They were constructing defensive works—he saw that everywhere along the French coast. But he could not envision the Germans moving huge numbers of troops, tanks, and armored equipment across the Channel.

Still, the officials from the Propaganda Ministry kept pushing the correspondents to write and broadcast that an invasion was imminent. Telephone lines and radio facilities would be made available. There would be no censorship. "I began to grow very suspicious," Shirer wrote. "I think the Germans want us to launch a scare story about an imminent invasion of Britain."

When the group arrived in Brussels, a high-ranking German officer told them: "We naturally cannot tell you the invasion date. But we are relaxing military censorship in order to allow you to report what you have seen the past few days on the Channel." Shirer told the officer he had not seen any barges that could transport an entire army, and the officer said there were things he could not show the correspondents. "But I believe you have seen enough to convince you that we are ready to invade," he told Shirer.

At the hotel, Shirer was shown a phone line reserved for him. "I would have no part of it," he wrote later. "To broadcast now and say that the Germans were all set to invade would be not only a lie, but do the beleaguered British a terrible disservice that could be fatal.... It suddenly occurred to me that we American correspondents...were faced with a decision that had consequences far more serious than we had ever experienced. The decision was not difficult for me. I would not broadcast."

With no work to do, Shirer went to the hotel bar and then to the restaurant, where he had a hearty dinner. He returned to his room at approximately 10:00 P.M. A few minutes later, as he prepared to go to bed, he answered a knock on his door and was greeted by an official from the RRG and one of the military guides who had escorted the group the previous few days.

"We've got an excellent line for you to Berlin," the radio man said. "When do you want to broadcast?"

Shirer told them he would not broadcast at all. Asked why, he said, "Because I do not believe, from what I've seen, you're going to invade, at least for now."

After the two Germans left Shirer's room, Fred Oechsner, the United Press bureau chief in Berlin, knocked on his door. He showed Shirer cables he had received from the home office in New York demanding to know why he had not filed a story on the imminent invasion of England as the other correspondents on the trip had with their wire services. Oechsner was certain he would be fired as a consequence but told Shirer he could not write that story because he did not believe it was true.

"How did you handle it in your broadcast?" Oechsner asked Shirer.

"I didn't broadcast," Shirer answered. "For the same reason you didn't cable anything."

As Shirer wrote years later, Louis Lochner, the Associated Press bureau chief in Berlin, and Pierre Huss, a wire service correspondent, filed stories that night predicting a German invasion of England. Shirer and Oechsner were disgusted. "Pierre, it seemed to me, had always played the Nazi game a little," Shirer wrote a half-century later. "Louis too, if only to get a beat, a scoop. I did not envy them."

*   *   *

When he returned to Berlin, certain that the Germans would call off any plans to launch an invasion of England from ports along the French coast, Shirer began assessing where he stood with the censors and what he needed to do in order to satisfy his internal demand that he not report propaganda. He would not be used by the Germans, even if that put him in a bad place with Paul White, the CBS manager in New York. As he had been since arriving in Berlin in August 1934, Shirer was fully aware of how thin the ice was beneath his feet.

In July the Propaganda Ministry had ordered Ralph Barnes, the Berlin correspondent for the *New York Herald Tribune*, out of the country, along with an assistant who also occasionally worked for Shirer. Barnes, one of Shirer's oldest friends in Europe, was no longer welcome to cover the German government. Barnes's sin was to have written a story for his newspaper suggesting that the German government was not all that friendly with the Soviets in Moscow, which ran counter to the official line in Berlin. It was read by a German, living and working in New York City or Washington, D.C., who reported back to Berlin. In his diary entry when he heard that Barnes was to be expelled, Shirer wrote that, in addition to the offending story, he was certain that the bureaucrats in the Propaganda Ministry loathed the *Herald Tribune* itself. To Shirer's eye, the *Herald Tribune* was the only New York newspaper with a Berlin bureau that insisted its correspondents maintain their independence from government officials.

The afternoon before Barnes boarded a train that would take him to the coast and then aboard a ferry to England, he and Shirer walked through the Tiergarten, Shirer's favorite place in Berlin. He had loved it since his arrival six years earlier and always found paths to walk that seemed fresh to him, and now he was with his friend. Neither knew, of course, but it would be the last time they saw each other. While Barnes was upset about having to leave the country, he was determined to cover it from another location. Shirer, for his part, was proud of Barnes for showing "more integrity than any of us who are allowed to stay."

Later in July, a second American correspondent was ordered out of Germany. Maxwell Corpening, who liked to be referred to as Captain Corpening, of Shirer's former newspaper the *Chicago Tribune*, arrived in Berlin and wrote a story for his paper about Germany's offering peace terms to the British. The story was immediately attacked by the Propaganda Ministry as false.

By late August, dealing with German officials and censors was the least of Shirer's concerns. The city was hot, its people tense as they awaited the certain arrival of British bombers bent on punishing Germans in their capital city for the attacks on London. On the night of August 19, Shirer, seated in his small studio at the broadcast center, jumped up when the air-raid alarms erupted. In less than a minute he was to speak into the microphone. A censor seated next to him to make sure Shirer followed the approved script indicated he could go on the air, even as dozens of people began rushing down staircases to the safety of the basement.

As Shirer waited to speak, a seventeen-year-old Englishman shouted and banged on Shirer's studio window. Shirer knew the boy had come to Germany with his mother to work for the Nazis. The German censor ignored the boy and indicated Shirer could begin his broadcast. Shirer knew enough not to mention that the air-raid alarms had sounded.

"This is Berlin," he began, quickly summarizing the previous day's bombing campaign by the Germans against London. "This evening's papers and even the early editions of tomorrow morning's newspapers are still playing up yesterday's attack. They all headline the final score as given out today by the High Command: 147 British planes destroyed against thirty-six German machines missing. The total number of British planes shot down in the last eight days is given in Berlin as 732."

Shirer reported that the German commander in the Netherlands had issued stern warnings against giving shelter to "enemy soldiers" and had declared that sabotage against the Germans would not be tolerated. Shirer went on to say the Germans would punish entire towns and villages where saboteurs lived, but the censor deleted a line in which Shirer intended to say that the Germans would take hostages of their own in retaliation.

The next afternoon Shirer was back on the air, and this time, after his "This is Berlin" opening, he mentioned the previous night's air raid. The censor again deleted sections of Shirer's script, which infuriated him. But there was nothing he could do about it except refuse to broadcast. "Afterward I went out to watch the excitement, but there wasn't any," he said into the microphone. "A few anti-aircraft guns roared in the distance, some searchlights went into action, but that was about all. Later it was explained that two bombers came over and cruised over a suburb without dropping any bombs. Later, say the Germans, one of the planes was picked up by the searchlights at Brunswick, and shot down in flames."

Early on the morning of August 25, British bombers appeared directly over the city. The sirens went off at 12:20 A.M. as Shirer sat in his office in the short-wave station preparing a script in the presence of one of the censors. Moments after the sirens sounded, the German antiaircraft guns positioned around the city exploded en masse, shaking the building. Shirer could hear the low thud of bombs hitting the ground—as far as he knew, the first the British had dropped on Berlin.

As the attack commenced, Shirer and one of the censors from the Propaganda Ministry argued. "About midnight I got into a heavy argument with K., censor from the P.M. [Propaganda Ministry] as to whether British planes could penetrate the Berlin defenses and reach the heart of the city," Shirer wrote in his diary. "I maintained that at night they could, and probably would visit us now that the Germans had dropped bombs on the center of London. He was dead certain they wouldn't because they couldn't. If it were at all possible, he argued with some vehemence, they would have been all over here long before now. Hardly were the words out of his mouth before the siren blew and the guns started sounding off."

To reach his studio from the short-wave station, Shirer walked out of one building and dashed madly across an open lot to another building and a series of sheds where the broadcast studios were set up. As he ran, the antiaircraft guns positioned around the broadcast buildings and other government build-ings exploded. Pieces of twisted metal fell out of the night sky and landed all around him. "It sounded like falling hail," he wrote. "I hesitated in the shelter of the doorway for a moment. In a couple of minutes my broadcast would begin. I made a dash for it."

Once he reached his studio, Shirer sat in front of his microphone, the sounds of the attack all around him. One of the German engineers told him to lean close to the microphone so the noise of the attack could not be heard on American radios. Shirer began: "This is Berlin. We're having an air raid alarm here at the moment. The sirens went off some time ago, about midnight, and afterward you could hear the big antiaircraft guns going into action, and see the searchlights trying to pick up the British planes. More details are not yet available."

When he finished with his broadcast, Shirer attempted to run back across the open lot to his office in the short-wave building but was stopped by a guard. Shirer had with him a flashlight lent to him by Sigrid Schultz earlier in the evening, and he was anxious to give it back to her, since she was shortly to give her own broadcast. The guard ordered Shirer to stay in the building, explaining that shrapnel was "falling like rain drops" and he could get killed. Shirer refused, pushing past the guard and making his way along the sides of the sheds that sat along the edges of the lot in order to reach the main building where Sigrid was waiting for him.

When he was halfway across the lot, "all hell broke loose, guns all around firing with everything they had. A rain of shrapnel came tumbling down." Shirer hugged the sheds trying to avoid the falling metal and made a mad dash for the safety of the nearest building, where he found Sigrid waiting for him. He handed her the flashlight, and in full flight she started out across the lot, hoping to reach the studios on the far side. Halfway across she stumbled and fell hard onto her knees, shrapnel falling all around her and noisily bouncing off the ground and the roofs of surrounding buildings. She picked herself up and continued to run as Shirer, stepping out into the lot to see if she was all right, heard the engine roar of the British bombers directly overhead, the searchlights desperately trying to pick them out.

The next day's Berlin newspapers gave the bombing raid six lines of an official communiqué, which caused Shirer to laugh out loud. The government-controlled papers spoke in big headlines of "the cowardly British attack" against civilians. Shirer, knowing from Murrow in London of the destruction and deaths in that city from the German bombing campaign, threw down the papers in disgust. The people of Berlin knew the truth even if their papers were going to pretend otherwise. "There is not a line about the explosive bombs we all heard," he wrote in his diary. "Nor is there a word about the three streets in Berlin which have been roped off all day to prevent the curious from seeing what a bomb can do to a house."

The government, of course, knew the reality that British planes had made it across occupied Europe and struck Berlin in the early morning hours. Someone Shirer called "X" in his diary told him the British had dropped one hundred bombs on the city, seventy of them incendiary bombs meant to start large fires.

On the night of August 29, the British returned, and the government press conceded that there were a number of fatalities on the ground. Shirer, watching the attacks from his vantage point in central Berlin, guessed that the British were trying to destroy the airport at Tempelhof along with a major nearby rail junction. This concerned him, for the obvious reason that the British would want to destroy government buildings—he worked in a government building—and because, if the airfields at Tempelhof were destroyed, it would reduce the possibility of his being able to flee the country if he had to.

For Shirer, the fear of being killed in a nighttime bombing raid, or being trapped in Germany as the war escalated and unable to join his family in Switzerland, was made worse by his daily struggles with the censors. They read his scripts and crossed off sentences, paragraphs, and entire sections. *You can say this, you can't say that.* None knew the difference between the truth and the government version as written and approved by the bureaucrats in the Propaganda Ministry and reprinted in the city's newspapers. On the night of one bombing of the city, the censors ordered Shirer not to mention that it was underway. He knew what Murrow did during bombing raids in London— describing them vividly as they happened—and he admired his colleague for it, but it would be impossible for Shirer to accomplish the same thing here. Shirer lost his temper, but he complied and when his broadcast was over, he was ordered to the bomb shelter in the basement of the building. When Shirer refused to go to the cellar, the censors rounded up two policemen to escort him.

*   *   *

As September 1 arrived, the one-year anniversary of the German assault on Poland, Shirer was certain he could not continue to stay in Berlin without risking his life more than he already had. On more than one occasion, as he returned to his room at the Adlon Hotel after an early morning broadcast, he saw fires burning along the city's skyline from the night's attacks. The hotel—at the intersection of two busy central Berlin streets, Unter den Linden and the Wilhelmstrasse, which was lined with government buildings including the Chancellery—could easily be struck, if not on purpose then by mistake. On several nights he stood on the roof of the broadcast center and watched the mad circling of the dark sky by the German searchlights and heard the deafening explosion of the antiaircraft guns. "There was nothing you could do against the night bomber but pray that its bombs would not fall on you," he wrote years later.

As he prepared to broadcast to America on the anniversary, the censor warned Shirer not to refer to Germany as the aggressor. "Please remember it was Poland who attacked us first," the censor told him. As they argued, the air-raid sirens sounded, and the antiaircraft guns positioned around the government buildings roared as bombers appeared overhead.

"How do the Germans feel today, after one year of war, you may ask?" Shirer said in his broadcast.

Well, judging by the front-page editorials in such leading papers as the *Völkischer Beobachter*, the *Frankfurter Zeitung* and the *Deutsche Allgemeine Zeitung* today, they have a clear conscience that the war was forced upon them by Britain, that they have a righteous cause, that they've done pretty well in a year of fighting, and that victory stands not far off. That is the official view, to be sure, but it would be a mistake to assume that it is not also the view of the great mass of the German people....

Well, how fare the German people, you may ask, after a year of war? Take food. On the whole, right now they are probably better fed than a year ago. Butter, bacon and eggs imported from Denmark, and vegetables imported from Holland have helped. Also, Germany's own stocks of food are still, I take it, very sizeable. Germans will not starve this winter. The situation in occupied Holland, Belgium and France is not so rosy. I don't know where their food is going to come from this winter. The official German standpoint is that if they suffer, it will be the fault of the British blockade.

Late in September, Shirer covered a speech by Hitler in the big Sportpalast in which he promised to punish Britain for its air attacks on Berlin. The crowd became hysterical when Hitler vowed to drop hundreds of thousands of kilograms of bombs on London in retaliation. "'We will stop the handiwork of these air pirates, so help us God,' Hitler shouted. At this point the poor imbeciles sprang to their feet, the better to screech out their barbarian yells of approval."

Hitler's lies—he said in his speech that Britain had tyrannized the Continent and that Germany was fighting for its freedom—and the lies of all the government officials Shirer dealt with on a daily basis continued to take their toll. "Lies. Lies. I'm getting tired of the censorship restrictions on our telling even a modicum of truth to America," he wrote in his diary. "And yet our American offices insist on our staying here, though they know our position. Personally, I shall not do it much longer."

Making his own situation worse with the authorities, Shirer turned down official offers of guided tours of the capital meant to show how well the Germans were dealing with the nightly attacks. He saw it as nothing but propaganda, and he would have nothing to do with it. "This attitude of mine greatly resented," he wrote in his diary. "AP and INS and buro chiefs which have played the Nazi game completely from the start were welcomed because they write only what will not displease the Nazi lords."

When officials at the broadcast center handed him a new kind of microphone that was supposed to keep out the sounds of the air attacks, Shirer reacted angrily. He knew the attacks were heard in New York because one of the CBS broadcasters there, Elmer Davis, had commented on the sounds, and the Germans had listened to his broadcast and responded accordingly.

To put additional pressure on Shirer to comply with their rules, the Germans required him to submit his work to three censors: one from the military, a second from the Foreign Office, and a third from the Propaganda

Ministry. One night the arguing with all three was so intense that Shirer missed his broadcast; the following evening, Tess called him from Geneva to tell him that Paul White had called her to ask why Shirer had not broadcast. Making Shirer look worse in New York, White told Tess he had received a cable from Berlin saying, "Regret Shirer arrived too late tonight to broadcast."

Shirer felt he had another person lined up against him: Paul White. "God knows I had had constant difficulties with the Germans," Shirer wrote years later. "But I was surprised to meet with a considerable lack of understanding at CBS." Earlier, when Shirer had complained to White that he would not broadcast if it was nothing but German lies, White had cabled him to make his position clear: "Bill, we thoroughly understand, sympathize condition in Berlin, but feel we must carry on with broadcasts even if only reading official statements and newspaper texts."

Writing a half-century later in his memoir, Shirer's anger still boiled. "CBS would have to get someone else for that menial chore," he wrote. "I replied to White I could hire a pro-Nazi American for $50 a week and no expenses to read that crap."

The night of September 11 brought the largest and most severe British bombing of Berlin. Three incendiary bombs fell near the Adlon Hotel, and a number landed close to the American embassy. A series of bombs hit a nearby train station and the Reichstag building. Shirer found himself in the middle of the attack as he left the broadcast center after the all-clear had sounded. He drove as fast as he could in a borrowed car and slammed on the brakes when he skidded into debris on the road, narrowly missing a bomb crater that would have swallowed the car.

The following day, Shirer boarded a train in Berlin for the long ride to the Swiss border, where Tess would be waiting for him. He had made up his mind to tell her that he could not stay any longer in Berlin. He also wanted to clarify his position with Paul White in New York, and he did not want to have that conversation over the phone in Berlin. As much as he yearned to be with Tess and Eileen in Geneva, Shirer worried that he was leaving Berlin at precisely the wrong moment. Rumors abounded in the city and among the military that the invasion of England was planned for the night of September 15, when the moon would be full and the tide right.

"I'll chance the trip anyway," he wrote in his diary.

CROWDED BUSES

On his way across Germany on a blacked-out train heading for the Swiss frontier, Shirer went over in his head what he wanted to tell Paul White. His thoughts came down to a simple statement: unless the Germans relaxed the censorship in Berlin and let him speak his mind, and explain on American radio what was going on in Germany, he would get out. He was determined to be candid with White, as White had always been with him. He had proved himself as Murrow's representative in Berlin. White could not criticize the work. He was approaching White not from a position of weakness but its opposite.

Shirer had been in Vienna for the *Anschluss*, in Munich for Neville Chamberlain's "peace in our time" meeting with Hitler, in Prague when the Germans occupied the Sudetenland, with the German Sixth Army as it bored its way across Belgium and into France, on the majestic boulevards of Paris after the city had fallen to the Germans, and in the woods of Compiègne for the French surrender. He had made broadcasting history, and he was cocky enough and sure enough of his own credentials to know it and to speak candidly to White.

Prior to his arrival in Switzerland and after dozens of late-night phone calls, Shirer and his wife had worked out a plan whereby Tess and Eileen would leave Europe for America. They had discussed this before, of course, but leaving Geneva for Lisbon—across France, which was then at war with Germany—would have been perilous. The French surrender and the end of fighting, and now the German occupation of Paris, northern France, and the Atlantic coastline, changed that fundamentally. To Shirer's mind, it seemed possible that Tess and their child could safely make their way across France, into northern Spain, and from there into Portugal. He tried desperately to come to some sort of solution in his mind, in favor of the plan at one moment and then arguing against it in the next. If Germany invaded England from French seaports, then this plan would fail. He could not get his mind around his and his family's future in the event of such an expansion of the fighting. What if Britain fell? What would Europe look like? But Shirer, as he had believed all along since visiting the coastline himself, saw no real possibility for a massive German invasion across the Channel. It would take too many boats of all kinds to ferry the men and equipment, and with Germany so far unable to destroy British airpower, such a massive movement of ships would surely be destroyed at sea.

Lisbon was the last port on the Atlantic from which his wife and daughter could board a passenger ship or an airplane for America. Tess was at first reluctant to make such a journey, but she was assured it was the best plan they could follow at the moment. More fighting would close more doors of escape. Shirer could envision a scenario in which he and his wife and daughter would spend the rest of their lives in Hitler's Europe. He would do anything to avoid that. Shirer promised he would follow her, with the goal of being together in New York by Christmas.

Shirer found Geneva a joy. He played with Eileen all day and sat up late each night with Tess talking about what they wanted for themselves in the future. Each dreaded the morning when Tess would take him to the rail station for the long trip back to Berlin. As he enjoyed his family, rumors spread through the city that the Germans had been overwhelmed by British air and sea power and that an invasion had been thwarted with an enormous loss of life. Shirer did not believe it, and it was quickly proved to be false.

It came as a surprise to Shirer when Tess explained on one of their evenings together that she would rather stay in Europe. Starting a new life in America, while not unappealing, did not fully engage her. Nor did she fancy the idea of living in the United States while her husband worked in Europe. But Tess's desire to stay in Europe, closer to her husband, didn't make sense. There was much to be worked out and not a lot of time in which to do it. And first he had to come to an agreement with Paul White.

Shirer called White and asked him to book seats on a passenger plane from Lisbon to New York for his wife and daughter. White agreed to do it but said it would be difficult to arrange. He promised to get Tess and Eileen to New York by Christmas, which was nearly three months away. At that point, Shirer told White he preferred to be with them when they left Europe.

"Bill, we understand your feelings," White said. "But we want you to stay in Berlin. We think you're doing a wonderful job."

Weary of having to explain his situation, Shirer launched into an account of the difficulties of working in Berlin and covering the German government. He tried to explain what it was like to deal with a government that lied about everything, in a country in which informing on your family and friends was encouraged and where enemies of the state were locked up in concentration camps or had their heads chopped off. "He had not the slightest inkling of what trying to work in the Nazi madhouse was like," Shirer wrote of his conversations with White. "Despite several hours on the transatlantic telephone over three days White and I did not quite solve our differences."

When the conversations were over, Shirer summed up what they had agreed to in a letter to White: "I realize that the next few weeks may decide the issue of the war, and that it is not the best time to pull out because of censorship.... For that reason I am going back to Berlin to have another crack at the job. But if there is a stalemate this winter and the censorship is not relaxed, I personally cannot remain there and do Nazi propaganda."

On the morning of September 18, Shirer boarded a train that would take him back across Germany to the capital city. Saying goodbye to Tess and Eileen had been wrenching, but he held on to the hope that they could both get to the United States safely and that he could join them by Christmas. No matter how he left the discussion with Paul White about his next few months in Berlin, Shirer had made up his mind that—barring an enormous change in Germany and how the Nazis ran the country—he would gather up his belongings and leave.

Shirer settled in on the train, reading and sleeping uneasily as the line of passenger cars moved toward the Fatherland. He kept up his diary, typing out his notes and writing on the backs of loose paper, in pocket diaries and calendars, in pencil and ink. He had taken Blanche Knopf's advice to heart and was faithful about the diary, hoping at some point to present it to her and her publishing company in New York City as a record of his work in Nazi Germany. He would end it when he left. It would be his "Berlin diary," his first book, and would give him much to talk about with John Gunther. He could only hope Knopf would find it interesting and publishable.

In the darkness of his first night on the train, somewhere between Basel and Frankfurt, Shirer was awakened in his berth by the porter's shouts. As he pulled himself up in the cramped quarters, he heard the *thump-thump-thump* of distant gunfire as an antiaircraft battery opened up against British planes. Thankfully, nothing came of it, and the train proceeded, arriving at the big Potsdamer Bahnhof in Berlin near the Brandenburg Gate on time. Stepping off the train, he found himself in a large group of wounded soldiers being removed from a rail car. He assumed they were airmen involved in the bombings of London. Many had serious burns.

On a siding, a Red Cross train stretched out of the station and down the track to the Landwehr Canal, where the body of the murdered Rosa

Luxemburg had been dumped in 1919. Shirer was puzzled as to why there would be so many wounded soldiers now, more than three months after the French surrender. "Can it be that the tales I heard in Geneva had some truth in them after all?" he wrote in his diary, quickly dismissing any thought that the Germans had failed in an attempted invasion of England. He was certain they had given up on an invasion and would instead concentrate part of their army on North Africa.

Berlin felt a less gloomy place to Shirer after four days in Switzerland. There had been only one air raid in his absence, which disappointed him greatly. "They really think the British planes can't get through," he wrote. "Morale tumbled noticeably in Berlin when the British visited us almost every evening."

His view that the British bombing of Berlin had so far been ineffective was confirmed a day or two later when he and two American colleagues drove out of the city center to the big Siemens Electrical Works. "We drove slowly around the plant, but could find no trace of any damage," he wrote. "The thousands of workers filing out after the afternoon shift seemed well fed and quite contented." Returning to Berlin, Shirer passed another long Red Cross train unloading scores of wounded Germans.

Over the next few days, Shirer battled with the censors, who removed large sections of his broadcasts about bombing raids. Meanwhile, Shirer found it more and more difficult to read the headlines in the daily newspapers, which he found so dishonest as to be laughable. One night when he wanted to read some of the headlines on his broadcast, one of the censors ordered him not to, saying he would be misleading his listeners. "Censorship of our broadcasts is growing daily more impossible," he wrote in his diary.

"I ask myself why I stay here.... For the last few months I've been trying to get by on my wits, such as they are; to indicate a truth or an official lie by the tone and inflexion of the voice, by a pause held longer than is natural, by the use of an Americanism which most Germans, who've learned their English in England, will not fully grasp, and by drawing from a word, a phrase, a sentence, a paragraph, or their juxtaposition, all the benefit I can. But the Nazis are on to me."

Shirer knew his broadcasts were listened to in the United States by Germans or their spies. Anything found offensive was then written up in a report that was forwarded to the Propaganda Ministry with his name prominently stamped on the envelope. The Nazis were actively following everything he said and how he said it, all with the goal of eventually finding an excuse to expel him from Germany. Shirer resented it greatly, as he also resented the "go along to get along" crowd among the other correspondents, with whom he had fallen out of favor.

Summing up his beliefs in the pages of his diary, he wrote: "The Foreign Office and the Propaganda Ministry keep receiving reports from the United States—not only from the Embassy at Washington, but from their well-organized intelligence service throughout our country—that I'm getting by with murder (which I'm not) and must be sat upon." He knew, apparently through friendly contacts in the ministry, that Kurt Sell, a German journalist based in Washington, compiled reports on what correspondents wrote for their newspapers and said on the air. In his diary, Shirer wrote that Sell "has several times reported unfavorably on the nature of my broadcasts."

Every day Shirer went to his small studio in the broadcast center he dealt with three censors, and it would have been these officials who read Sell's reports from the United States. As much as Shirer resented being spied on, he had an odd friendship with two recently appointed censors for the Propaganda Ministry. They were "Professor Lessing, who long held a post in an American university, and Herr Krauss, for twenty years a partner in a Wall Street bank. I cannot fool them very often. Personally, both are decent, intelligent Germans, as is Captain Erich Kunsti, former Program Director of the Austrian Broadcasting System and now my principal military censor. But they must do what they are told."

While Shirer had made up his mind to leave the country and follow his family to the United States, he held out a small measure of hope that Lessing, Krauss, and Kunsti would at least allow him a small measure of independence. As naïve as this was, Shirer thought if he could get across most of what he wanted to say in his broadcasts, he would be willing to stay in Berlin, as Paul White had made clear he wanted him to do during their phone conversations from Geneva.

"I haven't the slightest interest in remaining here unless I can continue to give a fairly accurate report," he told himself in his diary. "And each day my broadcasts are forced by the censorship to be less accurate."

Adding insult, a young German had been placed inside Shirer's studio. It was this man's job to call New York on the radio transmitter in preparation for Shirer's going on the air and reading his script. Now, rather than just following the script as Shirer read it to make sure he didn't change the wording, the German was underlining some words and sentences. "He was trying to note down, I take it, which words I emphasized, which I spoke with undue sarcasm, and so on," Shirer wrote. "I was so fascinated by this discovery that I stopped in the middle of my talk to watch him."

*　*　*

X came up to my room in the Adlon today, and after we had disconnected my telephone and made sure that no one was listening through the crack of the door to the next room, he told me a weird story.

—William L. Shirer, diary, September 21, 1940

Who X was—an influential German journalist, a party official, someone high up in a ministry or the military?—Shirer did not reveal in his diary on the night he made the entry. Shirer had already begun to think of ways of getting all his personal papers—diaries, letters, official correspondence, and maps—out of the country when he left. To risk his diary's being read by the Gestapo and a name being revealed from his diary horrified him. Shirer did not reveal X's identity in his diary at the time, and he did not do so forty-four years later when he published the second installment of his memoirs, *The Nightmare Years.*

"He says the Gestapo is now systematically bumping off the mentally deficient people of the Reich," Shirer wrote in his diary. "The Nazis call them 'mercy deaths.' He relates that Pastor Bodelschwingh, who runs a large hospital for various kinds of feeble-minded children at Bethel, was ordered arrested a few days ago because he refused to deliver up some of his more serious mental cases to the secret police....Must look into this story."

The program X knew of was an effort directed out of Hitler's Chancellery to gas Germany's mentally and physically disabled persons, including young children. It was run out of an office at Tiergartenstrasse 4 in Berlin—because of the address, it was known as the T-4 program. It began in the spring of 1939 and resulted in more than 70,000 murders. While it was happening, it was enough of an open secret in the country to be denounced by church leaders. X knew of it, but he also knew of the arrest several days before of Pastor Friedrich von Bodelschwingh.

While Shirer had heard reports of widespread murders in Poland after the 1939 invasion, now he was being told that the Nazis were also murdering the disabled, including children, perhaps on a large scale. While he makes very little in his diary about X's revelations beyond a single, one-paragraph entry—and he only referred to it in a footnote in his memoir—the news almost certainly strengthened his determination to leave Germany.

Meanwhile, the nightly British attacks on Berlin resumed and intensified, striking industrial and other targets in and around the city, setting fires that could be seen for miles. Shirer could not tell his listeners in the United States anything about them, and his broadcasts more and more took on the tone of a man reading heroic headlines from the German newspapers and from official communiqués, or relating the details of his interview with a German airman who had flown on a bombing raid over London.

The longest bombings of the war occurred the night of September 25, lasting from before midnight until 4:00 A.M. and hitting targets on the outskirts of the city. This time, just as Shirer finished his broadcast, the air warden in the broadcast center forced him down a flight of stairs to the cellar. With him were William Joyce and Joyce's wife, Margaret, and the three of them found their way to a tunnel beneath the building where they drank schnapps from a bottle Joyce had in his coat pocket. Shirer was amazed at how easily Joyce went about his life in Berlin working for the Nazis. Left alone by the warden, Shirer and the couple made their way back to Joyce's office to watch the bombardment.

As the bombing went on, Shirer quizzed Joyce about his loyalties. He found him an oddly likable man. "He argues that he has renounced his British nationality and become a German citizen, and that he is no more a traitor than thousands of British and Americans who renounced their citizenship to become comrades in the Soviet Union, or than those Germans who gave up their nationality after 1848 and fled to the United States.... He has a titanic hatred for Jews and an equally titanic one for capitalists," Shirer wrote in his diary. He referred in his diary to another English traitor, an actor named Jack Trevor, who also broadcast propaganda for the Germans, as also being consumed by hatred of the Jews.

Shirer was taken by Joyce's passion for National Socialism and his disregard for the consequences of his actions if the Germans were to lose the war. He acted as though he did not much care if the British hanged him for treason. He explained to Shirer that the Germans were involved in a "sacred struggle to free the world," an explanation Shirer found bizarre. There were three Americans working for the Propaganda Ministry—more would come later—and Shirer wrote their names down in his diary as if he were indicting them himself for high treason.

* * *

By mid-October, after weeks of unrelenting bombings of Berlin, Shirer made up his mind to return to Geneva to help Tess pack for the long bus trip across France to Spain and then Portugal. It was now or never, and his many hours spent thinking up scenarios by which, if the war worsened, his family could still get out had brought him nowhere. While Tess preferred to stay in Switzerland, Shirer worried that the Germans would refuse to sell the country coal to keep their homes warm. Food supplies had also been greatly restricted.

"Life in Switzerland this winter will be hard," he wrote.

As he planned for his family's leaving Geneva, he also solidified his own plans. "I shall follow in December," he wrote in his diary.

I think my usefulness here is about over. Until recently, despite the censorship, I think I've been able to do an honest job of reporting from Germany. But it has become increasingly difficult and at present it has become impossible.... You cannot call the Nazis 'Nazis' or an invasion an 'invasion.' You are reduced to re-broadcasting the official communiqués, which are lies, and which any automaton can do. Even the more intelligent and decent of my censors ask me, in confidence, why I stay.... With my deep, burning hatred of all that Nazism stands for, it has never been pleasant working and living here. But that was secondary as long as there was a job to do. No one's personal life in Europe counts any more, and I have had none since the war began.

On the morning of October 18, Shirer boarded a plane in Berlin that took him to Munich. From there he boarded a second plane that took off under thick clouds across the high, snow-covered Alps for Zurich. Once airborne, the passenger plane was approached by two German fighters, which flew close enough that Shirer was convinced they would touch the wings. He knew he would feel better, physically and emotionally, once he was out of German airspace, but getting there on this day was another matter.

Once the fighters had flown off, Shirer allowed himself a moment to breath a sigh of relief until, looking out the windows, he noticed that the plane had flown into thick clouds that obscured the sky above them and the high mountains below. How would the pilot find the Zurich airport? As the passengers held on for dear life, the pilot put the plane into a steep dive as he looked for a break in the clouds so he could determine where they were. Confused and lost, the pilot just as quickly put the plane into a steep climb, and all Shirer could imagine was the plane plowing into a mountain peak and exploding into flames.

When the plane seemed to turn back toward Munich, Shirer sank into his seat and tried to shake off feelings of deep gloom. "Then another plunge, this time a deep one, and suddenly it was dark and the thought that we were probably going to make an emergency landing in Germany depressed me, for a few minutes before, I had felt free of the Reich at last," he wrote in his diary. "Now we were diving at a steep angle. The pilot signaled to adjust the safety belt. I gripped the seat hard."

And then, just as suddenly, Shirer could see fog lights flashing on the ground, "and the familiar roof tops, and the city lights sparkling—this could be no city of blacked-out Germany, this could only be Zurich—and in a minute we were on hard ground," he wrote.

* * *

Five days after arriving home in Geneva, Shirer drove Tess and Eileen to a bus depot in the city. The morning was cold and clear. The people waiting to board were quiet, standing by their bags, emotional and frightened by what lay ahead in occupied France. Shirer had worked it out in his head that the bus would take two days and two nights to reach Barcelona. Once in Barcelona,

Tess and Eileen would board a train to Madrid, where they would change trains and proceed to Lisbon.

As they waited, the depot began to fill up with people clutching their belongings. Soon, by Shirer's estimate, a thousand men, women, and children waited anxiously to board two buses. At most perhaps one hundred would board. It would be another week before a bus was scheduled to leave Geneva for Spain. He overheard anxious conversations about flooding in the Pyrenees that had swept away roads. Would the buses leave at all? Shirer knew Tess should bring only a few belongings, but also food and water. There would be no stopping for food in France, no chancing encounters with German authorities demanding to look at identity papers. These were refugees, not tourists. The goal was to bring along enough gas—extra tanks were strapped to the sides of both buses—and to proceed as quickly as possible to the Spanish border.

Listening to the accents, Shirer discerned that hundreds of the people hoping to board the two small buses were German Jews. He was reminded of the Vienna airport on the night he flew to London to broadcast news of the *Anschluss*. Anxious, frightened Jews desperate to flee Austria had packed the terminal. Now, here in Geneva, he was seeing it all over again.

As Tess and Eileen and others began to board the buses, the mood in the vast crowd rose to near hysteria. People begged for seats. *Please! We need seats on the bus! Please!* Tess told her husband there were reports in Geneva that the French were turning over German Jews who had fled to France to the Gestapo—*without even being asked*. As he stood with his wife, holding his daughter in his arms, Shirer overheard a number of the Jews expressing great fear that, if they managed to get seats, the French might pull them off the buses and turn them over to the Germans. And what if they got through France, all the way south to the Spanish border, and the guards there removed the Jews and turned them over to the Germans?

If you get into Spain, you will be fine, Shirer told Tess. I will join you by Christmas, he reassured her.

A Warning from a Friend

With Tess and Eileen gone, Shirer's mood sank. He was overwhelmed with questions: What if the Germans stopped the buses and wouldn't let all the passengers proceed? What if they seized everyone on board and detained them indefinitely? Or sent all the passengers to Germany? Two buses overflowing with refugees—running *away* from the Germans—seemed like a set-up for problems. What he hoped for was that the buses would proceed across France to the frontier with Spain without any German or French officials demanding to know who was on board. That seemed an impossible wish. Surely a moral issue lay at the heart of Shirer's worries, one that had an echo to Shirer and the other correspondents living and working in Berlin and watching the government harass and disenfranchise the country's Jews, seeing it all happen in front of them: that Tess and Eileen would get through, but that all the Jews on the buses would be seized and, in front of them, removed and taken away.

Shirer's friend Joe Harsch joined him in Geneva the day after the buses departed, and the two took the train to Bern, where they hoped to catch a flight to Berlin, a city of gloom and darkness and everything Shirer loathed. Shirer stared out the windows, enjoying the sunlight and the snow-covered mountains, knowing the landscape would turn dark when he crossed into Nazi Germany, as if a black curtain dropped at the frontier. In Bern he and Harsch boarded flight that, to their horror, landed in a thick fog in Munich and was ordered grounded, unable to proceed to Berlin. Shirer, frustrated and impatient, decided not to wait for authorities to clear the plane for takeoff, so the two men bought seats on the night train for Berlin, risking, once again, attacks by British fighters.

With hours to kill before the train left, the two men wandered the city's beer halls, where National Socialism had taken root and where it had staged the failed coup in November 1923. Three days later, in Berlin on October 28, Shirer made two diary entries. The first, "No word from Tess," revealed his worry five days after his wife's and daughter's departure from Switzerland. The second showed his great relief: "Cable from Tess from Barcelona. Arrived there all well. She wired in German. Suppose that's the most politic foreign language to use there now."

The trip had gone smoothly across France until the buses tried to cross the Pyrenees into Spain. There, French authorities removed the German Jews from the two buses and prevented them from entering Spain. Everyone else on the buses sat in their seats and watched it transpire. If Shirer was horrified at the news of passengers being questioned and the Jews removed, he did not note it in his diary.

* * *

In Berlin, Shirer bided his time. There was no need to rock the boat, to push a grievance with the censors. It was time to bite his tongue. He hoped to be gone in early December, and the very last thing he wanted was to draw the scrutiny of the authorities. He did not want to be questioned at the broadcast center or stopped on a street corner or while walking in the Tiergarten. Worse would be to have his room at the Adlon Hotel searched. *What's this, Mr. Shirer? You met with someone you called X in your hotel room? It's right here in your diary.* Suspicions would lead to delays in his departure. As the days passed, he felt more and more anxious that something would trip him up.

Before he had left for Geneva to see Tess and Eileen off, a "close friend" who worked at the RRG had pulled him aside and whispered that he was being watched. Even before this Shirer had felt that he was under surveillance. After his return from Switzerland, the same person, a woman, told him of the contents of highly confidential cables sent from the German consulate in Washington to the Propaganda Ministry in Berlin that mentioned Shirer's name. She was sufficiently high up in the ministry, or on the staff at the broadcast house, that she had read them. She explained what was in them and went further to detail the reaction to them in Berlin.

"She was worried," Shirer wrote more than forty years later in the third installment of his memoirs. "The Gestapo, the Propaganda Ministry, the Foreign Office and even the military, she said, were beginning to build a case of espionage against me."

While she had been somewhat circumspect in their previous conversations, she now told him that he should leave Berlin "soon—while there was still time. Specifically, she said, the German embassy in Washington and especially the military attaché there, were cabling that they were convinced I was a spy and that I was getting out secret intelligence by use of code words in my broadcasts. She also told me the Gestapo was increasing its surveillance of me, and that I should be careful whom I saw, including her. I trusted her—one of the few Germans I did. All the more reason I dared not confide her warnings to my New York office or even to my diary, for fear of jeopardizing her very life....I had no intention of letting the Nazis frame me as a spy."

By early November, Shirer's plans to leave the country in a month had firmed up to the point that his mood shifted dramatically. He confidently wrote in his diary on November 5: "If all goes well, I shall leave here a month from today, flying all the way to New York—by Lufthansa plane from here to Lisbon, by Clipper from there to New York. The very prospect of leaving here takes a terrible load off your heart and mind. I feel swell. It will be my first Christmas at home in sixteen years."

To relax, Shirer went to whatever musical venues he could find in the city, including a performance of a Bach concerto conducted by Wilhelm Furtwängler. When he returned to his room at the Adlon, before writing in his diary about the day's events, Shirer played an accordion he kept with him until someone banged on the wall for him to stop. He followed the news in the United States as best he could, feeling a great sense of relief when President Roosevelt was elected to a third term. Shirer knew from Nazi officials that the Berlin government was hoping Wendell Willkie would win.

Nearly every night, the British bombed in and around Berlin, or in other German cities. Late in November, Shirer went to a dinner in a suburb in southwest Berlin. Two "well-known German figures" were there, one of them a "high Nazi official," presumably from the German broadcast system. The two officials told jokes about Goebbels, "whom they both appeared to loathe." Later in the evening, British bombers appeared overhead, and a wave of explosions rocked the city. One landed close by, and Shirer and other guests dived into a bedroom in panic.

Soon his plans had solidified to the point that he marked a date on his calendar for his departure: December 5. To leave the country, he would need an exit visa, which had to be stamped by the Foreign Office, the Gestapo, and customs officials. He also needed entrance visas for Spain and Portugal. Providing he received all the approvals he needed, there was the issue of his diaries and papers. He had begun packing his personal documents in large trunks, along with books and other property, but knew the trunks would be inspected, first by the Gestapo and later by customs officials at Tempelhof.

In his room at the Adlon on nights after his broadcasts, Shirer carefully separated those papers he was unwilling to pack in the trunks and risk having seized. Some he burned in the fireplace, a task that pained him greatly. Others he took to friends in foreign embassies, asking them to pack the papers in diplomatic pouches for confidential shipment out of Germany. Shirer hoped he could get them later, but there were no guarantees. As far as he knew, the Gestapo might search these pouches too or might have spies in the embassies who read them. He knew for certain that taking a chance that his most important papers would be seized when he tried to fly out of the country was even riskier. Better to lose some than all of them.

Some days, before he went to the broadcast center he walked in the Tiergarten, a beautiful place he was certain he would miss and hoped one day he could return to in a different Germany. He looked at people's faces and listened in on their conversations, hoping to take with him on his departure something that could help him remember the people themselves and how they lived under the Nazis. He walked by the building where he and Tess had first lived when they arrived in Berlin in 1934. Some nights after his work was completed, he went to the Taverne and sat by himself at the bar, looking at the corner of the restaurant where the foreign correspondents had once gathered to talk and drink and eat. Now it was empty, everyone he had worked with gone or expelled or reassigned back to the United States. Sigrid Schultz was still there, as were a few others, most of whom he had fallen out of favor with, and he alone knew he would be departing from Berlin soon. It was his secret, never to be divulged.

The nightly bombings concerned him. What if the runways at Tempelhof were destroyed? He calculated over and over in his head that he would take the train to Munich or another German city and fly out from there. It was all so iffy, though. All his plans depended on so many moving parts that a single night of bombings, a refusal from a government office, and the whole contraption could crash down. Hanging over all of it was the fear, growing each day, that he would be arrested and jailed until the Germans wanted to trade him for someone picked up in the United States. That could be months, or years. He shivered at the thought.

Through it all, he worked, reporting to the broadcast house daily, talking to officials, attending press conferences, speaking with Murrow on the phone and sending cables to Paul White in New York. Toward the end of November, when he hoped he would be gone in less than two weeks, he attended a dinner at a diplomat's house. When the phone rang, the butler informed Shirer that the caller had asked for him. It was "one of the girls at the Rundfunk saying that the British bombers were ten minutes away and that I had better hurry if I wanted to broadcast that evening."

He ran to his car and began the arduous drive toward central Berlin. He drove past air wardens wildly waving their arms for him to get off the street.

Less than two miles from the broadcast center, he heard the air sirens sound. His first thought was to pull off, kill the lights in the car, and wait it out. But he continued. Driving by uniformed police officers waving their lamps at him, he negotiated the cars that had stopped in the road until he was blocks from the center. Then he abandoned the car and ran the final distance.

Before the end of November, Shirer reached out to whoever would speak to him and might know about what the source X had told him of "mercy killings" of the mentally and physically disabled. "How many have been executed probably only Himmler and a handful of Nazi chieftains know," he wrote in his diary. "A conservative and trustworthy German tells me he estimates the number at a hundred thousand. I think that figure is too high. But certain it is that the figure runs into the thousands and is going up every day."

Shirer said he was informed of the existence of "peculiar death notices" running in small-town newspapers across the country. The places of death in these notices were all the same—"the chief headquarters for the 'mercy killings.' I am also informed that the relatives of the unfortunate victims, when they get the ashes back—they are never given the bodies—receive a stern warning from the secret police not to demand explanations and not to 'spread false rumors.'"

Another German—Shirer again labeled him X—told him "that relatives are rushing to get their kin out of private asylums and out of the clutches of the authorities." As to why the Germans were doing the killings, Shirer ventured three guesses: to save food, to experiment on how to kill large numbers of people with poison gas, and because the deaths fit Nazi philosophy. Shirer wrote that he doubted the second explanation but accepted the third. As he noted in a footnote to his published diaries, word of the "mercy killings" spread outside Germany, and, on December 6, 1940, the Vatican condemned them.

As December arrived, Shirer wrote longer and longer entries in his diaries that read more like essays, summing up his years in Germany and all that he had learned about the German people. He saw the Germans as deeply flawed—they wanted security and would give up their freedom to someone who provided it for them—and were willing and eager to go along with Nazi plans for conquest. Shirer did not buy the notion that Hitler had corrupted an entire nation but wrote that Hitler as the all-powerful leader of a police state made it all possible.

"It is not correct to say, as many of our liberals at home have said, that Nazism is a form of rule and life unnatural to the German people and forced upon them against their wish by a few fanatical derelicts of the last war. It is true that the Nazi party never polled a majority vote in Germany in a free election, though it came very close. But for the last three or four years the Nazi regime has expressed something very deep in the German nature and in that respect it has been representative of the people it rules."

Of the German people, he wrote, "Almost joyfully, almost masochistically, they have turned to an authoritarianism which releases them from the strain of individual decision and choice and thought and allows them what to a German is a luxury—letting someone else make the decisions and take the risks, in return for which they gladly give their own obedience.... The German has two characters. As an individual he will give his rationed bread to feed the squirrels in the Tiergarten on a Sunday morning. He can be a kind and considerate person. But as a unit in the Germanic mass he can persecute Jews, torture and murder his fellow men in concentration camps, massacre women and children by bombing and bombardment, overrun without the slightest justification the lands of other peoples, cut them down if they protest, and enslave them."

* * *

Shirer counted the days and the hours until he would leave Germany. He went to several events and parties, some held in government offices with officials he had worked with since being hired by Murrow. He was there to say goodbye, even if he could not tell anyone. By December 3, the Foreign Ministry had still not approved his exit visa. He did his last broadcast that night, going home to the Adlon Hotel with a great feeling of anticipation that he was on the eve of his departure, but he also worried that something would come out of nowhere and ruin his plans. The thought of having to stay in Germany, with his family now en route to the United States, sickened him to the bone. A wave of nostalgia came over him as he waited for all the approvals he needed. Good luck and a strong sense of his own fate had followed his every step. He had been in Europe since he was twenty-one years old. He concluded that "it was here, on the old continent, through a decade and a half, that I had really grown up and come to feel at home."

On the morning of December 4, word reached him that his paperwork was complete. His passport and exit visa had been stamped, and he was now free to leave the country. "Nothing to do now but pack," he wrote in his diary with the joy of someone who saw his plans coming together just as he had hoped.

His pal from Chicago, Wally Deuel, had also received his official paperwork to leave the country. Deuel planned to fly out of Tempelhof on December 4, a day ahead of Shirer, but lost his nerve when the weather turned cold and icy. Further alarming Deuel, three passenger planes had crashed in as many weeks because of ice and snow, killing everyone aboard. Deuel could not bear the thought of climbing aboard a big plane at Tempelhof and risking his life, so when the weather turned for the worse, he left Berlin for Stuttgart by train, hoping to escape the weather and find a city from which it was safe to fly.

"Hope I have better luck," Shirer wrote in his diary, the same day he learned that his paperwork had been approved. "I must leave all my books and most of my clothes here, as baggage accommodation on the plane is limited. Ed Murrow promises to meet me at Lisbon. My last night in a blackout. After tonight the lights…and civilization!"

Now that he had his exit visa, Shirer had one day to come up with a way to save his most precious paperwork—his diaries, his letters and correspondence, official and personal, along with clippings, postcards, cables, telegrams, pocket diaries, calendars, restaurant and hotel receipts, tourist brochures, and book reviews. He'd made carbons of so many letters that he needed boxes for all of them. Some pages of his diaries he had already burned, others he had given to friends in the Swedish and American embassies.

He worried most about the diaries. They were, of all his property, the most important to him. "There was enough in them to get me hanged—if the Gestapo ever discovered them," he wrote.

In his room at the Adlon, Shirer came up with a plan to store all his papers in two big trunks. He placed the most important pages of his diaries at the bottom of each trunk. On top of them he stacked pages of his broadcast scripts, all marked with the distinctive stamps of the censors. They looked official, acceptable. Shirer hoped the Gestapo or customs authorities at the airport would see the stamps and not go any further. On top of the scripts he placed military maps he had acquired during the invasion of the Low Countries and France, all of which he had acquired from high-ranking officers. Like the stamped scripts, they were official and, Shirer hoped, would suggest to someone who opened the trunks that the owner had high-ranking friends.

When he was done packing, he picked up the phone in the room and called Gestapo headquarters on the Alexanderplatz. "I have a couple of suitcases full of my dispatches, broadcasts and notes that I am taking out of the country," Shirer explained. "I am flying off at dawn tomorrow from Tempelhof. There will be no time for officials at the airport to go over the contents. Could you take a look now, if I brought them over? And put a seal on the trunks so I won't be held up at the airport?"

"Bring them over and we'll take a look," the official said.

When Shirer hung up the phone, he felt a shiver of panic. He was certain that, by walking into Gestapo headquarters and asking them to approve his trunks for shipment out of the country, he was inviting his own demise. The Gestapo would surely find his diaries. "That would be the end of me," Shirer wrote. "Maybe I had just better begin to flush them down the can."

Rejecting that idea, Shirer hoped the Gestapo would take the military maps—*Who do you think you are, trying to take these out of the country?*—but stop when they saw the stamped broadcast scripts. "Nothing impressed German cops more than official stamps, especially by the military.... That would make a Gestapo official sit up and take notice. It would give me prestige in his eyes, or at least make me less suspect, foreigner though I was. I was going to gamble on their inspection ending there, before they dug deeper....I was going to gamble too that they were not high enough up to be aware of exactly who I was, and that when they learned, I would be out of the country, out of their reach."

On the afternoon of December 4, Shirer hailed a cab and lugged the two trunks to the Alexanderplatz. Inside Gestapo headquarters two men opened up the trunks and, as Shirer had hoped, were shocked by the sight of military maps that had been the property of the High Command. Having gone over the routine in his head a hundred times, Shirer apologized profusely, acting as though he had been caught off guard and shocked at his own stupidity. *I am so sorry. I forgot they were in there.* He explained his role covering the German Sixth Army's great advance into France.

I shouldn't be taking those out of the country, he explained, and handed them over to the two officials.

"What else you got in here?" one of the men asked, reaching deeper into the trunk.

"The texts of my broadcasts," Shirer said, pointing out the official stamps from the High Command and the Foreign and Propaganda Ministries. He could see how impressed the officials were. It all looked so official and gave the contents of the trunk, at least the part the two men were looking over, the appearance of acceptability. Each man leaned over the suitcases examining the stamps on the scripts.

"I felt myself beginning to perspire," Shirer wrote. "I had deliberately got myself into this jam. What a fool!"

"You reported on the German army?" one of the men inquired.

Smiling, embracing the German victories, Shirer said, "All the way to Paris and to the armistice at Compiègne. A great army it was, and a great story for me. It will go down in history!"

The two men were done. The officials wrapped the two trunks with tape and marked their own stamps on them. Shirer thanked them and carried the two trunks out to the street. Standing on the curb, he felt a wave of relief pass over him. When the cab came, he told the driver to go to Tempelhof, where he carried the trunks inside and checked them in at the luggage room, telling officials there that he would be back in the morning for a flight to Spain.

Shirer awoke before sun-up the next morning, December 5. His exhaustion was severe, as if he had not slept in weeks or maybe longer, maybe all the way back to August 1934 when he first arrived on the train in Berlin and was greeted by the Gestapo. Weeks of bombing attacks on the city, months of arguments with the censors, running through the streets to avoid falling shrapnel, riding with a triumphant army into France—it had drained him completely, as if the only things left in his body were old bones.

Sitting on the edge of the bed, he could feel the fatigue and the stress in his body and the lingering effects of too many whiskeys over the previous nights. He'd lived too long like this and he wanted it to end, finally, on this day. Peering out his hotel window into the blackness of a Berlin night, he was shocked to see that a snowstorm had come up during the night, whipped by strong winds. It could only spell trouble at the airport. For a moment he felt his hopes, pinned on an easy exit, disappear. He was determined to make a go of it. So he cleaned up and changed his clothes and grabbed his suitcase. As he walked through the handsome lobby of the Adlon Hotel, he could not help but feel that it had been a welcoming place for a man doing the sort of work he did. When he reached the street, he stepped into a blizzard. A cab pulled up, and he told the driver to do his best to get to Tempelhof.

"As my taxi skidded through the familiar route to Tempelhof I wondered if my plane would take off in such weather," Shirer wrote years later. "If the flight was canceled it might mean I would be stuck here for weeks. The plane to Madrid and Lisbon was booked weeks ahead."

When he reached the airport, he saw that others were there to board planes out of Germany. Couples stood off by themselves whispering to each other. Some looked worried that the weather would not improve and the plane would be grounded and they'd be forced to return to their homes. That was all Shirer thought as he went to the luggage room to retrieve the two trunks he'd dropped off the day before. A porter threw them on a cart, along with Shirer's suitcases, which held the few clothes he was leaving with and a handful of books. Now he had to pass through customs, and, once again, he needed a lucky break so the officials would not open up the two trunks, sealed with tape by the Gestapo, and take away his diaries and him along with them.

A customs official, wearing the insignia of the Gestapo, went through the luggage first, and then told Shirer to open the two trunks.

"I can't," Shirer said. "They're sealed—by the Gestapo."

"Where were those bags sealed?" the official asked.

"At Gestapo headquarters at the Alexanderplatz," Shirer said.

While one official told Shirer to wait, a second picked up a phone. When the man hung up, he picked up a piece of chalk and marked both trunks as approved to leave the country. A porter helped Shirer get the luggage and two trunks to the Lufthansa counter.

"Where to?" the man at the counter asked.

"To Lisbon," Shirer said.

Once the bags were weighed and checked, Shirer sat in the terminal with the others and waited out the weather. Soon the sun was up, revealing the white, windblown landscape. The runways were thick with fresh snow. He knew from years of travel that the tower would not clear his airplane to take off without some visibility. He recalled Wally Deuel refusing to fly out of Berlin in bad weather for fear of icing and the plane going down. Shirer couldn't decide which was worse, taking off in a blizzard and risking a crash or having to stay behind in Germany for days or weeks or, God knows, maybe months.

Fighting off the tension, Shirer went to the cafeteria and ordered coffee and breakfast and sat in a corner, brooding. "I started to glance at the morning papers I had bought automatically on arriving at the airport," Shirer wrote. "I usually picked up first Hitler's own paper, the *Völkischer Beobachter*, full of propaganda though devoid of news. It gave the Nazi line, as the Führer himself probably determined it. I glanced at the front page. The usual bullshit. I tossed it down on the table."

He thought: *I don't have to read this trash anymore.* "I had only to hold out this one more day, and the whole nightmare for me would be over," he wrote.

Worried, he watched the snow until finally, for no reason that seemed connected to any improvement in the weather, his flight was called. He walked to the windows and could see workers loading the baggage into the airplane. Bundling up against the cold and snow, he crossed the tarmac and found his seat on the plane, and in a few minutes the engine hummed and the propellers turned. As the plane lifted off the snowy runway, Shirer could make out the house where he and Tess had lived. He closed his eyes and hoped for the best.

As planned, the plane's route was to be Berlin to Stuttgart, then on to Lyon, Marseille, and Barcelona. It was an all-day flight in a Junkers thirty-two-seat passenger plane in good weather. Shirer kept track of the day by writing diary updates on scraps of paper and on the pages of his datebook. En route to Stuttgart, Shirer stared out the cabin windows and watched as the wings iced over, along with both starboard engines. "The stewardess, though she tried to hide it bravely, got frightened, and when a stewardess on a plane gets frightened, so do I," he wrote.

A Lufthansa official seated next to Shirer, staring out his window at the ice building on the wings, had sweat pouring down his face. "Clumps of ice breaking off from the motors hurled against the side of the cabin with a terrifying crack," Shirer wrote. "The pilot, hardly able to control the plane, tried to climb, but the ice was too heavy."

As the pilot tried to control his plane, he turned it around, dropping lower and lower in hopes of finding warmer air that would melt the ice coating the wings. The Lufthansa official, Shirer wrote, turned to him. "Can't go any lower or we'll hit a mountain," he said. "Can't use the radio because the blizzard blots it out."

Stammering, Shirer said, "Perhaps we could land some place."

"Not around here," the man said. "Ground visibility is zero."

With the weight of the ice only growing, the plane kept falling, and, as he looked out his window, Shirer could see a section of autobahn below them. Then, suddenly, the pilot dropped even farther and a runway came up under him, and he put the plane down on snowy asphalt. He had landed the Junkers at the Dresden airport. The passengers were escorted off the plane and into the terminal, where Shirer found a seat in a small cafeteria, his hands shaking and his stomach twisted into knots. Lowering his head almost to the table, he felt lucky to be alive. He pictured Tess receiving a telegram in America from the airline informing her that her husband, William L. Shirer, had been aboard a flight that iced over and crashed into a mountain, all passengers burned beyond recognition. *Nothing could be found of his body or property, Mrs. Shirer.*

The next day, December 6, the plane took off in significantly improved weather. Shirer's mood brightened as he came to believe he would soon be out of German airspace and away from the Nazis. The plane flew from Stuttgart to Lyon, where it landed to refuel. The airfield was dotted with German military aircraft. On a far side of the field sat a row of French military airplanes, unused in the battle six months earlier.

Seated near Shirer, an official from the German Foreign Office who saw the German warplanes on the ground shouted, for all the passengers to hear, "*La Belle France!* And how we've destroyed her. For three hundred years at least!"

Airborne again, the plane flew over the Pyrenees and down the Spanish coast. From his seat, to his great joy, Shirer could see Lloret de Mar, the tiny fishing village where he and Tess had lived after he had been fired by the *Chicago Tribune*. The plane landed in Barcelona, and Shirer walked to the terminal to stretch his legs and look around. He had not been in the city since he and Tess lived on the Spanish coast, and he remembered it as a joyous place. Now, Fascism had brought nothing but misery. A horsedrawn wagon—there was no gas or oil for automobiles—took Shirer and other passengers to the Ritz Hotel, and along the way he saw frightened, hungry faces. A man he encountered told him that Barcelona and Spain had been crushed. "There is no food. There is no organization. The jails are jammed and overflowing. If we told you about the filth, the overcrowding, the lack of food in them, you would not believe us. But no one really eats any more. We merely keep alive."

When Shirer returned to the airport after a brief meal at the hotel and after going to the Swedish embassy to collect the diaries he had entrusted to a friend who had flown with them from Berlin to Barcelona, he and the other passengers were met by Spanish officials who ordered them into a tiny, airless room. "The chief of police has not washed his hands for a week," Shirer wrote. "His main preoccupation is our money. We count over and over for him our silver, our paper money, our travel checks. Finally, as darkness falls, he lets us go."

As Shirer waited, Wally Deuel stepped off a plane from Stuttgart and joined him in the terminal. He told a horror story of being delayed in Stuttgart because his exit visa had run out. Believing he would not be able to leave Germany for weeks if not months, Deuel finally persuaded a police official to issue him a new exit visa. Deuel was exhausted, frustrated, and, like Shirer, desperate to get out of Germany, through Spain to Portugal, and onto a boat to the United States. The following day, December 7, Shirer, Deuel, and dozens of other passengers boarded a Lufthansa flight from Barcelona to Madrid. There they were met by chaos. It seemed as though the airport was run by a mob of uniformed idiots, bullies, and government hacks with their hands out. Nothing worked, nothing ran on time. Men shouted orders to each other, and no one did anything in response. Airport authorities grounded the flight to Lisbon, and Shirer sank into a chair, believing he had come all this way only to be stuck in the hell of Franco's Spain.

"Then they decided one of three scheduled flights could be made to Lisbon," Shirer wrote. "They told me I could go, then that I couldn't go, then that I must catch the 4:00 P.M. train, then that the train had left. All the while shouting officials and passengers milled about the place. There was a restaurant but it had no food. In the end they called the passengers for the Lisbon plane. Only a group of Spanish officials and the German diplomat would be allowed to go. I asked for my baggage. No one knew where it was. Then an official came tearing up to me and tugged me towards a plane."

The plane at last took off for Lisbon. There, Portuguese officials told Shirer he could go no further since he did not have a ticket to leave the country en route to the United States. After hours of argument, they relented, and Shirer proceeded to the Lufthansa counter, where to his relief he found his trunks had arrived from Berlin intact, the Gestapo tape and seals still affixed to them. It seemed like a final piece of good luck on the long night of his German journey. He was so happy that he did not care any longer if the Portuguese authorities told him he could not leave the country. He collected his belongings and took a cab into the heart of the city, where every hotel overflowed with refugees. They occupied hotel lobbies and bars and crowded the streets, speaking a host of languages from countries under German occupation.

The driver turned west to the resort town of Estoril, where Shirer, exhausted to the bone, found a room in an oceanfront hotel. "I still felt so elated I would have gladly slept on the beach," he wrote years later. "I washed up, changed my shirt, had a good dinner—a local wine the waiter recommended was excellent—and spent the evening strolling through the town and along the beach, staring at the lights. They seemed so blinding—and beautiful—after a year and a half in blacked-out Berlin."

When he returned to his room, desperate for sleep, the phone rang. "It was Ed Murrow in London. He had been trying to get me in every hotel in Portugal. He had wangled a seat on a plane that would be arriving the next afternoon. 'We need to talk,' he said, 'and toss down a few, before you go.'"

* * *

At midnight the next day, Murrow's plane dropped out of the darkness over the ocean and landed in Lisbon. He had left London in spite of the war, pushing away fears that his plane would never get across open ocean to Portugal. Shirer knew it was a great compliment to him that Murrow would attempt such a trip. Waiting for him like an anxious older brother was Shirer, who'd arrived hours before to make sure he was there whenever the plane, on a route away from London and occupied France, landed safely. Murrow's plane had left London after darkness had fallen, following night after night of heavy bombing, fires burning across the city like giant torches, so that Murrow could join his friend. Shirer could imagine Murrow gripping his seat as the plane lifted off and turned away from London to fly south, his colleague peering out the small cabin windows to see if German bombers were airborne over London.

They had grown exceptionally fond of one another. One had endured the bombings in Berlin, the other the all-out German assault on London. Shirer knew Murrow had thrown caution to the wind and broadcast live accounts of the attacks, something Shirer was not allowed to do in Berlin. During one broadcast from the street, Murrow's office had been destroyed; soon after arriving in Portugal, a telegram brought word that his new office had been destroyed by bombs. Both men tempted fate, but it was Murrow who risked death each night the Germans appeared overhead.

As Murrow stepped off the plane, Shirer happily looked him over. Murrow wore an elegant English suit under an overcoat to ward off the chilly night air, his dark hair slicked back away from his handsome face, a cigarette in his fingers. Seeing his friend, perhaps Shirer was reminded of their first meeting, when Murrow summoned Shirer to the Adlon Hotel for martinis and dinner to talk about Shirer's coming to work for CBS. Murrow had taken a chance on Shirer, and Shirer knew it. Despite the hour and the deep fatigue felt by both men, they stayed up the rest of the night, seated on the outside terrace of a seaside café, talking about their lives and the war. Shirer spoke about the remarkable French collapse, a subject he never tired of, and one that fascinated him nearly above all else. He spoke of being at Compiègne and broadcasting live to America as the surrender papers were signed, and of Paris, its streets empty, and the sight of Germans marching behind a drum corps in the shadow of the Arc de Triomphe. Hitler in Paris! When the sky brightened to the east, they got up and went to their rooms. They slept in. After a late breakfast, they visited one of the local casinos and gambled.

Murrow's goal before Shirer boarded a ship for the United States was for both men to do a broadcast from Lisbon. During the day, they sat in Shirer's hotel room and typed out drafts of scripts until they agreed on one. Murrow had spoken to Portuguese authorities prior to his arrival and believed they would approve the broadcast, but at the appointed time of 2:00 A.M., they had not given their consent. When 4:00 A.M. passed without official approval, it looked as if Murrow would have to cable CBS and tell him they could not go on the air.

As they waited impatiently for the government to okay the broadcast, Shirer tried to purchase a ticket on the Pan American Clipper but was told the seaplane could not take off because of bad weather. Unwilling to wait and eager to be home with Tess and Eileen by Christmas, he inquired about a berth on a passenger ship, the SS *Excambion*. It was scheduled to depart Lisbon on December 13. If all went well—if the weather improved, and if a German submarine did not order them to halt on the high seas—he would just make his Christmas deadline. But he had to get on board the ship first.

A large crowd of refugees—well-dressed men and women with their belongings in suitcases and trunks, families with young children, single men and women traveling by themselves, groups of unsupervised children—were hoping to board the ship for the United States. It could take only one hundred and fifty passengers, and Shirer was determined to be one of them. He went to the ship's onshore offices to introduce himself to the local manager, who told him he would try to get him aboard but that Shirer might not have a bed to sleep on for the crossing. More than three thousand refugees were jostling for room on the boat. Some begged, others pleaded and offered bribes. Shirer knew that the Duke and Duchess of Windsor, he the former king of England, had left Lisbon a few months earlier on the *Excambion's* sister ship, the *Excalibur*. Lisbon had become something of a stepping-off point for well-off refugees fleeing the Germans. In his own way, by his own actions, Shirer was one of them, and he vowed he would sleep on the ship's deck if he had to.

Murrow and Shirer spent the next two nights dining together and visiting the casino. They found the gaming rooms "full of a weird assortment of human beings, German and British spies, male and female, wealthy refugees who had mysteriously managed to get a lot of money out and were throwing it about freely, other refugees who were obviously broke and were trying to win their passage money in a few desperate gambles with the fickle roulette wheel, and the usual international sharpsters you find at such places. Neither Ed nor I had any luck at roulette and we adjourned to the ballroom, where the same kind of people were trying to drown whatever feelings they had in drink and jazz."

On the night of December 12, the two men sat up until well after midnight believing the authorities would let them do their joint broadcast. They sent their script over to the censor, who phoned them at midnight to say he was having a hard time translating it and perhaps he would be done next week. Angry and frustrated, the two men went back and forth with the censor and the CBS office in New York and, when nothing came of it, gave up and left the studio and went to bed in their hotel rooms.

December 13, a Friday, dawned cold and breezy, fitting weather for a gloomy man to board a ship that would take him across the ocean. The two men spent the day together, both quiet and sad, knowing Shirer would have to be at the dock by sundown to board the ship. In his diary, Shirer let out his emotions: "All day both of us depressed at leaving, for we have worked together very closely, Ed and I, during the last turbulent years over here and a bond grew that was very real, a kind you make only a few times in your life, and somehow, absurdly no doubt, sentimentally perhaps, we had a presentiment that the fortunes of war, maybe just a little bomb, would make this reunion the last."

At the dock the ship sat at its berth, waiting to take its passengers to a world far different from the one it was about to leave. Walking through the crowd, Shirer counted fifty refugee children, mostly French, but some Austrians, Czechs, and Poles. They ranged in age from six to twelve and would be sleeping on mattresses or cots in an empty room on board. They were the face of Europe at war, and he could not help but think of Tess and Eileen fleeing the Continent and reaching safety in America. He wondered who these children were and what had happened to their families. "Their parents are either dead or left behind in a Europe shivering and half starving," he wrote in his diary. "Probably most of them will never see father or mother again."

There was also a group of young Norwegian women; a philosopher from Brussels on his way to a teaching position at the New School in New York City; an American recently released by the Gestapo in France; a group of Jews, "some still showing their suffering, some confident again"; and some American businessmen. Shirer and Murrow walked along the dock, talking, pausing at a dockside bar used by workers, where a woman poured strong drinks into cups.

When darkness settled over the port, and just as the gangway was being pulled up, Shirer paused, stared at Murrow for a long, sad moment, and reached out and hugged him tightly. "I climbed aboard and Ed disappeared into the night," he wrote in his diary.

Under a full moon, the sea sparkled. Shirer stood at the rail of the ship and watched it pull away from the coastline, the lights of Lisbon slowly fading away. Seated in a chair on the deck, wrapped in a blanket to ward off the damp cold, he wrote a few parting thoughts in his diary. "Beyond Lisbon over almost all of Europe the lights were out. This little fringe on the southwest corner of the Continent kept them burning. Civilization, such as it was, had not yet been stamped out by a Nazi boot. But next week? Next month? The month after? Would not Hitler's hordes take this too and extinguish the last lights?"

When he finished, he went to the ship's bar, where five other American correspondents, including Wally Deuel, were celebrating their return home. They ordered a round of a favorite drink called an old-fashioned and toasted their good fortune that they would be in the United States for Christmas. But Shirer was restless, and the toasts felt awkward, out of place. Hoping he might see Europe in the distance, he went back up on the deck. It was there, he wrote, but "a long, dark, savage night had now settled over it."

THE RUINS

If Shirer thought life moved in a circle, bringing the traveler back to the beginning of his story, then he knew with certainty that he would one day return to Berlin. He had become William L. Shirer there, and this alone would draw him back. His story needed an ending. He did not know when he would return, but he would—he was sure of that—and he also knew that Germany would be destroyed before he returned. There would be very little left of it. How else to excise the evil? The country and its people had to pay for bringing Hitler to power. The *people* were guilty. Their history brought them to Hitler. These were beliefs he would carry with him for the rest of his life. When he was in his eighties and in poor health, Shirer would make one final trip to Germany to speak his mind.

* * *

On a cold late-fall day in November 1945, four years and eleven months after he had left, Shirer looked out the windows of a military plane at the destroyed city of Berlin below. "And as far as you can see in all directions, a great wilderness of debris, dotted with roofless burnt-out buildings that look like mousetraps with the low autumn sun shining through the spaces where windows had been," he wrote in *A Native's Return: 1945-1988*, the final installment of his memoirs.

He was not the same man he had been on the day he left, when he was fearful of his own arrest and worried that the Gestapo would seize his diaries. Those people had been destroyed, their leaders dead or imprisoned. He was still a CBS newsman, but he was also the author of *Berlin Diary*, published in 1941 and based on the diaries he had smuggled out of Germany. The book sold

600,000 copies in a year. In part because of the success of the book, CBS had kept him on staff and given him a Sunday morning news and analysis show on the radio, in spite of the view held by Paul White that Shirer should not have left Berlin.

With his CBS friend and colleague Howard K. Smith, Shirer wandered the mountains of rubble in Berlin for several days. When he tried to sum up his feelings in the pages of his diary after a long day of examining the remains of government buildings, Shirer could hardly sum up the moment. "How can you find words to convey the picture of a great capital destroyed almost beyond recognition; of a once mighty nation that has ceased to exist?"

In a borrowed US Army jeep, the two set out to find familiar streets and buildings, but so little remained whole that it was nearly impossible. The famous landmarks were gone. "The building on the Tauentzienstrasse, between the Wittenbergplatz and the Gedächtniskirche, where on our arrival in Berlin in 1934 Tess and I had rented on the top two floors a spacious studio from a Jewish couple, he a sculptor and she an art historian, had been bombed to the ground level," he wrote.

Berlin's major squares, where broad, handsome boulevards had once come together, had been obliterated; the stores Shirer had frequented, such as the K.D.W. department store, but also the pubs and restaurants and cafés, were gone. The huge multi-story department store, which was within walking distance from the Shirers' apartment, had been owned by Jews and turned over to "Aryan" owners after 1933. An Allied bomber crashed into it in 1943. Nearby, only the stately columns remained of the big Protestant church "where the Kurfürstendamm turns half-right into the Tauentzienstrasse, my old street." Great hotels, movie houses, the trendy shops along the Kurfürstendamm were all rubble. Lines of women wearing rags and looking like convicts in a chain gang piled bricks so paths could be cleared. The city looked as if the war had ended yesterday, not seven months ago.

They found the Adlon Hotel battered but standing, the nearby American embassy nothing but rubble. Someone with a sense of optimism about the German future had tacked a sign on the door of the Adlon advertising a tea service at five o'clock in the afternoon. Shirer and Smith climbed over the rubble and walked down a flight of stairs to what had been a bomb shelter. There, like actors on the stage, Shirer found "veteran waiters I had known and Jimmy the barman, all three dressed in tattered dinner jackets." When they emerged, the light was almost gone from the sky, and a deep darkness had settled over the blasted landscape. They walked down the Wilhelmstrasse where government buildings and Hitler's Chancellery had once stood, now nothing at all but mountains upon mountains of bricks and debris. A stern Russian soldier stood guard in front of the ruins of the Chancellery, under which in his Führerbunker Hitler had killed himself on April 30, 1945.

Writing in his diary, parts of which later became a book titled *End of a Berlin Diary*, published by Alfred A. Knopf in 1947, Shirer gave one of his few clues as to who in the German government had supplied him with information. "I've found Hilda, who saved my neck on many an occasion when I was here during the war," he wrote on November 13. "Though as Aryan as they come, she had fallen in love with a Jew, who had escaped to a neighboring country. When it was overrun by the Germans, she gave him up for dead.... She had sustained me at many moments when hope seemed lost."

Hilda was almost certainly the woman Shirer described in his diary in the fall of 1940 who told him the Gestapo was making a case against him as a spy and that he should leave the country. From the way he wrote his entry—"I've found Hilda"—it sounds as if he went looking for her, rather than chancing upon her. Seeing her again, he told her he would try and help her determine the fate of her lover.

In mid-November, after two weeks in Berlin, Shirer and Smith made their way to Nuremberg, where the Allies had established a criminal court to try the major figures in the Nazi government. Shortly after 9:00 A.M. on November 20, Shirer took his seat in the press box, not far from the twenty-two former Nazis on trial. On a brown composition book, Shirer wrote: "When I came in defendants already there, lined up in box left to right. First row, l. to r., Göring, light gray uniform. Hess, also thinner, normal looking, light brown suit. Keitel. Rosenberg. Frank. Frisk. Streicher.... Doenitz. A bunch more."

He knew who all of them were. He had met several of them at official functions and briefings. He had been on a first-name basis with Hans Fritzsche, who headed the news division in the Propaganda Ministry. Shirer could not imagine why he was in the docket with the others. At the monthly beer parties for foreign correspondents at the Adlon Hotel, Shirer had met Göring, Alfred Rosenberg, and Heinrich Himmler, who had committed suicide in May 1945. He listened to their crimes when the indictment was read out.

To Shirer's great luck, the prosecution introduced thousands of captured German documents that explained the origins of the war, detailed key meetings, and laid out the case against the Nazis on trial for massive crimes against humanity. While he was in Nuremberg observing the proceedings, Shirer was hit with a bad flu and spent several days sleeping on a cot in a room in an abandoned palace provided for the journalists. On the morning of November 27, Smith shook Shirer awake to tell him word had come over the radio hookup to New York that Shirer's mother had died in Cedar Rapids. He had last seen his mother seven months earlier, after stopping in Cedar Rapids while en route back to New York from a speaking engagement in Nebraska. On the afternoon of April 12, 1945, he arrived at her home to find her weeping.

"He's dead," she said.

"Who?"

"The president."

Turning on the radio, Shirer heard that President Roosevelt had died at his retreat in Warm Springs, Georgia. Shirer rushed to a local radio station to speak about the death to a nationwide audience. He felt his own heart break at the news. After four terms in the White House and seeing the country through the Depression and the war, Roosevelt would not see its conclusion and aftermath. Shirer stayed with his mother as long as he could, and later in the day he took a taxi to Union Station for the train ride to Chicago and New York. Now, seated on his cot in a confiscated palace in Nuremberg, Shirer recalled this visit and choked back his tears. There was no way he could get to Iowa in time for his mother's funeral. When Tess cabled him, he learned that his mother had been talking to a neighbor and fainted and died twenty minutes later.

In his diary, Shirer wrote, "Tossing on this cot today, the grief recalling a thousand family pictures of the past, I thought of that time in our little Iowa town during the first German war when mother went into the downstairs bedroom and found her mother cold and dead." In a cable to his brother, John, in which Shirer said he could not be in Cedar Rapids for the funeral, he wrote, in part: "I would have liked to say a few words recalling her integrity, her courage, her wisdom, her self-sacrifice, her too great modesty and the wonderful inspiration she was to us."

Not the Ed Murrow He Had Known

By 1947, Shirer had worked for CBS for a decade. He could well have thought that year that he was among the best in the business and had firmly established himself. Praise had been heaped on him for his work in Europe. "Our mutual friend William has been doing the best sustained job of radio reporting that has ever been done in the history of this mad medium," Murrow wrote Tess Shirer in the fall of 1939, after the German assault on Poland.

Shirer had grown critical of anti-Communist sentiment in the United States. He had no love for Communism at all but saw the effort against so-called Communists in government and the arts to be nothing but witch hunts. An April 1942 diary entry shows Shirer accusing the FBI of organizing a "reign of terror" against perceived Communists who he said were being run out of their government jobs, "many of them expert and irreplaceable in their fields and trying to help win the war."

That spring, an FBI agent called Shirer at his office and asked about his friend Wally Deuel. Wasn't he a Communist? Shirer lost his temper and slammed down the phone. A few days later, an FBI agent who had been in Shirer's graduating class at Coe College arrived in his CBS office to inquire about the political sympathies of Joe Barnes, who had worked in Moscow for the *Herald Tribune*. The agent said Barnes had been overheard saying he was happy the Russians were pushing back against the Germans along the eastern front. Shirer lost his temper, and the agent left the office.

If his views, however benign, had become a problem to his employer, Shirer did not suspect it. So when, on Monday, March 10, 1947, an executive at a Madison Avenue advertising agency called Shirer to tell him he was being dropped as the host of a Sunday evening radio news broadcast, Shirer wondered why. The executive explained that the sponsor, a soap and shaving company, wanted a younger audience and a different format. He did not believe the explanation, and he was even more suspicious about why CBS had not told him about this before the ad agency called. And what about Murrow? He was vice president of news—he had to have known this was coming.

Even more puzzling to Shirer was his show's high rating. "Could it be, I began to wonder, that the sponsor, though pleased with the ratings, didn't like my supposedly liberal view of the news?" he wrote in his memoirs. "The era of McCarthy lay just ahead, but already there were signs foreshadowing it. I had not taken the change of climate as seriously as perhaps I should."

There had been criticism of Shirer's program, but he had discounted it until now. He had heard that Cardinal Spellman, the influential archbishop of New York, had complained about him. He suspected that the ad agency executive had also complained behind Shirer's back that Shirer was too liberal in his views. The sponsor and the agency were trying to silence him, Shirer concluded. He hoped that as CBS executives—in particular Murrow—heard what had happened, they would back him.

"It was therefore with considerable confidence that I phoned him," Shirer wrote, "told him my sponsor was dropping me despite good ratings, that there were other advertisers waiting to buy my Sunday spot, and would he advise me whether the program belonged to me or the sponsor? To put it bluntly...would he and Paley allow an advertiser to throw me off the air? To my surprise, Ed, who began to sound somewhat officious as our conversation proceeded, said he would get back to me—in a day or two. I next called Paley. He was brisk and businesslike. He said the decision about my Sunday broadcast was up to Murrow. Ed was in charge of CBS News."

Shirer waited a week for his friend to call him. When he didn't, Shirer wrote him, asking for his decision. Several days later, Murrow—"crisp and cool, most unlike the Ed I had known for ten years"—called Shirer to say he would be replaced on the Sunday night news broadcast with another person. "He offered no explanation," Shirer wrote.

The Shirer archive in Cedar Rapids has boxes of files containing letters and other written material about the events surrounding what Shirer believed was his firing by the network. Shirer saved carbons of his letters, hundreds of letters to him, press releases, and newspaper clippings related to the end of his

career at CBS. He had saved everything that crossed his desk in hopes, perhaps, of some day making sense of what had happened to him.

At the end of March, Shirer sat in front of the microphone for the last
time and read a statement he'd spent all weekend typing and retyping. He had
cleared the statement with Murrow the day before and then called him Sunday
morning to assure him he would not deviate from it. When Murrow picked up
the phone, he was angry and accusatory, as Shirer related in his memoir.

"You son-of-a-bitch!" he shouted. "You better not try anything funny
today. You better stick to the script—or else."

"Look at all the experience I've had in sticking to scripts. In Berlin.
Remember?"

"For your information," Murrow said, "I've got things fixed so we can shut
you out in a split second."

"Just like in Berlin," Shirer responded.

At the end of the broadcast, Shirer read the approved statement. "This
is my last broadcast—on this program and on this network. The issues
involved...are too involved to go into at this moment. I realize full well that
you tune in on this program to hear news and news analysis, not a debate on
a disagreement between CBS and me which we have not been able to resolve.
In conclusion, I would like to say this: to you who have followed these Sunday
night broadcasts since 1941—through the years of the war and the beginning
of a good peace, I express my appreciation for your kind interest."

After the broadcast, Shirer released his own statement to the press: "In
view of certain circumstances and statements connected with my replacement
as a news analyst on the Sunday 5:45 P.M. program over CBS—a move that
was first communicated to me by the advertising sponsor, though the final
decision, I am ready to believe, was made by CBS—I feel that the Columbia
Broadcasting System has brought my usefulness on its network to a sudden end
after ten years of regular broadcasting from here and abroad. I am therefore
resigning."

Almost immediately after Shirer left the studio, the Associated Press sent
out a story. The clipping, torn and faded, sits in a file in his archive. "William
L. Shirer, news commentator for the Columbia Broadcasting System who said
last week his regular Sunday broadcasts were being dropped as an attempt to
'gag' him for his liberal views, announced tonight his resignation from the
network."

Shirer's leaving CBS fundamentally altered his future. Years later, as a
very old man, he told a television interviewer that the firing turned him into
the book writer he had always wanted to be. For years he grappled with who
was to blame for his leaving the network. Maybe he was overly confident
in his place in the network and the world, he wondered, and had too much
hubris. Some of his colleagues argued that he had not been fired at all but

had resigned. His pride got in the way, they said, and his account of being gagged for his liberal views were the rantings of a man who wanted what to some was a demotion to be recast as something heroic. It was far better for him to be the victim of a conservative witch hunt than a man demoted to an uncertain future. Whatever the truth, the firing—if it was a firing at all—was the most critical turn in the road for Shirer, far more critical than what he experienced after being fired by Colonel McCormick at the *Chicago Tribune*.

His treatment by Murrow cut him deeply. "Beyond the issues involved in my case there was a very personal matter: the destruction of a great friend-ship," he wrote. "Ed Murrow had hired me in Berlin in 1937 when I was out of a job, and for that I was grateful.... Murrow had been an interesting, inspiring, and forthright man to work with. And he had proved to be, I had thought, a close and loyal friend."

The Big Book

By 1950, Shirer was living on a farm in Connecticut with Tess and their two daughters, Eileen and Linda, struggling mightily to pay his bills and stay afloat. He sold stories to magazines and was paid for speaking engagements, but there was far too little money to keep the family going, and every month was a strug-gle. He hoped to find a way back into radio or the new medium of television, but nothing materialized. It felt as though his name was on a blacklist.

All the letters Shirer saved and filed that are now part of the Shirer col-lection at Coe College show that at this time his marriage to Tess was under siege, their relationship sinking under the weight of rancor and bitterness. He told the story, often in embarrassing detail, in his third memoir. "We began to clash over other aspects of our deteriorating financial situation. As our affairs grew steadily worse, Tess seemed to resent my inability to earn enough to keep us in a comfortable state, free of worry. It was a husband's duty, she kept say-ing, to support his family.... As with so many other spouses everywhere, our squabbles over money, or rather the lack of it, began to erode a long and pretty solid marriage."

To Shirer, as he entered old age, looking back on his life from the conve-nience of distance, the many years he spent with Tess after their marriage in Vienna had been solid and rewarding. He remembered the good times they had shared, the children born and raised, the many travels, and the worries over sickness and forced separation.

His final memoir, *A Native's Return*, is a book he perhaps should not have written. Here, a reader learns that, in 1941, a year after his return to the United States from Germany and the year *Berlin Diary* was published to great com-mercial success, Shirer began a relationship with a woman named Tilly Losch.

Shirer was now a well-known writer, on top of his career as a broadcaster. He can easily be pictured as a man with a big ego and a fair amount of hubris. Like Tess, Tilly was Austrian. Shirer had seen her in 1929 on the stage in London when she had a part in a Noel Coward play. She was also an acclaimed ballet dancer and an exotic beauty. On a summer evening in 1941, she came to his office in New York with a group of film directors, and they went out for late-night drinks. A relationship blossomed quickly—they told each other they were in love—and he talked about leaving Tess, but he could not bring himself to break up his family, and the relationship ended. On Christmas Eve 1975, Tess showed Shirer Losch's obituary in the *New York Times*. She had died of cancer.

By the early 1950s, the Shirers could barely live on his income from books, magazine articles, and freelance book reviews. The difficulties brought on by lack of money made his bitterness over leaving CBS and his treatment by Murrow far worse. To keep the family afloat, his only option was to dream up another book idea and hope for a decent payment. That idea came in 1954 when he decided to take the captured German documents he had seen at Nuremberg in 1945, examine them further, and write the definitive book about the Nazis' rise to power and ultimate defeat. A title came to him quickly: *The Rise and Fall of the Third Reich*.

Shirer was not a historian or an academic, but he set out to write a history that would anchor his reputation. As envisioned, it would be a big book in size and scope. He would construct it based on the German records and, beyond these, use his own memory as an eyewitness and also the accounts of others who had been there. As he viewed German history, he would blame the Germans themselves for the evil of the Nazis. The poison ran all the way from Martin Luther to Adolf Hitler. As he saw it, no one in America was better suited to write this book than he. The war had been over for barely a decade when he got started; everything was fresh. He had already spent considerable time going through the records, many of which were in the National Archives in Washington, and he had made extensive notes. By 1955 he was in front of the typewriter at his farm in Connecticut.

A biographer will someday write the story of the enormous hurdles Shirer had to climb to sell the book—Simon and Schuster finally agreed and paid Shirer a $10,000 advance—and then to research and write it; how he went broke well before the book was done and had to beg grants and loans in order to finish it; how, after his name appeared in *Red Channels*, a publication that named suspected Leftists in television and radio, his freelancing efforts all but ended; and how the massive book (1,245 pages) was panned by the academic historians, many of whom had neither the talent nor the work ethic to write a similar book. *The Rise and Fall of the Third Reich*, published in October 1960, won for Shirer the National Book Award and sold one million copies in hardback.

An Old Friend Wants to Apologize

The split with Murrow in 1947 remained for Shirer a cause of anger and pain for years afterward. It was not just the firing by CBS and the end to his career. That left Shirer deeply scarred and asking himself what might have been and sent his life and his family's into turmoil. What truly pained him was the simple truth that it had been Murrow who played the key role in his demise. To Shirer, it was a wrenching betrayal almost equivalent to a man's cheating on his wife, which Shirer knew something about.

One of the themes of Shirer's life from his college graduation in 1925 to his leaving Berlin in 1940 was his powerful sense of optimism and his faith in good luck. He had seen himself on a mission from the moment he drove away from Cedar Rapids in his uncle's car en route to Paris. He was a man who persevered, who hit bumps but then had a saving grace come along and pluck him out of harm's way. It had always worked out. Getting fired and having perhaps the closest friend he had ever had in his life play a role in it shattered a lot of Shirer's good nature and hopeful outlook. Shirer's view that Murrow had turned on him was the deepest wound of his life.

It may have been a similar wound for Murrow. As Shirer described it in *A Native's Return*, Murrow returned to broadcasting after Shirer left the network and made an even bigger name for himself with the success of *See It Now*, a news program Murrow produced with Fred Friendly. By 1957, Murrow had fallen out with William Paley. Murrow, Shirer wrote, became a sad, exhausted, and embittered man.

"I ran into Ed one day on Madison Avenue," Shirer wrote in his memoir. "It was a cold, dark day in December 1960, shortly after the publication of my *Rise and Fall of the Third Reich*, on which I had worked day and night for ten years. I had not seen Ed during that time. We had never become reconciled. I had not sought or wanted reconciliation, though I heard from mutual friends that he did. What had happened thirteen years before had receded in my memory but it could never be undone."

Murrow congratulated Shirer on the great success of the book. "It's a tremendous achievement," Murrow told him. "Far greater than anything we've done on the air. You ought to be proud of yourself."

They talked about the "old days," but Shirer was reluctant to go too far with the conversation. He could not take his eyes off Murrow's face. "His deeply lined face was emaciated; his trim body seemed shrunken. A cigarette dangled from his lips. He coughed."

Murrow talked haltingly about CBS. "I'm through at CBS," he said. "Washed out. In the end, I got what you got. I remember you told me I would. I should have known it."

The men parted, two actors on a once grand stage, and went their separate ways. Four years later, in August 1964, Janet Murrow phoned the Shirer house in Connecticut. She was with her husband on their farm near Pawling, New York. Janet had once been very close to Tess and was godmother to the Shirers' daughter, Linda. Janet told Tess that her husband very badly wanted to see Bill, asking in an almost pleading voice if Bill and Tess could drive over to the Murrow farm the next day. They could have lunch, Janet explained. The Shirers had heard that Murrow was dying of cancer. A lung had been removed. Tess accepted the invitation.

"As we drove over to Pawling the next day—it was one of the loveliest days of the summer, pleasantly warm, dry and sunny—I told Tess that I would not discuss, nor let Ed discuss, our break. I had heard again recently that he wanted a reconciliation," Shirer wrote in *A Native's Return.*

The wound was too deep, and Shirer was too stubborn to let his former colleague say what he wanted to say before he died. Shirer presented an unflattering portrait of himself on the car ride to Pawling, a man unwilling to accept the confession of a dying friend. Shirer did not write what Tess said to him as they drove, but it would not be hard to imagine her telling him to reconsider, to let Murrow say what he wanted to say and, if he asked, to offer forgiveness and reconciliation. But she could not talk him out of it.

When they arrived at the farm, they found Murrow pale and weak, "a mere shell of the man we had known in our youthful, golden years in Europe together." His face was thin, his body further shrunken, his cheeks hollow. "Though he had given up smoking, he coughed a great deal and seemed to have trouble breathing," Shirer wrote.

The four sat for lunch and talked about Europe. Shirer could see Murrow was "a bit on edge." He had something he wanted to say. Instead, they talked about "the good and crazy times together in Berlin, Geneva, Vienna, London, and the first year in New York after we came back from the war."

When lunch was finished, Murrow told Shirer he wanted to drive around the farm in his old jeep and show his friend how beautiful the land was on a summer day. Shirer, uneasy that Murrow "wanted to get away from Janet and Tess so that he could have a heart-to-heart talk with me about the past," suggested the tour would be too much for Murrow. But Murrow insisted.

In the jeep, it took all of Murrow's strength to steer over the rough farm roads. He perspired heavily, stopping every once in a while to catch his breath. On one of those stops, as Murrow tried to control his coughing, he "started to say something about the old days together. I changed the subject as quickly and as gracefully as I could. We fell silent and Ed drove back to the house."

Later in the day, the Shirers said goodbye and drove back to Connecticut. The two men would never see each other again. Eight months later, on April 27, 1965, Murrow passed away.

LEAVING TESS

With the great success of his big book, Shirer felt whole again, financially and intellectually. Within a few short years of the book's publication, its big sale to the Book-of-the-Month Club, and its appearance in paperback, Shirer and Tess were fighting the kinds of bitter battles that almost always ended in separation and divorce. They had been married for almost forty years, but the decades together and all they had been through as a couple did not help them now. Nor did it help when Shirer fell in love again. Or thought he had fallen in love again.

Her name was Virgilia Peterson, and Shirer had first met her in 1932 at a Christmas party in Vienna at the home of John and Frances Gunther. She was also a writer who liked being around other writers, and had been on the judges' panel that awarded the National Book Award to *The Rise and Fall of the Third Reich*. In *A Native's Return*, he wrote gushingly of seeing her again in New York in 1965 and how his "resistance crumbled" when they could not stay apart. He called her Gilly and regarded her as sophisticated and polished.

Shirer wrote that, in early 1966, not long after Peterson's husband died of cancer, they fell in love. His description of their relationship is silly and melo-dramatic, beneath a man of his age and stature. "It seemed absurd, unreal. We could not understand it. And we fought to repress it.... But it was no use," he wrote. They would rendezvous at the weekend Connecticut home of friends a short distance from the Shirers' farm. Shirer wrote that, although he was in love with Gilly, he still could not leave Tess.

When Christmas 1966 came around, Shirer promised he would get out of his home and meet her at the farmhouse. But he wanted to be with Tess and their two daughters, who would be home for the holiday. It snowed hard on Christmas Eve and into the next day, and Shirer stayed at his home, while Gilly drove over bad roads to the farmhouse hoping Shirer would meet her. He never arrived. There, on Christmas Day, Gilly, alone, swallowed enough sleeping pills to end her life.

The following fall, 1967, Shirer moved out of the house. He and Tess were formally divorced in 1970. After the papers were signed in the courthouse in New Haven, Connecticut, Shirer wrote her a letter, which he included in his memoir. It reads, in part:

> *Dear Tessie:*
> *It was very sad for me, the parting yesterday in the heat of ugly New Haven.*
> *Whatever has happened it was depressing to come to an end after so long a time of a*

shared life that saw so much over many continents that was meaningful and exciting and joyous.... Despite all our problems and the impossibilities of the later years, we had a rich life together and fuller than most people will ever have or know. This cannot be lost, no matter what happens.

Don't Let Them Forget Their Guilt

Shirer made one final trip to Berlin, in the spring of 1985. Angry that President Ronald Reagan had scheduled a trip to a German military cemetery in Bitburg, West Germany, where SS troops were buried, Shirer accepted an invitation from CBS to travel there and offer his own views. He was eighty-one years old, his vision failing.

"The president of the United States was going to honor such murderers, along with other war dead," a baffled Shirer wrote, adding that he was particularly upset that Reagan had said that the German soldiers buried at Bitburg were "as much victims of the Nazis as those done to death in the German concentration camps." This flew in the face of Shirer's own firsthand experience and all of his research in the German documents for his big book. That opinion also fit nicely into what he saw as a thoroughly dishonest German view of the past, in which the Germans positioned themselves as Hitler's opponents and victims and not his enthusiastic supporters and enablers.

In a letter to the *New York Times*, published on April 25, 1985, Shirer castigated Reagan, saying the German troops he had followed into France were enthusiastic followers of Hitler and the Nazi program. None were victims, he wrote. The following month, he flew to Germany. As Shirer interpreted the mood in the country, the Germans no longer wanted to be reminded of their ugly past. They wanted the international community to let them off the hook and to see that Nazism and its actions were the work of one man and not a people. In Berlin, Shirer took a room in a hotel on the Kurfürstendamm. On a stroll on his first night in the city, he passed a Jewish community house, where two policemen had been posted. Later, a group of protesters gathered in front of the building, and a German rabbi spoke to the crowd in opposition to Reagan's visit to the military cemetery.

As Shirer recounted in his memoir, the president of the Federal Republic, Richard von Weizsäcker—whose father Shirer had known as an official in the German Foreign Office in the 1930s—gave a speech at the time of the visit in which he asked why the Germans had ignored the war against the Jews. The speech showed that the government was not running from the past. Shirer had gotten the German mood wrong.

Weizsäcker's eloquent words could well have been addressed to the American correspondents who had been based in Germany in the Nazi years prior to the start of the war and who did not write in a serious, aggressive fashion about the German government's policies against the Jews. For those journalists it would have been better to cover the horror aggressively and be thrown out of the country than not to write about it at all or to write about it in timid, sparing words. No doubt some did not report what was happening right in front of them because they believed they couldn't for fear of being expelled. Some, without question, did not care. Still others no doubt thought there was a larger, more important story to pursue. They made choices, Shirer among them.

"There were many ways of not burdening one's conscience, of shirking responsibility, looking away, keeping mum," Weizsäcker said to the German Bundestag. "All of us, whether guilty or not, whether old or young, must accept the past."

A few weeks prior to Reagan's visit, German Chancellor Helmut Kohl said that the Germans must reconcile themselves with their past. "A nation that abandons its history forsakes itself," he said. Both Weizsäcker's and Kohl's speeches were quoted in Shirer's final memoir, as if he were acknowledging his error.

The morning Shirer left, Berlin was warm and dry. At the airport he sat in a waiting area, watching the clock and reading, anxious to get home. It is easy to imagine this old man, his white hair spilling over his ears and down his neck, lost in thought and introspection, looking back on the long arc of his life. He keenly felt his age and the burden of his work all these years and the weight of decisions made and decisions avoided. Perhaps he thought of Tess and their decades together. Had he done right by her? He knew for certain that this was his last trip to Germany. He would stay home now and await his own death.

AUTHOR'S NOTE

This book, the story of William L. Shirer's six years as a foreign correspondent in Berlin in the 1930s, is not a scholarly work. I am a journalist, not an academic, and this story is about a journalist at work, based on the books, memoirs, diaries, notes, personal letters, and correspondence of the journalist himself. My goal from the beginning was to write more of an adventure story than a book of history.

During the six years he was based in Berlin, Shirer was a witness, through a small window, of the day-to-day events from his arrival in the summer of 1934 to the snowy night he flew out of Berlin in December 1940, en route to a meeting in Portugal with his colleague and friend Edward R. Murrow. On board Shirer's plane were years of his personal papers, packed into trunks he managed to trick past the German police and customs authorities. These papers, and many others he collected in his life, are the anchor of a first-class archive in the Stewart Memorial Library at Coe College, in Cedar Rapids, Iowa. Shirer, who spent part of his youth in Cedar Rapids, graduated from Coe College in 1925. During the course of my research on this book, the custodians of this archive at Coe were Richard Doyle, Jill Jack, and Sara Pitcher. No archive could have more dedicated caretakers.

The collection is the foundation of this book. I have borrowed liberally from Shirer's personal papers, in many places using his own words and in others paraphrasing him or using my own interpretations of what he meant. The thousands of papers filed in the archive show what Shirer did and thought on a certain day, where he was, and what he believed lay ahead for him. He wrote down everything, it seems, probably to create the kind of record he knew he would need later if he wrote his memoirs but also because spilling out his thoughts on paper was part of his personality.

There are deeply personal letters in the collection; some are painful to read, as they reveal the turmoil in Shirer's life at different times, but particularly when he was older and divorced from his wife, Tess. Other letters, written when he was younger, show the kind of journalist he was—at times angry and frustrated, tenacious, opinionated, resentful of authority, ambitious, conspiratorial, unforgiving, and unwilling to make deals to further his career.

I have mined as much of the collection as possible to support the narrative of this book. That includes diary pages he filed away and those he used in the writing of *Berlin Diary*, his first book, which was published in 1941 by Alfred A. Knopf. When I could, I used diary entries rather than Shirer's memoirs, which were mostly written nearly a half century after the events he describes and are thus not as reliable. In his diary entries, Shirer wrote what he saw—but he only saw, in large part, what German authorities allowed him to see; he was told, with some significant exceptions, only what German authorities wanted him to know. A great deal of the information passed on to Shirer and the other foreign correspondents covering Hitler's government was false—the official lies of the government. His work as a journalist, as is true with any journalist, was to learn the truth, if only a small piece of it, while working at odds with censors and manipulative government officials. In the end, he found that process so demoralizing that it became the major reason he left Berlin in 1940.

While Shirer's work in Berlin was extraordinary, his view of the history unfolding in Germany during those years was not the same as that of Victor Klemperer, the German professor, born a Jew, who had served his country in the army during the Great War. Klemperer converted to Christianity and married a Protestant and remained in the country throughout the second German war. Klemperer also kept a diary, which was published after the war. It shows the insults and horrors and doom all around him that descended on Germany like a great, black night after Hitler came to power in January 1933. It is no small point to say that Klemperer wrote about his and his wife Eva's lives as Germans, lives lived on very thin ice, while Shirer wrote about others' lives from the safety of his position as an American correspondent.

Shirer had high-ranking and influential sources within the government, but many of them, perhaps all of them, could not have predicted that by the middle of 1941 and into the spring of the following year, their government would have already murdered hundreds of thousands of Jews and established extermination centers along main rail lines to murder millions more under factory conditions. While based in Berlin, Shirer did not see that coming. In that way, he and other American as well as British correspondents missed the central story of Germany and World War II.

Only a small number of Berlin-based foreign correspondents wrote much at all about the Nazi efforts against the Jews during the years from Hitler's coming to power to the start of the war in September 1939. Each of these correspondents, including Shirer, had to make choices about what to write, with the real risk of expulsion hanging over their heads. This is not to offer an excuse for why they did not write more about official harassment and disenfranchisement of Germany's Jews—and, in November 1938, state-sponsored violence—but it was a factor.

In a real way, each of these correspondents faced a choice—how much of the Nazis' official programs against the Jews should they try to cover? Some did not write about these efforts because they just didn't care about what was happening to the German Jews. Guido Enderis of the *New York Times* Berlin bureau seems to fit into this category. The work of Laurel Leff, a former journalist and now a faculty member at Northeastern University, shows how Enderis went out of his way to avoid writing about the German government's policies against the Jews.

She also shows in her book *Buried by The Times: The Holocaust and America's Most Important Newspaper* that the *Times's* coverage of the exterminations after the war had commenced was woefully inadequate. Leff's research has brought her to the conclusion that, for most of the Berlin-based foreign correspondents at work in Germany during the 1930s, what was happening to the Jews wasn't that important to them.

Some American correspondents were harsh anti-Semites and openly pro-Nazi. An American colleague of Shirer's, Robert Best, who reported from Vienna, went to work for the Germans and was arrested after the war and put on trial in the United States for treason. Shirer testified against him in a Boston courtroom. Best was convicted and sentenced to prison, where he died. Donald Day of the *Chicago Tribune* went to work for the Germans in 1942 as a propagandist. Unlike a group of other Americans and Englishmen who went to work for the Germans, Day somehow avoided prosecution after the war. He justified his work in a bizarre book that he completed while working for the Nazis, whom he describes as doing a great service for "Western civilization" by going to war against the "Jewish-Bolshevik" menace. His book, published in the United States in 1982 under the title *Onward Christian Soldiers*, has a chapter called "Jews" that reads like something Joseph Goebbels might have written.

It is almost too strange to be true, but one of Day's sisters was Dorothy Day, the Catholic convert who spent much of her life in the Catholic Worker movement helping the poor. She has been proposed for sainthood, something her brother, who broadcast for the Nazis on an English-language radio station in Berlin as Americans were being killed by the thousands in western Europe—and as Jews were being murdered by the millions—could never have understood.

For the other foreign correspondents, questions about the focus of their work can't be answered today. It is impossible to get into their heads. As for Shirer, while I had many questions about the fact that he hardly mentioned the German government's official policies against the Jews in his letters and diaries, correspondence in his archive at Coe College, written in the summer and fall of 1938 between Shirer and a Vienna photographer named Helene Katz, helped to answer some of these questions. They also helped me to get inside his head, and to understand him better, as he worked to get her out of Austria and to safety.

From his unique post, Shirer saw many things that horrified him. He stood near Hitler and heard his threats. He attended parties at which high-ranking Nazis entertained foreign correspondents. It's clear he found them a loathsome group and a grave threat to democracies everywhere. It was only after the war—after he sat in the courtroom in Nuremberg, after he read many of the captured German documents kept in the US National Archives in preparation for writing *The Rise and Fall of the Third Reich*, and after he read the accounts of the Eichmann trial in Jerusalem—that he realized that what he had seen during his six years in Berlin was through a very small window. I believe he made a pact with himself while he was in Berlin—to write as best he could under difficult conditions, to keep going as long as he could, and to report as thoroughly as was possible. He could not do it all. By all appearances, he did the best he could.

Many journalists have worked under conditions of official government deception, lies typed out daily in press statements, and reaped great results. David Halberstam and Neil Sheehan covered the war in Vietnam while working against military censors and government officials angered at the two journalists' stories about the state of the war effort. Both men were denounced by American officials. They kept writing.

There are many journalists working in countries around the world who write stories that anger their governments. They swim against the current that other journalists float comfortably along in. Two courageous Israeli journalists, Amira Hass and Gideon Levy, write what they see in Israel and in the occupied territories. Hass has lived in the territories so she can better understand the day-to-day lives of Palestinians under the Israeli occupation. Both continue to file stories; their newspaper, *Haaretz*, continues to publish them.

A former colleague of mine at *Newsday*, Roy Gutman, won the Pulitzer Prize for writing about concentration camps in Bosnia. No government official typed out that story on a press release and handed it to him, along with a map showing just where to look for the evidence. Concentration camps! Could he have done more important work as a journalist? This is not a book about journalism as it is being practiced in America circa 2011. There is no sermon embedded in the narrative of this book. It is a story about a single journalist at work.

The expression "the good German" has since the end of World War II come to apply to those "good" Germans who opposed Hitler and worked against his policies. In Berlin, as I see it, Shirer was "the good American." Whether he could have done more—whether he could have written serious, in-depth stories about the German government's drive against the country's Jews, whether his editors would have shown any interest in these stories—is a question that can't be answered today. The role and responsibilities of a journalist covering a vast human catastrophe is the theme that lies at the heart of this book. The expression the "good American" applies to all journalists working under horrific conditions who are still writing for American newspapers or broadcasting for American radio or television networks.

ACKNOWLEDGMENTS

Many people aided me in the research for this book. First and foremost, I want to thank the wonderful staff of Stewart Memorial Library at Coe College in Cedar Rapids, Iowa. I am particularly grateful to Richard Doyle, Jill Jack, and Sara Pitcher for their assistance in helping me navigate the William L. Shirer collection. Each time I visited the library to work in the collection, the staff graciously invited me to their regular events in the library, including lunches and parties, and refilled my coffee cup—as long as I kept it away from the archives. Rich even lent me one of his bicycles so I could ride the extensive network of trails built atop an old railroad bed in Cedar Rapids. Our relationship began as research librarians helping a journalist; we ended this project as great friends.

I am very grateful to John Chaimov, a gifted professor at Coe College, who introduced me to one of his students, Nina Carlson, who helped translate documents found in the Shirer collection that related to the desperate efforts of a Viennese photographer named Helene Katz to flee Austria in the fall of 1938. Nina's and John's work with these documents shed light on the fate of a Jewish woman, just one of so many caught up in the hatred and madness after the *Anschluss* in March 1938. John and Nina brought the story of Helene Katz out into the open. They saved her name. There is something noble about that.

I want to thank the staff at the United States Holocaust Memorial Museum in Washington, D.C., and particularly senior historian Ann Millin. In Vienna, a number of researchers helped me, including Katja Maria Chladek, David Forster, and Susanne Uslu-Pauer; Austrian journalist Anton Holzer also helped with interviews he conducted with a friend of Helene Katz's. I am grateful to David Lewin and Lilian Levy in London; in New York, Valery Bazarov, the director of the Hebrew Immigrant Aid Society's History and Location Service, helped me trace Katz's movements; in Jerusalem, Shaul Ferrero at Yad Vashem helped me to discover that there were two women from Vienna named Helene Katz—one who was deported to Poland and murdered at Belzec, the second the photographer whose letters to William L. Shirer were found in the Shirer collection archives. If anyone who reads this book can help me learn the fate of the photographer Helene Katz after she fled Austria, please let me know.

I want to thank two wonderful friends, Donald Mace Williams and his wife, Nell Williams, for their very careful reading of the manuscript as it limped along toward completion. I do not know of two better people to work with on a book than Don and Nell, nor two sharper eyes. I also want to thank Michael V. Carlisle and Ethan Bassoff at Inkwell Management for enthusiastically getting behind the book's proposal and finding it a home at Palgrave Macmillan, where Luba Ostashevsky and her team masterfully guided it to publication. The copyediting of Georgia Maas and the very careful attention to detail by production manager Donna Cherry were superb.

Lastly, I want to thank William L. Shirer's and Tess Shirer's two daughters, Linda Rae and Eileen Inga Dean. Their support of the preservation of their father's huge archive, and of serious research into it, is a lasting testament to their parents. They have kept their parents' memories alive. There is something noble about that.

NOTES

The heart of the research that informs the narrative of this book comes from material archived in the William L. Shirer Collection (WLSC) in the Stewart Memorial Library at Coe College in Cedar Rapids, Iowa. I have read hundreds of pages in the collection, including Shirer's letters, diary entries, cables, telegrams, and other correspondence. Shirer's voluminous writings—in diary entries, letters, and thoughts he jotted down on scraps of paper and pocket calendars and in three memoirs he published—have allowed me, in a number of places in this book, to express what I believe were his thoughts, his moods, his hopes, and his fears at different times of his life while he lived and worked in Europe, from the summer of 1925 to December 1940.

—Steve Wick, January 2011

CHAPTER 1 THE WRITER

The account of William L. Shirer's daily routines when he and Tess lived in Spain is from his second memoir, *The Nightmare Years: 1930–1940* (Boston: Little, Brown and Company, 1984). Dozens of letters in the WLSC also speak to his day-to-day habits while in Spain.

4   **"Had so much grand music":** letter from WLS's mother, January 13, 1935, WLSC.

5   **"McCormick's a contemptible son of a bitch":** WLS, *The Nightmare Years*, pages 57–58. WLS's contempt for Col. Robert McCormick appears in numerous letters in the WLSC.

5   **On a warm spring day:** The accounts of WLS's graduation from Coe College in 1925, his borrowing of $100 each from his uncle Bill Shirer and from Harry Morehouse Gage, the Coe president, are told in his first memoir, *20th Century Journey: The Start: 1904–1930* (Boston: Little, Brown and Company, 1976), pages 17–29. Numerous letters in the WLSC also speak to Shirer's leaving Iowa for France.

6   **Shirer's reading habits:** WLS's youth in Chicago, the habits instilled in him by his parents, and his father's death at the age of forty-one are told in *Twentieth Century Journey: The Start*.

7   **Years later, the young Shirer would remember stepping off the train:** Ibid., pages 128–129. WLS gives a very good account of his early years in Cedar Rapids after his father's death and tells how his mother fostered his early reading of

newspapers and books. WLS's barely concealed contempt for many of the citizens of Cedar Rapids and their conservative political and social views are also on display in this memoir as they are in many of the letters in the WLSC.

7   **"Something in the literary ferment"**: Ibid., page 108.

8   **Similarly, a man living in Germany:** Victor Klemperer, *I Will Bear Witness: A Diary of the Nazi Years* (New York: Random House, 1998), pages 30–31.

8   **Soon after enrolling at Coe College:** The profound influence of Ethel R. Outland, a Coe journalism professor, on Shirer is told throughout his letters in the WLSC and in *Twentieth Century Journey*.

8   **"She could not stand sloppy thinking and especially sloppy writing"**: *20th Century Journey*, page 208.

9   **"The city editors of the Post":** letter to Shirer, not dated, but presumably 1925, WLSC.

10 **"They had struck me as a romantic tribe":** *20th Century Journey*, page 34.

10 **"I yearned for some place":** Ibid., page 21.

11 **"Morning after morning":** Ibid., pages 50–51.

CHAPTER 2   HIS LUCK HOLDS

WLS's account of his summer in Paris, his search for a job, and the unexpected chance to stay in the city and work for a newspaper are in *20th Century Journey: The Start, 1904–1930* (Boston: Little, Brown and Company, 1976). Numerous letters in the WLSC also speak to his first few months in Paris and the beginning of his journalism career.

14 **They visited the Louvre:** *20th Century Journey*, page 57.

14 **"...ribbons of light..."**: Ibid., page 57.

14 **"I'm sorry":** Ibid., page 59.

14 **Shirer took note of his journalistic shortcomings:** Ibid., page 59.

15 **Dear Mr. Shirer:** Ibid., page 60.

15 **"You're not going to take it":** Ibid., page 61.

15 **"How's your French":** Ibid., page 61.

17 **"Most of the American writers on the Left Bank":** Ibid., page 229.

17 **"Hemingway did not join in the discussion":** Ibid., page 230.

18 **In one of his letters to Simon:** letter to Charles Simon, 1926, no month or day, WLSC.

19 **In his first few months in Paris:** *20th Century Journey*, page 232.

19 **"The rooms were rather spacious":** Ibid., page 235.

CHAPTER 3   THE AMERICAN CORRESPONDENT

22 **Somewhere while he was reporting:** *20th Century Journey: The Start, 1904–1930* (Boston: Little, Brown and Company, 1976), pages 268–269.

23 **When the show ended that summer:** Ibid., pages 274–279. In addition, there are numerous mentions of Grant Wood in the letters archived in the WLSC.

25 **Hoping to make the move from reporter...to a foreign correspondent:** Ibid., pages 323–339.

28 **The publisher's mother:** Ibid., page 351.

28 **"Don't fall for all those Socialists":** Ibid., page 488.

29 **"This guy Shirer is as heavy as a bride's cake":** letter from McCormick forwarded to Shirer, dated February 28, 1928. Rest of letter referring to "sentences so long..." is handwritten on same note, WLSC.

29   **Williams, who signed his letters "ww," went so far:** letter to Shirer from Wythe Williams, dated January 31, 1928, WLSC.

29   **Shirer and Gunther quickly grew close:** *20th Century Journey*, page 438. Shirer also writes of meeting Marcel Fodor and other journalists, including Robert Best, Webb Miller, William C. Bullitt, Dorothy Thompson, and her husband, Sinclair Lewis.

30   **That first winter in Vienna:** *20th Century Journey*, pages 491–492.

CHAPTER 4   THE LONG TRAIN HOME

WLS's account of his journey to India and Afghanistan is in his *Gandhi: A Memoir* (New York: Simon & Schuster, 1979) and *The Nightmare Years: 1930–1940* (Boston: Little, Brown and Company, 1984). Supplemental materials related to this period, including letters and cables, also come from the WLSC.

32   **"No problem with the visa":** *The Nightmare Years*, page 5.

32   **"Soldiers lugged in a large wobbly table":** Ibid., page 7.

33   **"Each day as I waited vainly":** Ibid., page 14.

34   **On December 29, the paper published an advertisement:** Ibid., page 21.

34   **Safely back in India, Shirer resumed...writing letters:** John Shirer sent his brother the Coe College *Courier*, dated November 1930, which extolled Shirer's trip to Afghanistan, WLSC.

35   **After Shirer had returned to India, McCormick cabled:** dated November 17, 1930, WLSC.

35   **On January 9... McCormick cabled his correspondents:** dated January 9, 1931, WLSC.

35   **This appealed to McCormick, who cabled Shirer to return to Vienna "via Babylon":** *The Nightmare Years*, page 29.

36   **"She was bundled up in a heavy winter coat":** Ibid., page 40.

CHAPTER 5   HIS LUCK HOLDS AGAIN

The account of Shirer's marriage to Tess Stiberitz, his return to India, and her trip to join him in India come from *The Nightmare Years: 1930–1940* (Boston: Little, Brown and Company, 1976).

38   **Shirer bought a ticket on the Frontier Mail:** *Gandhi: A Memoir* (New York: Simon & Schuster, 1979), pages 15–29.

38–39   **At some point when she was covering the vibrant Vienna theater scene:** the possible friendship between an Austrian photographer named Helene Katz and the Shirers is based on a reading of letters among Katz, the Shirers, and the Gunthers in the WLSC.

39   **Conditions in her room were abominable:** *The Nightmare Years*, pages 43–44.

40   The account of WLS's firing from the *Chicago Tribune* upon his return to Vienna comes from Richard Norton Smith, *The Colonel: The Life and Legend of Robert R. McCormick* (New York: Houghton Mifflin Company, 1997), pages 303–309; *The Nightmare Years*; and from letters and correspondence in the WLSC. Smith, in his excellent book, draws a strong portrait of McCormick bullying and ultimately firing Shirer, as he did a number of his foreign correspondents, including Vincent Sheean, Henry Wales, Jay Allen, Floyd Gibbons, who had lost an eye covering World War I, and George Seldes. For a first-rate portrait of Allen, who died in 1974, see *We Saw Spain Die: Foreign*

Correspondents in the Spanish Civil War by Paul Preston (New York: Skyhorse Publishing, 2009).

40 **As he fell, the grip end of the ski pole:** *The Nightmare Years*, pages 52–53.

40 **On October 16, 1932, E. S. Beck…telegrammed Shirer the blunt message:** A copy of the October 1932 cable from Beck to Shirer, and Shirer's October 17, 1932, letter to McCormick, are in the WLSC. Shirer's October 17, 1932, cable to Beck is also in the WLSC, as are his letters that same month to Sigrid Schultz and John Steele.

41 **In a letter to his friend Nicholas Roosevelt:** dated January 11, 1933, WLSC.

41 **The same week he wrote to Roosevelt, Shirer sent off a letter to Claude R. Dawson:** dated January 9, 1933, WLSC.

41 **Soon after arriving in Lloret de Mar:** Ibid., pages 64–65.

42 **A letter to Shirer from his brother, John:** dated April 19, 1933, WLSC.

42 **Frederick Birchall of the *New York Times*:** dated June 5, 1933, WLSC.

42 **Harold E. Scarborough, the London correspondent:** dated August 22, 1933, WLSC.

42 **One letter went out to J. David Stern:** undated, WLSC.

43 **Other letters went out to Edwin L. James:** dated December 11, 1933, WLSC.

43 **"Paris has become the most expensive place":** dated April 21, 1933, WLSC.

43 **"I can make Central Europe interesting":** dated January 20, 1933, WLSC.

43 **"Being unemployed is no life for me":** dated August 3, 1933, WLSC.

45 **"Very naturally every one is indignant":** *New York Times*, July 23, 1933.

45 **After introducing himself to Wiegand:** dated January 15, 1934, WLSC.

45 **He visited with Eric Hawkins:** *The Nightmare Years*, pages 78–79.

46 **In mid-January…Shirer…wrote a long letter to Ethel Outland:** dated January 19, 1934, WLSC.

47 **Seated at his writing desk:** *The Nightmare Years*, pages 79–80.

CHAPTER 6   GESTAPO AT THE TRAIN STATION

WLS's account of his return to Paris, his work as a reporter covering the anti-government riots, and his move to Berlin to work for a Hearst wire service is told in his first published book, *Berlin Diary* (New York: Alfred A. Knopf, 1941) and in *The Nightmare Years: 1930–1940* (Boston: Little, Brown and Company, 1984).

49 **Victor Klemperer:** Victor Klemperer, *I Will Bear Witness: A Diary of the Nazi Years* (New York: Random House, 1998), pages 54–55.

50 **"With such a record of past national service":** Michael Burleigh, *The Third Reich: A New History* (New York: Hill and Wang, 2000), pages 281–284.

51 **Even before Hitler assumed power:** Oron J. Hale, *The Captive Press in the Third Reich* (Princeton: Princeton University Press, 1964), pages 59–69.

51 **That night, McDonald dined:** James G. McDonald, *Advocate for the Doomed: The Diaries and Papers of James G. McDonald, 1932–1935*, ed. Richard Breitman, Barbara McDonald Stewart, and Severin Hochberg (Bloomington and Indianapolis: Indiana University Press, 2007), pages 27–29.

For additional information on the foreign correspondents working in Nazi Germany, see Deborah E. Lipstadt's very strong *Beyond Belief: The American Press and the Coming of the Holocaust, 1933–1945* (New York: The Free Press, 1986).

55   **The next morning a letter:** WLSC. Shirer's return telegrams, dated August 12 and August 18, 1934, are also in the WLSC, as is Jay Allen's congratulatory letter to Shirer.

CHAPTER 7   BERLIN AND THE WORLD

Accounts detailing Shirer's arrival and early stay in Berlin and his coverage of the Nuremberg rally are from *Berlin Diary: The Journal of a Foreign Correspondent 1934–1941* (New York: Alfred A. Knopf, 1941), *The Nightmare Years: 1930–1940* (Boston: Little, Brown and Company, 1984), and in various places in the WLSC. As for the existence of Germany's concentration camps for enemies of the Nazis, many histories of the Third Reich show they were widely known to the public and openly discussed. The extermination centers—Belzec, Treblinka, Chelmno, and Sobibor in Poland—and what the German people knew of them remains a contentious debate among historians. This debate goes to the heart of the extermination enterprise—how and when it started, whether the order to begin it came directly from Hitler, or whether it unfolded at lower levels of his government as bureaucrats worked to please him and carry out what they believed were his wishes. Another debate goes to the question of whether the German people as a whole, driven by lethal anti-Semitism, were themselves the engines behind the extermination process—that the Nazis simply stepped out of the way and let the process run on its own citizen-generated momentum. Nothing—no physical evidence, no oral histories, no recollections of the Germans themselves, no courtroom testimony at numerous war crimes trials—has persuaded a group of kooks, conspiracy buffs, and hard-core anti-Semites of the existence of the gas chambers and the deliberate, organized murders of an estimated six million Jews by the German government. To these people, the gas chambers are not just a myth—they are a Big Lie. For a strong look at British pseudo "historian" David Irving's methods and distortions that were exposed in a London courtroom, see Richard J. Evans's *Lying About Hitler: History, Holocaust, and the David Irving Trial* (New York: Basic Books, 2001) and Deborah E. Lipstadt's *History on Trial: My Day in Court with a Holocaust Denier* (New York: Echo, 2005). Additional historical information comes from Evans' *The Third Reich in Power, 1933–1939* (London: Penguin Books, 2006). Ernst Hanfstaengl defected from Germany before war erupted in 1939 and eventually made his way to the United States. He died in 1975.

61   **The government's second party rally:** Evans, *The Third Reich in Power*, pages 123–124.

CHAPTER 8   TAUENTZIENSTRASSE

The accounts and quotes of WLS's and Tess's lives in Berlin and their social activities with government officials come from *Berlin Diary: The Journal of a Foreign Correspondent 1934–1941* (New York: Alfred A. Knopf, 1941) and *The Nightmare Years: 1930–1940* (Boston: Little, Brown and Company, 1984). Additional historical information comes from *Advocate for the Doomed: The Diaries and Papers of James G. McDonald*, ed. Richard Breitman, Barbara McDonald Stewart, and Severin Hochberg (Bloomington and Indianapolis: Indiana University Press, 2007). General von Reichenau died in a plane crash in 1942 while returning from the Russian front.

68   **In a letter, Josephine told her brother:** undated, but early 1935, WLSC.
69   **A letter from his mother:** dated April 26, 1935, WLSC.
69   **To a friend, Shirer wrote:** undated, WLSC.

69   **In late February, Shirer had written another friend:** dated February 23, 1935, WLSC.

CHAPTER 9   THE WATERING HOLE

References to WLS in Berlin, the encounter with the lawyer, and his social life at the Taverne come from *Berlin Diary: The Journal of a Foreign Correspondent, 1934–1941* (New York: Alfred A. Knopf, 1941) and *The Nightmare Years: 1930–1940* (Boston: Little, Brown and Company, 1984).

75   **The true oddball among them all was Martha Dodd:** Shareen Blair Brysac, *Resisting Hitler: Mildred Harnack and the Red Orchestra* (New York: Oxford University Press, 2000), pages 136–157.

76   **In mid-1935 Shirer wrote:** undated, WLSC.

76   **In late August, Dosch-Fleurot wrote to Hanfstaengl:** dated August 26, 1935, WLSC.

79   **In an undated letter addressed to "Herr Koehl":** WLSC.

79   **In August he wrote a friend:** dated August 20, 1935, WLSC.

79   **He wrote to his friend Nicholas Roosevelt:** this letter, Roosevelt's response, and Shirer's letter to his brother John are all August and early September 1935, WLSC.

CHAPTER 10   THE DIRTY LIAR

Accounts of WLS's activities in Berlin and his interaction with government officials come from *Berlin Diary: The Journal of a Foreign Correspondent, 1934–1941* (New York: Alfred A. Knopf, 1941) and *The Nightmare Years: 1930–1940* (Boston: Little, Brown and Company, 1984). WLS's worries about being spied on are clearly evident in his letters archived in the WLSC. An example is an October 14, 1935, letter, which shows that his outgoing mail was being opened, read, and resealed with a special government stamp.

82   **As historian Michael Burleigh has noted:** Michael Burleigh, *The Third Reich, A New History* (New York: Hill and Wang, 2000), pages 294–296.

Additional information about American correspondents in Berlin and their work and dealings with government officials comes from Deborah E. Lipstadt, *Beyond Belief: The American Press and the Coming of the Holocaust, 1933–1945* (New York: The Free Press, 1986). Lipstadt writes of a number of examples of how distrustful the correspondents were of the Nazis. She cites the example of Sigrid Schultz, who discovered that her housekeeper was a spy. The quote that begins "Those who today claim that the world should have recognized" is on page 146 of Lipstadt's book.

CHAPTER 11   PARADING DOWN THE WILHELMSTRASSE

WLS's accounts of his work as a correspondent in Germany come from *Berlin Diary: The Journal of a Foreign Correspondent, 1934–1941* (New York: Alfred A. Knopf, 1941) and *The Nightmare Years: 1930–1940* (Boston: Little, Brown and Company, 1984). For a closer look at the work of other Berlin-based correspondents, I consulted Laurel Leff, *Buried by The Times: The Holocaust and America's Most Important Newspaper* (New York: Cambridge University Press, 2005). Leff's excellent book takes a very close look at how American newspapers and correspondents covered the German war against the Jews. I also consulted Louis P. Lochner, *What about Germany?* (New York: Dodd,

Mead & Company, 1942) and Deborah E. Lipstadt, *Beyond Belief: The American Press and the Coming of the Holocaust, 1933–1945* (New York: The Free Press, 1986).

92   **In March…he wrote to the New York office:** dated March 10, 1936, WLSC.

<h3 style="text-align:center">CHAPTER 12   BAD WRITING</h3>

WLS's accounts of seeing Lindbergh again, watching developments in Spain, and meeting Thomas Wolfe for lunch come from *Berlin Diary: The Journal of a Foreign Correspondent, 1934–1941* (New York: Alfred A. Knopf, 1941) and *The Nightmare Years: 1930–1940* (Boston: Little, Brown and Company, 1984).

95   **He wrote letters to Mrs. Alfred A. Knopf:** they were written the third week of August 1936, WLSC.

<h3 style="text-align:center">CHAPTER 13   GET OUT OF THE COUNTRY</h3>

Accounts of WLS's work in Berlin come from *Berlin Diary: The Journal of a Foreign Correspondent, 1934–1941* (New York: Alfred A. Knopf, 1941) and *The Nightmare Years: 1930–1940* (Boston: Little, Brown and Company, 1984); additional material surrounding the execution of Helmut Hirsch was informed by the *New York Times* edition of June 5, 1937. Otto Strasser fled Germany after Hitler came to power and spent some of the war years in Canada. He returned to Germany in the 1950s. His brother Gregor was one of the victims of the June 1934 purge against Ernst Röhm and the SA.

103   **In February, Seymour Berkson:** dated February 26, 1937, WLSC.
103   **In mid-March, Bill Hillman:** dated March 16, 1937, WLSC.
104   **On a small slip of paper:** WLSC.
104   **Later, he would write…inside a 1940 leather-bound diary:** WLSC.

<h3 style="text-align:center">CHAPTER 14   DRINKS AT THE ADLON</h3>

WLS's accounts of meeting Murrow, returning to the Nuremberg rally, and going to work for CBS come from *The Nightmare Years: 1930–1940* (Boston: Little, Brown and Company, 1984) and *Berlin Diary: The Journal of a Foreign Correspondent, 1934–1941* (New York: Alfred A. Knopf, 1941), as well as additional material from the Shirer collection.

108   **A handwritten note jotted down on a scrap of paper:** WLSC.
109   **By the end of 1937:** *The Germany of that year:* Richard J. Evans, *The Third Reich in Power, 1933-1939* (London: Penguin Books, 2006), pages 555–575.
109   **At his home, Victor Klemperer:** Victor Klemperer, *I Will Bear Witness: A Diary of the War Years* (New York: Random House, 1998), page 237.
110   **Grateful to Murrow, Shirer sent him a telegram:** dated September 1937, WLSC.

Walter Duranty was Moscow bureau chief for the *New York Times* from the early 1920s to the mid-1930s. His coverage of the Soviet famine, for which he won the Pulitzer Prize in 1932, has been sharply criticized as taking the Soviet line. Shirer's good friend Webb Miller had an extraordinary career as a journalist, riding along with General Pershing into Mexico in the hunt for Pancho Villa, covering the front in the Great War, and the rise of Adolf Hitler in Germany. He died under mysterious circumstances on May 7, 1940, when he stepped off a train in London and supposedly hit his head.

Chapter 15 The Jewish Doctor

References to Helene Katz come from the Shirer collection. WLS's accounts of the dire situation in Austria, his daughter's birth, and Tess's grave health situation come from *Berlin Diary: The Journal of a Foreign Correspondent, 1934–1941* (New York: Alfred A. Knopf, 1941) and *The Nightmare Years: 1930–1940* (Boston: Little, Brown and Company, 1984), with supplemental information provided by the WLSC. Marcel Fodor was a journalist who, along with John Gunther, interviewed Hitler's family members for a story undertaken after Hitler came to power in Germany. For additional information, see Ken Cuthbertson's *Inside: The Biography of John Gunther* (Chicago: Bonus Books, 1992). Shirer testified at the Boston federal treason trial of Robert Best, who was accused of broadcasting propaganda for the German government. A jury convicted Best; he was sentenced to federal prison, where he died in 1952.

117 **On a scrap of paper years later:** WLSC.
118 **On another scrap of paper written years later:** WLSC.
118 **On another note:** WLSC.

Chapter 16 Clearing the Mountains

Shirer's account of conditions in Austria and his and Tess's flight to Switzerland are told in *Berlin Diary: The Journal of a Foreign Correspondent, 1934–1941* (New York: Alfred A. Knopf, 1941) and *The Nightmare Years: 1930–1940* (Boston: Little, Brown and Company, 1984).

121 **In his letter, T. G. Ferreby wrote:** dated March 20, 1938, WLSC.
121 **In a letter to a friend:** dated April 19, 1938, WLSC.
122 **Just before his daughter's birth:** dated January 10, 1938, WLSC.
122 **While Shirer had been praised...White now wrote Shirer:** dated March 16, 1938, WLSC.
122 **A full month later, White wrote again:** dated April 1938, WLSC.
122 **Shirer explained that he had tried to line up a replacement:** dated April 28, 1938, WLSC.
125 **Shirer summed up the horrors...in a letter:** dated June 28, 1938, WLSC.
125 **Fuhrmann wrote back:** dated June 21, 1938, WLSC.

Chapter 17 The Photographer

The remarkable letters exchanged among Helene Katz, the Shirers, and the Gunthers come from the Shirer collection. Additional research materials from archives in Austria and Israel are identified in this chapter; the names of researchers are identified in the Acknowledgments section. Katz took a portrait of John and Frances Gunther's son, John, whom they called Johnny. He died of a brain tumor at the age of seventeen in 1947. John Gunther told of his son's death in a book called *Death Be Not Proud: A Memoir* (New York: Harper, 1949). John and Frances Gunther divorced, and she died in Israel in 1964. Her personal papers are with the Jewish Women's Archive at the Radcliffe Institute for Advanced Study at Harvard University. The book I found the most inspiring as I tried to cobble together what little I could find on the life and fate of Helene Katz is *Into the Tunnel: The Brief Life of Marion Samuel, 1931–1943*, by German historian Götz Aly, translated by Ann Millin (New York: Metropolitan Books, 2007).

Chapter 18   Sigrid Wakes Him Up

WLS's accounts of his work in Prague and elsewhere leading up to the September 1939 German invasion of Poland come from *Berlin Diary: The Journal of a Foreign Correspondent, 1934–1941* (New York: Alfred A. Knopf, 1941); copies of his radio broadcasts are published in his *"This Is Berlin": Radio Broadcasts from Nazi Germany* (Woodstock, N.Y.: Overlook Press, 1999) and *The Nightmare Years: 1930–1940* (Boston: Little, Brown and Company, 1984). Where not specifically cited, the narrative has also been informed by letters, cables, and other materials from the Shirer collection.

138   **As Shirer went back and forth:** dated September 26, 1938, WLSC.
139   **In a telegram Shirer sent to Paul White:** dated September 1, 1938, WLSC.
142   **In a letter to a friend in Rome:** dated March 15, 1939, WLSC.

Chapter 19   Lies as Thick as Grass

WLS's activities come from *Berlin Diary: The Journal of a Foreign Correspondent, 1934–1941* (New York: Alfred A. Knopf, 1941), *The Nightmare Years: 1930–1940* (Boston: Little, Brown and Company, 1984), and *"This Is Berlin": Radio Broadcasts from Nazi Germany* (Woodstock, N.Y.: Overlook Press, 1999). Philip Johnson became one of the most celebrated architects of his day, hailed at the time of his death in 2005 by the *New York Times* as "architecture's restless intellect."

149   **In late September…Shirer received a letter:** dated September 29, 1939, WLSC.
156   **At their home near Dresden:** Victor Klemperer, *I Will Bear Witness: A Diary of the Nazi Years* (New York: Random House, 1998), pages 322–324.

Chapter 20   The Germans Are Out of Their Minds

WLS's accounts of the German invasion of the Low Countries and northern France, and his mood and views as he followed the army, are informed by the Shirer collection, as well as his diary entries in *Berlin Diary: The Journal of a Foreign Correspondent, 1934–1941* (New York: Alfred A. Knopf, 1941) and his broadcasts compiled in *"This Is Berlin": Radio Broadcasts from Nazi Germany* (Woodstock, N.Y.: Overlook Press, 1999).

Chapter 21   Riding in Staff Cars

WLS's accounts of the German army and the fall of France come from the Shirer collection, including copies of cables and diary entries, and *Berlin Diary: The Journal of a Foreign Correspondent, 1934–1941* (New York: Alfred A. Knopf, 1941) and *"This Is Berlin": Radio Broadcasts from Nazi Germany* (Woodstock, N.Y.: Overlook Press, 1999).

Chapter 22   War of the Worlds

WLS's remarkable experiences in France, his arrival in Paris, and his witnessing of the surrender and signing of the armistice are told in *Berlin Diary: The Journal of a Foreign Correspondent, 1934–1941* (New York: Alfred A. Knopf, 1941), *The Nightmare Years: 1930–1940* (Boston: Little, Brown and Company, 1984), and *"This Is Berlin": Radio Broadcasts from Nazi Germany* (Woodstock, N.Y.: Overlook Press, 1999), with supplemental material from the Shirer collection. The encounter with Carl Flick-Steger in the hotel bar is told in a bound diary for 1950, which is in the Shirer collection. When Shirer later returned to Germany after the war, he encountered Flick-Steger again. Now he was working for the Associated Press. General Charles Huntziger signed the armistice on behalf of the French government. While he did so under protest, he apparently had no difficulty signing the notorious "Statute on Jews" in October 1940 on behalf of the Vichy regime—laws that were passed without pressure from the German occupiers. The statute stripped Jews of any rights and allowed the French to deport them to German camps. It was reported in the fall of 2010 that Marshall Pétain, France's chief of state during the Vichy years, personally helped write this statute and toughened its original language against Jews. Approximately 76,000 Jews in France were deported by the Vichy government, and fewer than 3,000 survived. Huntziger died in an airplane crash in the fall of 1941, and Pétain died in 1951 on a French island off its Atlantic coast. Shirer refers to journalist Walter Kerr in several places in his diaries. Kerr was a well-regarded foreign correspondent for the *New York Herald Tribune*. He died at the age of ninety-one in 2003. (This Walter Kerr is not to be confused with Walter Francis Kerr, a famous New York theater critic.) Just how Shirer's historic broadcast of the French signing of the armistice was broadcast live via short-wave directly to the United States is not completely known. In *The Nightmare Years*, Shirer writes: "The German radio engineers at the Berlin end of our military telephone line from Compiègne threw the wrong switch. Instead of steering my broadcast to a recording machine at the *Reichs Rundfunk* for recording, they channeled it into a shortwave transmitter at Zossen, which sent it out automatically and instantly to New York."

CHAPTER 23   A LONG TRAIN RIDE TO TESS

WLS's time in Berlin during the British bombings of the city are told in *Berlin Diary: The Journal of a Foreign Correspondent, 1934–1941* (New York: Alfred A. Knopf, 1941), *The Nightmare Years: 1930–1940* (Boston: Little, Brown and Company, 1984), and *"This Is Berlin": Radio Broadcasts from Nazi Germany* (Woodstock, N.Y.: Overlook Press, 1999), with additional material mined from the Shirer archive. WLS's close friend Ralph Barnes was killed in a plane crash in Yugoslavia in 1940.

CHAPTER 24   CROWDED BUSES

WLS's recollections come from *The Nightmare Years: 1930–1940* (Boston: Little, Brown and Company, 1984) *and Berlin Diary: The Journal of a Foreign Correspondent, 1934–1941* (New York: Alfred A. Knopf, 1941), with supplemental information from the Shirer collection. William Joyce was hanged in London after the war. Shirer also met or knew of Americans working for the Nazis, including Fred Kaltenbach, who grew up in Waterloo, Iowa; Edward Delaney, who on German radio called himself E. D. Ward; a Philadelphia woman who called herself Constance Drexel; and Donald Day, a former correspondent for the *Chicago Tribune*. Day was a world class anti-Semite and a self-righteous fraud who spent the postwar years trying to convince himself and the few people who would listen to him that he was a truth teller. He died on September 30, 1966. It is very difficult to believe that Donald Day and Dorothy Day, a Catholic who believed her faith compelled her to help the poor and disadvantaged, were brother and sister.

CHAPTER 25   A WARNING FROM A FRIEND

This final chapter is anchored in information from the Shirer collection, *Berlin Diary: The Journal of a Foreign Correspondent, 1934–1941* (New York: Alfred A. Knopf, 1941) and *The Nightmare Years: 1930–1940* (Boston: Little, Brown and Company, 1984). The fate of the Jewish men, women, and presumably children removed from the two buses that carried Tess and her daughter to Spain is not known, nor are their names. If anyone reading this book knows of their fate, please contact me. The career of WLS's close friend Wally Deuel was extraordinary. After war broke out, Deuel joined the Office of Strategic Services. He later joined the new Central Intelligence Agency and briefed President John F. Kennedy in the White House. Deuel's son, Michael, was a CIA operative who was killed in Laos in 1965.

POSTSCRIPT

WLS exposes a lot of himself, professionally and personally, in the large number of letters he saved that are archived in the Shirer collection. Many of these letters written by WLS late in his life, after painful divorces from two wives, his struggles to stay afloat financially, and the extraordinary effort it took to research and write his books, reveal an aging man mired in bad, sometimes humiliating relationships and romances. Yet he saved these letters, believing, I suppose, that if he was going to save his personal papers, the only honest thing he could do was to save them all. He was not about to edit his own letters and correspondence. A large measure of joy returned to WLS when he was reunited with Linda and Eileen and when he married for a third time. This trove of letters and diaries, plus his second book of diary entries, *End of a Berlin Diary* (New York: Alfred A. Knopf, 1947), along with his second and third memoirs, *The Nightmare Years: 1930–1940* (Boston: Little, Brown and Company, 1984) and *A Native's Return, 1945–1988* (Boston: Little, Brown and Company, 1990), are the foundation of the material found in the postscript. For additional information about Howard K. Smith's work as a journalist in Berlin, see his *Last Train from Berlin,* first published in Great Britain in 1942 by the Cresset Press and in paperback by the Phoenix Press in 2000.

William L. Shirer, one of the very best American foreign correspondents of his era and a man whose life was a great adventure, died December 28, 1993, at the age of eighty-nine. There are shortcomings in every book centered on the work of an individual—what is told and what is left out. In this book, it is the lack of information about the life of Tess Shirer, who died in New York on January 25, 2008, at the age of ninety-seven. Perhaps one day a full biography will be written about the Shirers and will include her life and accomplishments, which were considerable.

Victor Klemperer and his wife, Eva, miraculously survived the Nazis and the war, and, as the war neared its conclusion, the Allied fire bombing of Dresden. He appeared after May 1945 like a man emerging from years trapped in a dark cave. His remarkable diary ends in June 1945 as he and Eva found the strength to return to their home, which had been "Aryanized" in the 1930s. The last line of his diary records, simply and sweetly: "In the late afternoon we walked up to Dolzschen."

BIBLIOGRAPHY

Along with the books listed below, the material archived with the William L. Shirer collection in the Stewart Memorial Library at Coe College in Cedar Rapids, Iowa, was of invaluable assistance in the preparation of this book.
—Steve Wick

Aly, Götz. *Into the Tunnel: The Brief Life of Marion Samuel, 1931–1943*. Translated by Ann Millin. New York: Metropolitan Books, 2007. 2004.

Brysac, Shareen Blair. *Resisting Hitler: Mildred Harnack and the Red Orchestra*. New York: Oxford University Press, 2000.

Burleigh, Michael. *The Third Reich: A New History*. New York: Hill and Wang, 2000.

Cuthbertson, Ken. *Inside: The Biography of John Gunther*. Chicago: Bonus Books, 1992.

Day, Donald. *Onward Christian Soldiers: 1920–1942: Propaganda, Censorship and One Man's Struggle to Herald the Truth*. Torrance, Calif.: The Noontide Press, 1982. From a manuscript written in 1942.

Deuel, Wallace R. *People under Hitler*. New York: Harcourt, Brace and Company, 1942.

Edwards, John Carver. *Berlin Calling: American Broadcasters in Service to the Third Reich*. New York: Praeger, 1991.

Evans, Richard J. *The Third Reich in Power, 1933–1939*. London: Penguin Books, 2006.

Fallada, Hans. *Every Man Dies Alone*. Translated by Michael Hofmann. Afterword by Geoff Wilkes. Brooklyn, N.Y.: Melville House, 2009. First published in German in 1947.

Gellately, Robert. *Backing Hitler: Consent and Coercion in Nazi Germany*. New York: Oxford University Press, 2001.

Hale, Oron J. *The Captive Press in the Third Reich*. Princeton: Princeton University Press, 1964.

Inglis, Fred. *People's Witness: The Journalist in Modern Politics*. New Haven and London: Yale University Press, 2002.

Kershaw, Ian. *Hitler, the Germans, and the Final Solution*. New Haven and London: Yale University Press, 2008.

Klemperer, Victor. *I Will Bear Witness: A Diary of the Nazi Years*. New York: Random House, 1998.

Leff, Laurel. *Buried by The Times: The Holocaust and America's Most Important Newspaper*. New York: Cambridge University Press, 2005.

Lipstadt, Deborah E. *Beyond Belief: The American Press and the Coming of the Holocaust, 1933–1945*. New York: The Free Press, 1986.

Lochner, Louis P. *What about Germany?* New York: Dodd, Mead & Company, 1942.

McDonald, James G. *Advocate for the Doomed: The Diaries and Papers of James G. McDonald, 1932–1935*. Edited by Richard Breitman, Barbara McDonald Stewart, and Severin Hochberg. Bloomington and Indianapolis: Indiana University Press, 2007.

Payne, Stanley G. *The Collapse of the Spanish Republic, 1933–1936*. New Haven and London: Yale University Press, 2006.

Preston, Paul. *We Saw Spain Die: Foreign Correspondents in the Spanish Civil War*. New York: Skyhorse Publishing, 2009.

Riess, Curt, ed. *They Were There: The Story of World War II and How It Came About, by America's Foremost Correspondents*. New York: G. P. Putnam, 1944.

Safrian, Hans. *Eichmann's Men*. Translated by Ute Stargardt. Cambridge: Cambridge University Press, 2010.

Shirer, William L. *20th Century Journey. A Memoir of a Life and The Times, the Start: 1904–1930*. Boston: Little, Brown and Company, 1976.

Shirer, William L. *Berlin Diary: The Journal of a Foreign Correspondent, 1934–1941*. New York: Alfred A. Knopf, 1941.

Shirer, William L. *End of a Berlin Diary*. New York: Alfred A. Knopf, 1947.

Shirer, William L. *Gandhi: A Memoir*. New York: Simon and Schuster, 1979.

Shirer, William L. *A Native's Return, 1945–1988*. Boston: Little, Brown and Company, 1990.

Shirer, William L. *The Nightmare Years: 1930–1940*. Boston: Little, Brown and Company, 1984.

Shirer, William L. *The Rise and Fall of the Third Reich*. New York: Simon and Schuster, 1960.

Shirer, William L. *"This Is Berlin": Radio Broadcasts from Nazi Germany*. Woodstock, N.Y.: Overlook Press, 1999.

Smith, Howard K. *Last Train from Berlin: An Eye-Witness Account of Germany at War*. London: Cresset Press, 1942.

Smith, Richard Norton. *The Colonel: The Life and Legend of Robert R. McCormick*. Boston: Houghton Mifflin Company, 1997.

INDEX